For Joyce (CJ) Field, in memory of our journeys through the
Shtetlekh and forests of eastern Galicia in search of the truth.
"Yidn, shreibt un farschreibt!"

In December 1941, during the evacuation of the Riga ghetto, the 81-year-old
historian Simon Dubnow was shot. The story is told that Dubnow's last
words were an admonition to his fellow Jews: **'Write and record!'** (*Yidn,
shreibt un farschreibt*). It was a phrase written on walls and scraps of paper
in a last desperate act of defiance when the victims finally saw their
immediate demise. These 'words' can be found in many thousands of
locations, including Fort IX, Kovno, Bełżec, Sobibor and Treblinka death
camps, and on scraps of paper thrown out deportation trains destined for
destruction.

The real Oskar Schindler and his List:
Stepping Stone to Life

CODE NAMES: "Ing. Zeiler", "Osi", "Schäfer", "Otto":

Angehöriger des
"Generalkommandos VIII in Breslau; *Abwehr* Admiral Canaris"

A Reconstruction of the Schindler Story

by
Robin O'Neil

Photo courtesy of Radoslav Fikejz, Svitavy Museum, Czech Republic.

"The Real Oskar Schindler And His List"
Stepping-Stone to Life

A Reconstruction

By Robin O'Neil

A Publication of JewishGen, INC
Edmond J. Safra Plaza, 36 Battery Place, New York, NY 10280
646.494.5972 | info@JewishGen.org | www.jewishgen.org

The Real Oskar Schindler and His List

About JewishGen.org

JewishGen, an affiliate of the Museum of Jewish Heritage - A Living Memorial to the Holocaust, serves as the global home for Jewish genealogy.

Featuring unparalleled access to 30+ million records, it offers unique search tools, along with opportunities for researchers to connect with others who share similar interests. Award winning resources such as the Family Finder, Discussion Groups, and ViewMate, are relied upon by thousands each day.

In addition, JewishGen's extensive informational, educational and historical offerings, such as the Jewish Communities Database, Yizkor Book translations, InfoFiles, Family Tree of the Jewish People, and KehilaLinks, provide critical insights, first-hand accounts, and context about Jewish communal and familial life throughout the world.

Offered as a free resource, JewishGen.org has facilitated thousands of family connections and success stories, and is currently engaged in an intensive expansion effort that will bring many more records, tools, and resources to its collections.

Please visit https://www.jewishgen.org/ to learn more.

Executive Director: Avraham Groll

About the JewishGen Press

JewishGen Press (formerly the Yizkor Books-in-Print Project) is the publishing division of JewishGen.org, and provides a venue for the publication of non-fiction books pertaining to Jewish genealogy, history, culture, and heritage.

In addition to the Yizkor Book category, publications in the Other Non-Fiction category include Shoah memoirs and research, genealogical research, collections of genealogical and historical materials, biographies, diaries and letters, studies of Jewish experience and cultural life in the past, academic theses, and other books of interest to the Jewish community.

Please visit https://www.jewishgen.org/Yizkor/ybip.html to learn more.

Director of JewishGen Press: Joel Alpert
Managing Editor - Jessica Feinstein
Publications Manager - Susan Rosin

Credits for Book Cover

Front Cover:

Front cover photo courtesy of Rosalia Kornhauser (76335), Raanana, Israel.

Rosalia was interviewed by the author in 1992.

This photograph was widely distributed by Oskar Schindler to the survivors of his Emalia factory.

"The Real Oskar Schindler And His List"

Stepping-Stone to Life

Code names: "Ing. Zeiler", "Osi", "Schäfer", "Otto":
Angehöriger des
"Generalkommandos VIII in Breslau; Abwehr Admiral Canaris"

A Reconstruction
Robin O'Neil

In Memory: My Heroes in the Schindler Story

Viktor Dortheimer[1] 69124

Moshe Bejski[2] 69387

Josef Bau[3] 69084; (d)

Mrs. Rosalia Kornhauser 76335

Photo Credits: Author's Collection

The immediate and extended families of the above Schindler survivors were murdered in the Bełżec death camp and elsewhere.

List of Contents

Introduction

Oskar Schindler was a naive optimist, a chronic alcoholic, a lover of women outside his marriage to Emily Pelzl. The Jews he saved used to say, "Thank God he was more faithful to us than to his wife." Will the enigma ever be solved? Schindler is not here to tell us, and the survivors are uncertain and differ in their opinions. The establishment and Schindler's business associates in Krakow had opposing views of his ethics and would have preferred to sit on the fence and hope the Schindler story would retreat into the archives. Schindler's friends and enemies accept that he was a very unusual man. A few of the Jews that he saved maintain, after all these years, that they still consider him a Nazi and exploiter of Jewish slave labor. Others swear their love for the man. That he used Jewish slave labor to enrich himself is not questioned, nor are his endeavors to eventually save his Jewish laborers.

My introduction to the investigation of the Schindler story began in November 1989, with my arrest by guards at 4, Lipowa Street (Krakowskie Zaklady Elektroniczne 'TELEPOD'), Krakow, the former factory premises (Emalia) of Oskar Schindler. I had left the UK at 7am, and by 10pm, I was locked-up in Polish jail. This was the cold war period during which foreigners travelling in Eastern Europe were eyed with suspicion.

Entering Lipowa Street, Krakow, I was about to take a photograph of Schindler's factory (now the Warsaw Pact communications establishment) but had failed to notice the signs forbidding photography. Surrounded by guards, with a Kalashnikov up my nose, taken first to the central police station in Krakow where I was placed in a room where a photograph of the then Prime Minister (Tadeusz Mazowiecki), was displayed on the wall. Written across the profile of the P.M. in red, was "*Juden*".

After some hours I was escorted to the headquarters of the SIB (Special Investigation Branch) and interrogated for several hours. It was somewhat comical, as, despite all their efforts, they failed to find an interpreter. I had decided not to reveal my knowledge of the Russian language and just sat in the corner smoking my pipe and reading Tom Kenealley's novel *Schindler's Ark*. Eventually common sense prevailed: having examined my camera and film and failing at any point to communicate with me, they kicked me out of the front door.

However, it didn't stop there. I decided to return to the UK via Vienna where I was to report back to Simon Wiesenthal. Everything was fine but at the Czech-Austrian border I was unable to find my return travel visa and was again arrested by border guards and removed from the train to a holding depot where I joined several hundred other misfits for unlawfully entering the Czech Republic. I was sent back to Poland and a frantic search for emergency papers, and tried again, this time with success.

Early in 2008, while escorting a group of Catholic Nuns (from Notting Hill, UK) to Schindler's haunts in Krakow, I met the guard named Mietek, who had arrested me in 1987. Long retired, he was now a security officer at 4, Lipowa Street: housing The Schindler Museum! (On my return to the UK

I complained to the Polish Embassy about P.M. Mazowiecki's disfigured photograph and later received a letter of apology from the Polish Ambassador.)

Chapter One
Early Years 1908-1938

Figure 1: Oskar's parents, Hans and Francizka Luisa
Photo Credit: Aleksander B Skotnicki Collection

Oskar Schindler was born on April 28, 1908,[4] in Svitavy, a Moravian industrial town which, at the time of his birth, was part of the Austro-Hungarian Empire. Many ethnic Germans lived in Svitavy and the surrounding area, the Sudetenland. Oskar's parents, Johann[5] and Francizka,[6] had come to Svitavy from Silesia. Both were German. A sister, Elfriede,[7] born in 1915, was seven years younger than Oskar. The relationship between the two children was good. Oskar's relationship with his mother was, allegedly, also close; nobody, however, seems to know about his early relationship with his father. His father appears to have been a jack-of-all-trades but dealt mainly with farm machinery, traveling the area and plying his trade.[8]

In *Schindler's List,* Keneally draws our attention to the Schindlers' neighbors, one of whom was Dr. Felix Kanter, a liberal rabbi, who had two sons attending the same school as Schindler.[9] By all accounts, the children enjoyed a natural and free upbringing, participating together in the rough and tumble of daily life. Both Jew and Gentile assimilated into the social strata of the community. Keneally states that the Kanter family left Svitavy in the mid-thirties and was not heard from again.[10]

Figure 2: Oskar at three years   Figure 3: Oskar at five years

At the end of World War I, when Schindler was 10 years old, Svitavy became a Czechoslovakian town. Schindler's education took place at the local German grammar school. Expected to continue his father's business, he took the Realgymnasium course, designed to produce practical-based trades of all kinds suitable for the industrial requirements of the area. After being well into completing junior school in Svitavy (November 1925), because of some boyish misdemeanor (cheating in school exams), he was expelled from school and never graduated.[11]

Figure 4: Oskar at 12 years with his sister ElfriedePhoto Credit: Author's collection
Figure 2, 3 and 4 Photo Credit: Aleksander B Skotnicki Collection

In his early to mid-teens, Schindler's physically strong body soon outstripped his parents' efforts to clothe him satisfactorily. From the age of 16, he was renowned for his heavy smoking and frequent visits to the local drinking dens.[12] At 18, he had a heavy build and stood over six feet tall. There followed several brushes with the police. Arrested on several occasions for rowdiness, drinking and assault, he was well-documented with the judiciary.[13]

Figure 5: Oskar at 21 years
Photo Credit: Aleksander B Skotnicki Collection

Women were always to play a big part in the life of Oskar Schindler. By the time he was 19, and before his marriage, he had fathered illegitimate twins,[14] a fact that was not to become known until after his death in 1974. Further information revealed two more children born out of wedlock: on March 20, 1933, his daughter Edith Schlegelova was born from a relationship with her mother, Aurelie Schlegelova (born 1909); on December 20, 1934, a second child was born – a son named Oskar, who has been missing from the records since 1945. This Oskar may be the individual that Keneally met in Australia.[15] His taste in women gravitated towards the older in preference to the younger. He was to carry on his fraternizing with the opposite sex right up to the day of his marriage (and, of course, well after that), with near catastrophic results.

Schindler's main hobbies were anything mechanical. Johann Schindler encouraged his son's natural ability with motorbikes. He showed off his skills by competing in road races at a very high standard on specialized motorcycles. On May 13, 1928, he came in third in a road race in Brno, riding a 250cc Motto-Guzzi.[16]

Schindler's reputation as a gambler, drinker, and womanizer would appear to stem from this point of his development. One observer of Schindler in Svitavy at this time was Ifo Zwicker, a Jew and a resident of the town where Schindler was born and grew up. He knew Schindler well, as he was also with Schindler in the Emalia camp in Krakow. Interviewed some years later, he remarked:

> "As a Svitavy citizen I would never have considered Oskar Schindler capable of all those wonderful deeds. Before the war, everyone in Svitavy called him 'Gauner' (swindler or sharper)."[17]

After leaving full-time education, Schindler worked in the family business in Svitavy; and afterward he commuted to Brno, where he worked for an electrical company as a representative.[18] Bored with this work, he then became the manager of a driving school in the town of Mahren-Schonberg.[19]

It was towards the end of 1927 that Schindler first met Emilie Pelzl, born October 22, 1907, at her parents' house in the village Alt Moletein, in the area of Honeenstadt, northern Moravia, some 60 kilometers to the east of Svitavy. The family had lived in the region since the twelfth century, when they arrived as colonizers.[20] Emilie lived with her parents and her brother Frank in a comfortable farm environment in a middle-class district of the town. The Pelzl family made a good living as farmers trading in wheat, rye, and flax. There was also an orchard with many fruit trees, and they kept horses for riding and for the plough. Emilie Schindler's recollection of her mother was that she was always understanding and sympathetic with a kind word for all. Emilie worked in the family home, for which she was paid. Her love for the country far outweighed her love for her weekly piano lessons, which were compulsory.[21]

As she grew up, she began to notice racial and cultural differences. Even when she was young, she had felt an attraction towards gypsies – their appearance, their freedom, and independent lives. When the gypsies came to the town, she would go out of her way to talk to them and listen to their stories and songs. She could never understand the prejudice against them. Emilie recalls that on one occasion an old gypsy read her fortune: "An extensive life with much pain and suffering. There would be a man who would take me away from Alt Moletein; I would love him but never be happy by his side."[22] Emilie's grandparents lived close by and were a great influence in her upbringing. Her grandmother paid for a dressmaker to dress Emilie and, by all accounts, worried about Emilie's eating habits.

In 1914, when Emilie was seven years old, her father was recruited into the army. After the end of the war when he returned to their farm, he was changed. During his service, he had contracted an incurable case of malaria and developed a heart condition. He was subject to fainting fits without warning. At the age of 40, he was a broken man – ruined. He had returned as one of the many mutilated, maddened, sick, and hungry from a discarded army.

At 14, Emilie attended a convent. She disliked this part of her education. The nuns were unpleasant, the food was awful, and the whole atmosphere was one of disillusionment and regret. Emilie says that the nuns did not understand her. She was a free country spirit now encased in an introverted environment, with no purpose in sight. After one year, Emilie left the convent and continued her education at an agricultural college where she remained for three years. It was the happiest time of her life. Emilie made many friends. One was a young Jewish girl named Rita Goss.[23] Emilie and Rita discussed the racial intolerance that was sweeping the country. Rita Goss was brutally murdered by the commander of the German forces in Alt Moletein during the opening phase of the war.[24]

Emilie's relationship with her brother Frank strengthened because of her father's medical condition and withdrawal from normal life. She talks about finding her brother in the stables smoking a cigarette. He persuaded her to try the cigarette, which she did. They were to share many secrets over the years. One winter night, when she was with Frank out in the woods, she was in danger of passing out from the cold. Frank made a sled and pulled her on it to the safety of home, realizing the danger of hypothermia.

Her mother was now the mainstay of the family upon whom they all depended.[25] That Christmas was one to remember. Emilie marvels at her mother's puddings, with Christmas cake, homemade marmalade, cherry sponge cake, and her grandmother's huge goose full of apples and plums. This was the life of the well brought-up country girl of Alt Moletein.

She recalled:

> "Infancy and old age seem similar. When we are young, we perceive with an innocent eye; when we are old, we forgive without indulgent spirit. Old age is a second innocence, and our memories are simply shadows, allowing us to perceive a contented reality. The images of my countryside childhood are forever in my mind, but that idyllic image would soon be torn by war and by the arrival of a man who would take me away and share with me a life of happiness and misfortune."

It was a business trip for Oskar, accompanying his father to the Pelzl household to sell electrical equipment to Josef Pelzl. On that day, Emilie observed the two men as they spoke to her father: one, over 50, tall and well-built. The other, young, slim, with wide shoulders, blonde hair and blue eyes. On subsequent visits, Oskar paid a little more than casual attention to this young beauty. The business calls accelerated over the next few weeks; there was a flirtatious whirlwind courtship with a momentum of its own. Three months later, on March 6, 1928,[26] against the wishes of both families, they were married. Emilie Schindler says:

> "My father was ill and bad-tempered; my grandmother was suffering from old age, and my mother progressively tired by overwork. I was prepared to believe in words and emotions, and the protection his wide shoulders offered me. Now, I believe I would act differently."[27]

On the very day of the wedding, there was a disaster. The local police had received anonymous information that Schindler was already married. He was arrested and detained in the Svitavy police cells so that inquiries could be made. It transpired that Schindler had been cohabiting with a much older woman for three years, a fact that he denied to his new wife, Emilie. The allegation of bigamy was malicious, but the facts were correct and caused Emilie much heartache. She never forgave him.[28]

Figure 6: Marriage: Svitavy 1928
Photo Credit: Aleksander B Skotnicki Collection

After the wedding, the newly married couple moved into Oskar's parents' house at 24 Iglaustrasse, where they occupied the upper part of the house. Emilie was never happy with this situation and was in constant argument with Johann Schindler, whom she describes as an uneducated man who came home drunk on many occasions. She was kinder about Mrs. Francizka (Fanny) Schindler, who she says was a very elegant woman, but always ill. Elfriede Schindler (Oskar's sister), then 13 years old, was described by Emilie as looking like Johann: ugly, with chestnut hair and large brown eyes. Despite all this, Emilie helped Elfriede with her homework and generally made allowances for her.

One of the highlights of Emilie's early marriage was traveling to Prague on an errand for her husband. She was overwhelmed with the architecture and scenery surrounding Prague. Thereafter, everything declined. Her marriage was collapsing, and she became sadder and more disillusioned with life. Old man Pelzl had given Oskar 100,000 Czech Crowns, a considerable sum of money. Despite old man Pelzl's attempt to safeguard the dowry, Schindler bought a car and squandered the rest in the bars and clubs of Ostrava and Svitavy. Emilie challenged him over this waste, for which Oskar would ask forgiveness like a child who knew he had been caught in the act. Emilie, although very annoyed about her husband's stupidity and deceit, still thought of him as an affable, benevolent, magnanimous, and charitable person. She put his behavior down to the fact that he was spoiled by his mother because of the constant absence of his father. Her days were spent in domestic isolation. Schindler was without doubt a scatterbrain, an impulsive liar, and a playboy of immense charm.

Emilie led a comparatively sheltered life. She was a quiet convent-schooled girl but endowed with personality and humor. She was a well-educated young lady who spoke very directly and a woman of devout faith who attended mass twice a day.

She may well have been under the aura of her flamboyant husband, but she was subsequently never to be deceived again. However, throughout the tumultuous years ahead she would never hear a bad word against him and she remained loyal and supportive to the end. The marriage, as everyone had predicted, was one that Oskar would never quite adjust to. After a brief period of harmony, he reverted to the ways of a single man. Despite all this, the couple remained more or less together until their final separation well after the war.[29]

By the end of 1928, we find Schindler conscripted for military service in the Czechoslovakian army, where he served for 18 months.

Figure 7: Schindler in the uniform of the Czechoslovakian army in 1935
Photo Credit: Photo Credit: Aleksander B Skotnicki Collection

After completing his service, he returned to his old job in the electronics company M.E.A.S. in Brno. The economic climate had changed, and the company went into liquidation in 1931. The Schindler family business was also in financial trouble and that, too, went bankrupt in 1933.[30] Schindler went out on his own, running a poultry farm in the village of Ctyricetlanu, but gave up after six months, unable to make any money. After a short period of unemployment, Schindler worked in Prague at the Yaroslav Chemnitz Bank. His last period of serious employment was as a representative for the company Opodni Ustev, 30 Veveri Street, Brno, earning between 6,000 and 10,000 Crowns a month.

In 1935, Johann Schindler left his wife Franczika and the marriage collapsed, leaving the family in turmoil. A short time later Franczika Schindler died, resulting in further recriminations and splits in the family. By this time, Oskar had completely fallen out with his immediate family. He was not to see his father again until well into the war. He had only one other relative, an uncle named Adolph Luser, who had a publishing house in Vienna, whom he hadn't seen since 1929.[31]

Oskar, the reluctant husband, spurned Emilie and turned to other familiar pastures and into the web of espionage and treason.

**Figure 8: Emilie: Svitavy 1929   Figure 9: Emilie: Poland 1940
Photo Credit: Photo Credit: Aleksander B Skotnicki Collection**

**Figure 10: Oskar Schindler (at the wheel) Svitavy 1928
Photo Credit: Aleksander B Skotnicki Collection**

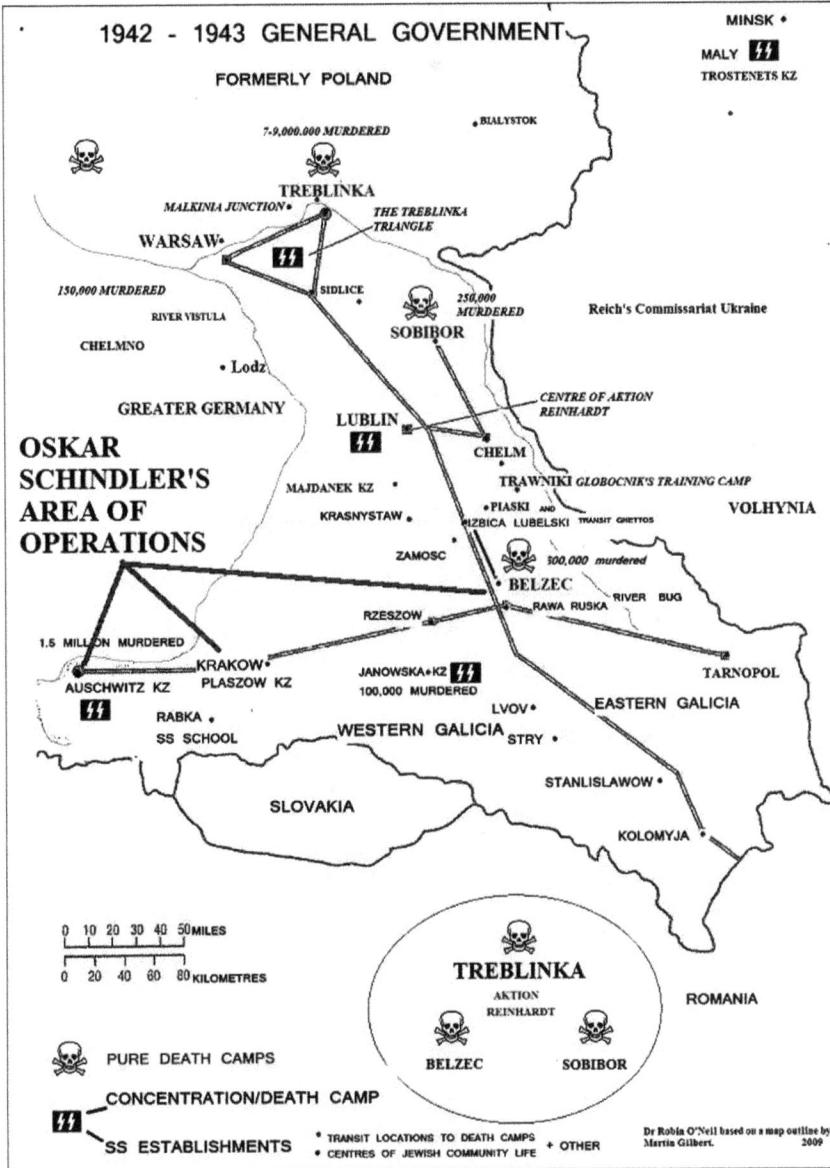

1942 - 1943 GENERAL GOVERNMENT

FORMERLY POLAND

MINSK •

MALY [SS] TROSTENETS KZ •

7-9,000,000 MURDERED

• BIALYSTOK

TREBLINKA

MALKINIA JUNCTION •

THE TREBLINKA TRIANGLE

WARSAW•

[SS]

150,000 MURDERED

SIDLICE

RIVER VISTULA

250,000 MURDERED

SOBIBOR

Reich's Commissariat Ukraine

CHELMNO

• Lodz

GREATER GERMANY

LUBLIN [SS]

CENTRE OF AKTION REINHARDT

CHELM

OSKAR SCHINDLER'S AREA OF OPERATIONS

MAJDANEK KZ •

TRAWNIKI GLOBOCNIK'S TRAINING CAMP

KRASNYSTAW •

• PIASKI AND IZBICA LUBELSKI TRANSIT GHETTOS

VOLHYNIA

ZAMOSC

500,000 murdered

• BELZEC

RIVER BUG

RZESZOW •

RAWA RUSKA

1.5 MILLION MURDERED

KRAKOW•

PLASZOW KZ

JANOWSKA•KZ [SS] 100,000 MURDERED

TARNOPOL

AUSCHWITZ KZ

[SS]

LVOV •

EASTERN GALICIA

RABKA •

SS SCHOOL

WESTERN GALICIA STRY •

STANLISLAWOW •

SLOVAKIA

KOLOMYJA •

0 10 20 30 40 50 MILES

0 20 40 60 80 KILOMETRES

TREBLINKA

AKTION REINHARDT

ROMANIA

BELZEC

SOBIBOR

[skull] PURE DEATH CAMPS

CONCENTRATION/DEATH CAMP

[SS] SS ESTABLISHMENTS

• TRANSIT LOCATIONS TO DEATH CAMPS

• CENTRES OF JEWISH COMMUNITY LIFE

+ OTHER

Dr Robin O'Neil based on a map outline by Martin Gilbert. 2009

Figure 11: General Government District
Photo Credit: Author's Collection

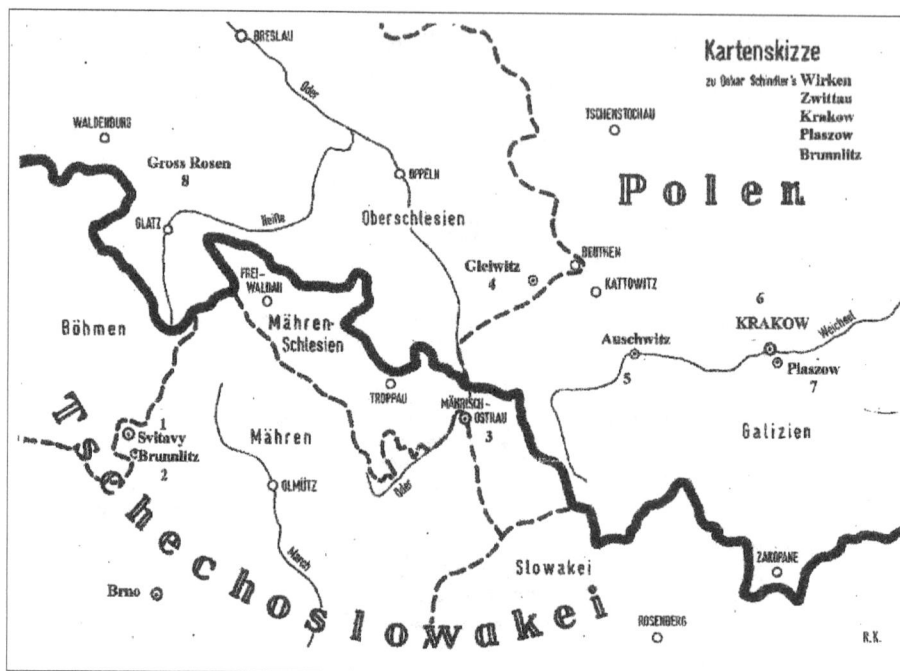

Figure 12: Schindler's area of wartime activity

Photo Credit: Author's Collection

1. Svitavy/Zwittau: Schindler's hometown
2. Brünnlitz: Schindler's factory
3. Mährisch-Ostrau: Schindler's Abwehr HQ.
4. Gleiwitz: Location that set off the Second World War
5. Auschwitz: Concentration/death camp
6. Krakow
7. Plaszow: Amon Goeth's Concentration Camp
8. Gross-Rosen Concentration Camp

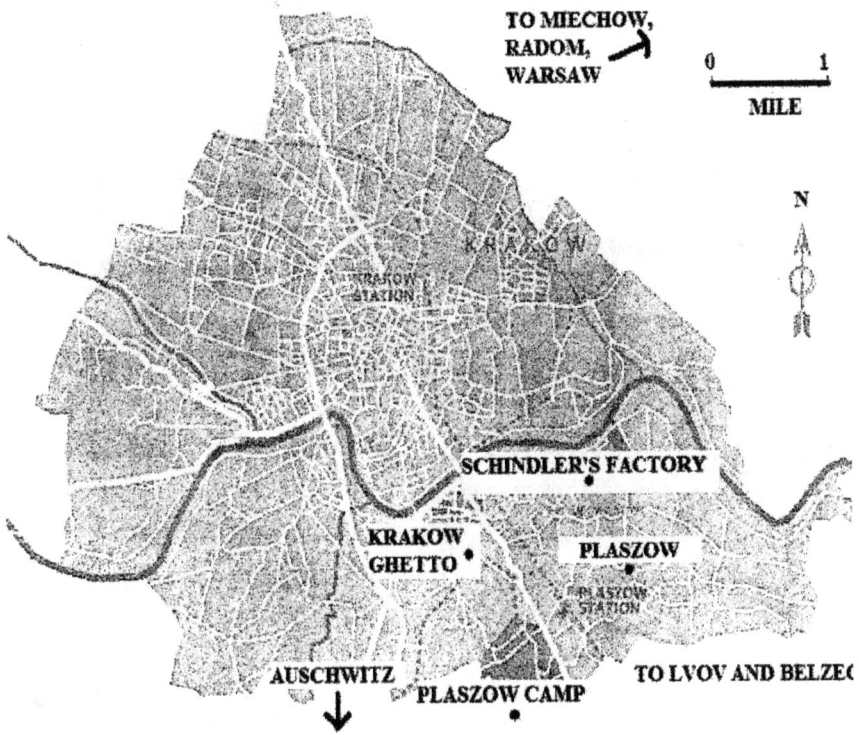

Figure 13: Schindler's Krakow
Photo Credit: Author's Collection

Chapter Two

Recruited into the Abwehr

Figure 14: Oskar and Emilie, agents of the Abwehr
Photo Credit: Svitavy Museum Collection

There are gaps in Keneally's book that have, in my opinion, resulted in a slight ambiguity, particularly regarding Schindler's dealings with the Abwehr in the period 1938-39. My purpose is to bring the events back on course and, where necessary, provide sources for the material already researched by Keneally. I will enhance the evidence from my own inquiries to ensure a clearer understanding of the man himself.

It was during this opening barrage of German military expansion that we come to the opening phase of Schindler's wartime activities, his recruitment into the Abwehr. Keneally touches on these activities, Spielberg implies them, and Steinhouse was not aware of them. Other writers and filmmakers who have worked with the Schindler story have relied on one basic source for their information – the novel and film, *Schindler's List.*

In 1935, the German intelligence agencies were collaborating with the security offices from Austria and Hungary. Czechoslovakia and Poland were high on the agenda for political infiltration, and it was at this time that Schindler became active and a spy for the Third Reich.

One of Schindler's first contacts with the Abwehr web of agents was on a business trip to Krakow when he met the Jew Simon Jeret (69506), the owner of a timber company in Zablocie. Jeret had introduced him to Amelia, a fellow agent of German Counterintelligence. Schindler and Jeret were to remain friends throughout the war and well into the peace. After the war Jeret became one of the closest friends of Oskar Schindler.

On June 24, 1937, Hitler signed the plan *Fall Grün* (Case Green – a preparation for war directive). Upon receiving the order, Canaris instigated a web of coordinated actions to penetrate Czechoslovakian security in Moravia, Bohemia, and the Sudetenland border areas.

The winter of 1936-37 was, for Schindler, the moment from which everything would radiate. The past would become insignificant and the future uncertain. New Year celebrations in 1937, in a select hotel in the suburbs of Berlin, would bring the unemployed and frustrated man from Svitavy face-to-face with the top echelon of the Wehrmacht Military Intelligence and with his own personal destiny.

It began in late December 1936, when, by chance, Schindler met an old girlfriend, Ilse Pelikan, whom he had known when he was a driving instructor in Mahrisch Schonberg. Ilse invited Schindler to a New Year's celebration to meet friends whom she identified as high-ranking officers of the German Wehrmacht.[32] We can only speculate what went on at this New Year's party, but knowing the character of Schindler and his love for pretty women and a good time, it is not difficult to imagine that towards the end of the celebrations he would have been at the center of things and by then known to all as "Oskar." The opening of Spielberg's film, *Schindler's List,* shows the easygoing Schindler mixing with high-ranking SS and Wehrmacht officers.[33]

According to Mrs. Sophia Stern, after the war, Schindler told her husband, Itzhak, that it was at this New Year's party that he had been introduced to a man very high up in German Intelligence Services, who was celebrating his fiftieth birthday and the second anniversary of his appointment as the Chief of the Abwehr. This man was probably Wilhelm Canaris.[34] When Schindler was in trouble with the SS in Krakow, it was the Canaris factor that afforded him immediate release.

Schindler's immediate acceptance by this elite company indicated to him what was to follow. Ilse Pelikan, knowing Schindler to be one of those committed Germans awaiting deliverance by the Führer, had invited him to work for the "better good of Greater Germany." Schindler knew he was being propositioned to become a gatherer of intelligence.[35] A few days later Schindler returned to Svitavy, dismissing his night out with Pelikan as just another good night out. Whatever Schindler thought of this offer can only be considered in the light of his subsequent actions.[36]

Figure 15: Schindler's boss: Wilhelm Franz Canaris
January 1, 1887-April 9, 1945
Photo Credit: Svitavy Museum Collection

Many months later, Schindler was to meet another lady from a previous friendship, Gritt Schwarzer, and hotelier in Rumberg, a village just inside the Czech border. Schindler had been closely involved with Schwarzer (just as with Pelikan) some years previously and was surprised to receive a letter from her. Schwarzer suggested they meet for old time's sake, and suggested the Juppebad Hotel at Ziegenhals, which required crossing of the Czech/German border. When Schindler said there would be difficulties because of security documentation, he was assured that it had been taken care of. He was about to be recruited into the Intelligence Services, the Abwehr.[37]

The political situation in Europe[38] was at boiling point. In March 1938, Hitler marched into Austria[39] to the welcome and open arms of the population. All eyes now turned to Czechoslovakia. Czechoslovakia was a state of nationalities, not a national state. Only the Czechs were genuine Czechoslovaks; the others were Slovaks, Hungarians, Ruthenes, and Germans, all national minorities. The three million Germans, Sudeten Germans, were closely linked to the Austrians by history and blood. The Anschluss had stirred them to ungovernable excitement. Hitler was threatening to liberate the German minority in Czechoslovakia and the German minority was beckoning him to do so.[40]

On March 28, 1938, Hitler received the Sudeten representatives and appointed Konrad Henlein, their leader, as his viceroy. They were to negotiate with the Czechoslovakian government. In Henlein's words, "We must always demand so much that we can never be satisfied."[41] Henlein's party was to be a third force in the politics of the country and would remain legal and orderly, preying on the disaffection of the German populace.

Schindler, like many of the Sudeten Germans, joined up with the party that promised plenty. He now worked as a salesman for his old employers, the Electrical Company in Brno, and moved about the area securing business from like-minded sympathizers of the New Order.[42]

Hitler had his eyes on Czechoslovakia, and the world that was watching seemed unable to deal with the situation. The momentum of German expansionism was unstoppable and Jews who had fled Germany and Austria to the safety of Czechoslovakia trembled and prayed to the Almighty.

Schindler's Abwehr activities can be divided into two distinct phases: first, his initial engagement on July 2, 1938; second, his activities in the Svitavy and Brno areas. This period was catastrophic for him, resulting in his arrest and death sentence. The second phase deals with his release from prison brought about by Hitler's takeover of Czechoslovakia in March 1939, when all political prisoners were released.

On July 1, 1938, Schindler set off from Svitavy for the Czech/German border to meet Gritt Schwarzer at the Hotel Juppebad. Despite assurances from Schwarzer, he was unable to cross the frontier without papers and sought the assistance of a local publican named Folkel. That night, Folkel showed Schindler the route across the border to avoid the German customs post. The crossing went via the rear of the local church, across fields and into Germany. Schindler telephoned Gritt Schwarzer at the Hotel Juppebad[43] and she arranged transport for him to the hotel. There he met Peter Kreutziger, an agent of the Abwehr, who opened up a docket on the table and addressed Schindler. He said, "Do you want to join us, the German Information Service?" The driving instructor and poultry keeper from Svitavy, lured by the money, power, and other promises well beyond his dreams, agreed to join.

Schindler must have been one of the ineptest spies recruited by the Abwehr. By July 18, 1938, he had been arrested and charged with capital offenses against the Czech State.[44] Schindler had made some very basic mistakes. His assignment was to obtain political and economic information that would be of use to the Wehrmacht: railway installations, fortifications, and troop movements on the Czech/Polish border around Ostrava. He was to contact like-minded sympathizers and use these contacts to obtain information. Results of his activities were to be filtered back via Gritt Schwarzer at the Hotel Juppebad.[45]

Schindler's first mistake was that he didn't move out of his immediate home area. He lived in Svitavy and worked in Brno. He was well-known to everyone, including the police. The naive Schindler approached his first assignment by recruiting a Sudeten German police officer named Prusa. Prusa worked for the Criminal Investigation Department in Brno and was an alcoholic, in debt, and separated from his wife. After several days, Prusa agreed to join Schindler. Abwehr Agent Kreutziger, Schindler, and Prusa traveled the area looking at likely targets for closer inspection.[46] Unknown to Schindler, Prusa had reported the facts to his superiors, which resulted in the Czech Security Service monitoring Schindler's activities. Schindler was set up, and on the evening of July 18, 1938, at the Hotel Ungar in Svitavy, Schindler and Prusa met in the bar of the hotel. During Prusa handing over material to Schindler, the Security Service arrested him. Schindler was taken to the Svitavy police station and on the following morning transferred in custody to Brno for interrogation.[47]

Figure 16: Hotel Ungar (now Hotel Slavia) where Schindler was arrested
Photo Credit: Svitavy Museum Collection

Immediately, the CSO[48] raided the Schindler home and searched for other incriminating evidence. Mrs. Schindler stated that the police returned on several occasions but were unable to find anything. Then, according to Mrs. Schindler, the police returned and went directly into the bathroom where, from behind a bathroom panel, they found plans of Czech military establishments.[49] Schindler made a deal whereby, cooperating with the CSO, he would receive certain considerations. It was apparent that he was under a great deal of pressure to cooperate. The CSO threatened to arrest his wife and father unless he cooperated fully. This he apparently did.[50]

Emilie Schindler contacted Kreutziger. He was aware of the arrest but declined to help. In August 1938, Schindler appeared before the court in Brno and pleaded guilty to offenses of betrayal against the State. He was sentenced to death. (The warrant and conviction of Schindler were never rescinded and attempts immediately after the war to arrest him were considered a priority. This is the reason he never returned to his hometown, Svitavy.)

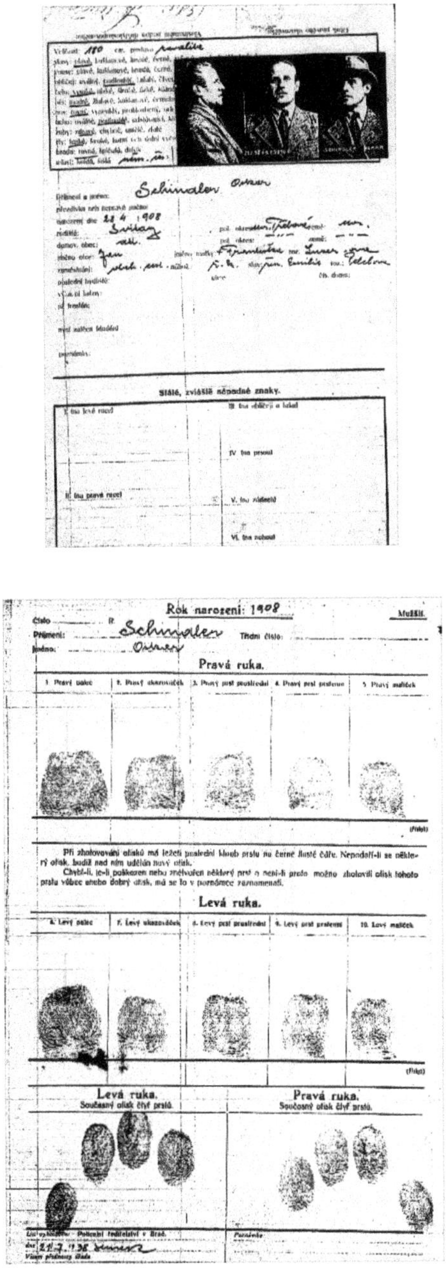

Schindler Oskar

Stálé, zvláště nápadné znaky.

Rok narození: 1908

Mužští

Příjmení: Schindler

Jméno: Oskar

Pravá ruka.

Levá ruka.

Levá ruka.
Současný otisk čtyř prstů.

Pravá ruka.
Současný otisk čtyř prstů.

Figure 17: Schindler's arrest documentation, Brno 1938

Photo Credit: Svitavy Museum Collection

In October 1938, Germany moved into the Sudetenland and all political prisoners were released. Having escaped the hangman, Schindler resumed his duties and was promoted to deputy commandant of the *Abwehr* in Moravska Ostrava on the Czech/Polish border.

After being released from prison, Oskar Schindler spent a short amount of time in his native Svitavy. Schindler was then ordered to relocate to Moravska Ostrava, where he took up residence in a flat on Sadova St. (Parkstraße). Along with Emilie, Schindler continued his work for the Abwehr, though this time with different assignments.

We now move into the second phase of his Abwehr activities, which encompass facts hitherto unknown. This period also clarifies the work of Schindler and the roles of Mrs. Schindler and Josef Aue.[51]

Chapter Three
Prelude to War

OSKAR SCHINDLER: STEPPING STONE TO LIFE

Figure 18: Oskar Schindler Krakow 1940[52]
Photo Credit: Svitavy Museum Collection

The Abwehr building in Moravska Ostrava[53] shared offices with sections of the Gestapo, SD, and Kripo. Karel Gassner was head of the Abwehr in Moravska Ostrava, with Schindler as his deputy. Schindler's team members in the field were Alois Girzicky, Ervin Kobiela, Hildegarde Hoheitcva, and Hans Vicherek, all of whom were engaged in collecting and assessing information from a number of sources with sub-agents acting on their behalf on the Polish border.[54]

When Emilie Schindler was asked whether her husband was a Nazi, she gave this reply:

> "My husband was not at all a Nazi. He had nothing to do with the SS; he worked for the Wehrmacht, for the German military. It had nothing to do with the Nazis. He had to join; otherwise, he could not have existed and lived at all. He never performed any function for the Nazis. He was directly under the protection of the German Wehrmacht, not the SS."[55]

Mrs. Schindler cannot be criticized for misunderstanding the question. She has always accepted that her husband was a member of the NSDAP (Nazi Party). Her problem was that in her understanding, Nazi was synonymous with SS (Shutztaffeln). But Mrs. Schindler was correct when she said, "He was directly under the protection of the German Wehrmacht."[56]

Schindler took his counter-intelligence work seriously. According to a memoir by Mrs. Schindler, her husband brought three cages of pigeons home to their flat in Moravska Ostrava to be used for carrying messages. He installed them in the loft and his wife was expected to feed and clean them daily. Schindler, characteristically, soon lost interest in this new venture and Mrs. Schindler, tired of looking after them, resorted to desperate measures; she opened the cages and allowed the pigeons to fly away. Much to her dismay, the pigeons returned to the roof of their apartment (as they do!) and she was soon getting complaints from neighbors.[57]

The Schindlers' apartment in Moravska Ostrava was run by their housekeeper, Viktorka, an excellent cook and loyal servant. Emilie recalls that at a dinner party at the apartment, an impeccably dressed high-ranking officer of the Wehrmacht arrived. He slowly took off his gloves, hat, and overcoat, and was shown into the living room, where he occupied a plush green velvet chair. Emilie's husband and the officer were engrossed in political talk most of the evening. Suddenly, the officer stood and toasted the Führer, and proceeded to throw one of Emilie's best crystal wine glasses against the piano, breaking it into many pieces. Emilie castigated the officer and chalked up her first act of defiance against the Third Reich.[58]

It is important to clarify the relationship between some of these departments and, in particular, the personal relationship between the Chief of the German Security Police (the SD), Richard Heydrich, and Wilhelm Canaris. From his headquarters,[59] Heydrich concentrated his efforts on those whom he considered to be the State's dangerous potential enemies: those within the Party and the police.

Heydrich forged a working relationship with his old acquaintance, Admiral Wilhelm Canaris, head of the Abwehr. Heydrich was convinced that within the Abwehr there were "reactionaries" – men with old ideas and attitudes who would need watching. But as the SD and the Abwehr were in the same business, they had to get along because a good working relationship was essential.

Although a professed National Socialist, Canaris was known to dislike the cruder excesses of the Nazis and was not reluctant to say so. In short, Heydrich and Canaris did not get on. Each was suspicious of the other and protective of his own power bases. An intermediary[60] was brought in, resulting in an agreement based on what has since become known as the "Ten Commandments." In essence, the document drew a line between the rival intelligence agencies of the Wehrmacht (Abwehr) and the SS. This uneasy truce shielded Canaris from interference by the SS and established the Abwehr's predominant role in espionage and counterespionage.[61]

It was Shindler's contact with Canaris that sent Oskar to Dachau concentration camp in the spring of 1939 where he observed the persecuted Jewish women and children. That experience opened his eyes and he decided that he had to find a way out for his Jewish friends.

"I felt obliged towards all my school mates with whom I had spent a wonderful youth time without racial problems."[62]

I believe that Canaris was crucial to the future activities of Schindler. Canaris surrounded himself with like-minded men with a commitment to the cause, but who opposed the excesses of racial persecution engineered by Heydrich and the SS. Canaris was Schindler's insurance and ace card which he used later in the war when he was in trouble.

Also living in Moravska Ostrava was an unemployed half-Jew named Josef Aue.[63] Brought up as a German-speaking Czech, he was now earning his living buying and selling Polish money. His main area of business was with the Jews who were leaving the country. Aue's main source of money changing was Mrs. Bohdanova, who owned a fur shop in Tesin, in the suburbs of Moravska Ostrava. Through Bohdanova, Aue was introduced to a man named Ing-Zeiler.[64] Zeiler told Aue that he was from the police and was aware of his money-changing activities. Zeiler pointed out that Aue was breaking the currency laws and could go to prison, but then suggested an alternative arrangement. Aue should work for him, to collect intelligence on the Polish border. Zeiler impressed upon Aue that it was his duty as a true German to comply with his instructions. Aue agreed.[65]

Josef Aue's first assignment was to travel to the area around Bohumin and gather reports of military activity by Polish soldiers and reports about the installation of fortifications. Aue made a complete mess of his assignment. He couldn't read the maps Zeiler had given him, so he made up a story and when he met Zeiler the following day in the Café Plaza he gave him false information. Zeiler was now aware that Aue was not capable of this type of work and suggested that he would find other work for him. For some months Aue disappeared from the scene and was not to re-establish contact with Zeiler until October 1939.[66]

Zeiler was, in fact, Oskar Schindler.[67] Aue was not to know this until after the invasion of Poland when he traveled to Krakow with Schindler. From archive material, we know that Schindler also used the cover names of Osi, Schäfer, and Otto.

The German High Command had opted for the invasion of Poland, but before this could be carried out, some pretext was necessary. This was conceived in the crudest melodramatic terms and was the work of Himmler's SS and Heydrich's SD.[68] Operation Himmler was launched by Heydrich, who summoned to Prinz Albrechtstrasse one of his highly trusted associates, a veteran street brawler from Kiel named Alfred Helmuth Naujocks. Naujocks had joined the SD in 1934 and held the rank of SS-Sturmbannführer. Five years later, Naujocks had become head of a sub-section of Section III of SD-Ausland under the control of SS-Oberführer Heinz Jost and became involved with the fabrication of documents for agents working abroad.[69]

The events leading to the invasion of Poland were outlined by Naujocks at the Nuremberg trials after the war. His task, he was told by Heydrich, was to make a staged attack on the German radio station at Gleiwitz in Upper

Silesia near the Polish border. The incident had to appear as an act of aggression committed against the station by a force of Poles. Documentary proof of Polish aggression would be made available along with German convicts decked out in Polish uniforms. The man who was to supply the necessary equipment for this operation was Schindler.[70]

Mrs. Schindler noted:

> "The following is an example of the activities we had gotten involved in. A Polish soldier was paid to get a Polish army uniform. It was then sent to Germany to serve as a pattern for manufacturing more Polish uniforms that spies of the Third Reich would wear as camouflage. When Germany invaded Poland, the SS were wearing these uniforms in the attack on the radio station but then blamed the Polish resistance for acts of sabotage."[71]

Schindler's apartment was filling up with large cardboard boxes: uniforms, weapons, identity cards, and even Polish cigarettes were being assembled. According to Mrs. Schindler, who was privy to her husband's activities, their greatest problem was with the Polish Counter-Intelligence Services, who were paying attention to their apartment.[72]

The role of the Gestapo emerged when Naujocks was ordered to Oppelin, a small Silesian town forty miles north of Gleiwitz. There, Heinrich Müller (Heydrich's SS representative) and SS-Oberführer Herbert Mehlhorn explained that the Gestapo had been ordered by Heydrich to provide a commodity referred to as Konserven (canned goods). The commodity in question turned out to be a dozen prisoners who were under sentences of death in concentration camps but who had been identified by Müller as expendable in the interests of the Third Reich.

At Nuremberg, Naujocks testified:

> "Müller declared that he had 12 or 13 condemned criminals who would be dressed in Polish uniforms and left for dead on the spot to show that they had been killed in the course of the attack. To this end, they had to be given fatal injections by a doctor in Heydrich's service. Later they would also be given genuine wounds inflicted by firearms. After the incident, members of the foreign press and other persons were to be taken to the spot. A police report would then be made. Müller told me that he had an order from Heydrich telling him to put one of these criminals at my disposal for the Gleiwitz Action."[73]

> The criminal in question, a Pole, was anesthetized and brought to the radio station, where he was then shot. The body was photographed on the spot for the benefit of the press. The attack on the station then went ahead. A Polish-speaking member of Naujocks' team broke into a broadcast in accented German and said: 'This is the Polish rebel force radio station: Gleiwitz is in our hands. The hour of freedom has struck!'" [74]

Müller had pretended to his Polish-uniformed prisoners in "canned goods" (code name for the operation) that they were taking part in a film and that, in exchange for their patriotic participation in the action, they would be pardoned and set free. The radio station secured, Naujocks and his men promptly retired. The dead bodies of the conscript actors were left on the scene. They were not the only witnesses to be disposed of, which goes some way in explaining why details of the affair did not leak out. All participating members of the SD, with the exception of Naujocks, were liquidated.[75] The entire affair was a source of immense satisfaction to the Berlin SS Mandarins. This was a highly successful operation between the SD and the Gestapo, as well with Canaris' Abwehr, represented by Schindler and his team.[76]

Hitler's plan to invade Poland was disguised by the code words *Fall Weiss*. At 4:45 a.m. on September 1, 1939, the war began. By September 6, Krakow was occupied by German units belonging to the 14th army of the Wehrmacht. General Sigmund List had secured the city, despite fierce opposition from the Polish forces.

On October 17, 1939,[77] Josef Aue, who had been avoiding Zeiler, met him by chance in a street in Moravska Ostrava. Zeiler invited Aue back to the Café Royal to talk about possible work. There, Zeiler introduced Aue to his Abwehr associates that included his present woman friend, a Pole named Marta.[78] Both Schindler and Aue witnessed the rounding up of Jews in the city and then watched them being marched to the railway station. The Jews were being deported by train to the Lublin region of Poland, an area initiated by the Nazis' Jewish resettlement policy. That same day the Abwehr in Moravska Ostrava was transferred to Krakow.

Reflections:

Before moving on to the greater part of this documentation, I will reflect on the facts and circumstances surrounding Schindler during this period. So far, what does the information tell us about the man – his personality, his judgment, and commitment to the Nazi Party? I will disregard his letter to Dr. Ball-Kaduri and deal with his motives and actions considering what was happening at the time.

From his early teens, Schindler was a flamboyant personality. He was a drinker, gambler, and womanizer. He was both sensitive and impulsive. He suffered a double blow when his mother died. Not only did he lose her, he also lost his father because of a massive row. In effect, when he was 28, he had lost both parents. Schindler lost his inheritance because of the economic climate and, for the first time in his life, he was without insurance. His marriage to Emilie Pelzl proved a mistake. He had reverted to the ways of a single man living in bars and clubs, reflecting on what might have been. His immoral nature, in the end, saved him and set him on course, albeit with a few disasters along the way.

His initial Abwehr experience exposed his character as naive, inept, and impulsive. Schindler was a quick learner and, by the time he had been released from prison, his persona was well equipped for his new posting. The political circumstances at the time allowed him a second chance. Schindler was well thought of by his superiors. He spoke German, Czech, Polish, and some Yiddish. He represented the Abwehr at secret meetings and acted as interpreter for senior ranks. He was considered a bold and capable informer with the result that he was privy to the most delicate and secret war decisions of the Reich.

What Schindler knew about the policies of Nazi Germany at that time is uncertain, but I conclude that Schindler's patriotism was in no way influenced by the Nazi racial ideology. For Schindler there was no "Jewish question." He was a member of the Nazi Party,[79] joining the movement on February 10, 1938.[80] He worked to support the war on behalf of his superiors.

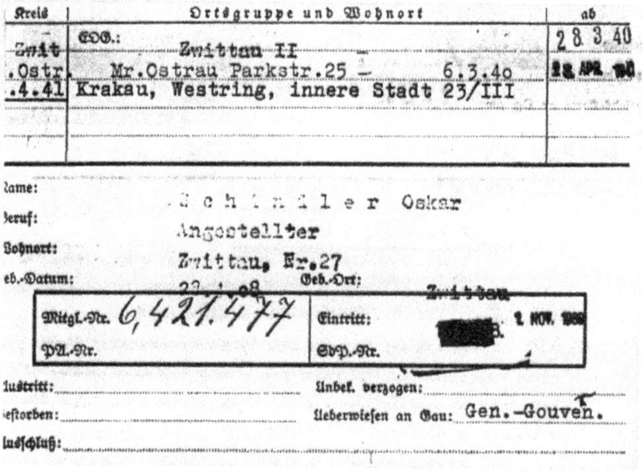

Figure 19: Schindler's Nazi membership card with address

Photo Credit: Svitavy Museum Collection

In my view, the crucial point was that Oskar Schindler was non-racial and a man of independent mind and would remain so throughout the duration of the war. Herbert Steinhouse sums it up by quoting from a letter he received from one of the Kanter boys (Schindler's Jewish neighbors in pre-war Svitavy) just after the war:

> "He was a Sudetenland fascist and a member of the Henlein Party which was later absorbed into the Greater Germany's Nazi Party. Schindler was a true believer in everything but one factor – that was the racial policy. He was a friend of many local Jews in Svitavy. Schindler was friendly with our family, particularly with my father the Rabbi. He would have talks with my father about sophisticated Yiddish literature in Poland and Czechoslovakia, about folk tales and the mythology and the

anecdotes and the ancient Jewish traditions of the villages of Eastern Poland and Moldova. And what all that showed, of course, was unlike the portrait painted later by the Spielberg film."

The Gleiwitz operation was acceptable to Schindler. It was all part of the prosecution of the war strategies. But had the deportation of the Jews from Moravska Ostrava raised a doubt in his mind? We will see how Schindler reacts when he is confronted with the reality of the German occupation in Krakow and the bloody work of SS-Hauptsturmführer Amon Goeth and the SS.

Chapter Four
Schindler in Krakow

Figure 20: Oskar Schindler: Krakow 1941
Photo Credit: Svitavy Museum Collection

Political Maneuverings

Within just one month of the German occupation, an independent Poland ceased to exist. On October 12, 1939, the General Government, with Krakow as its capital, was established. In the old Krakow Royal Palace, the Wawel, government meetings of the "New Order" headed by Governor Dr. Hans Frank,[81] were held.

The regional network of the General Government administration closely paralleled the regional machinery in the Reich. There were four District Governments in Poland in 1939.[82] The Governor of the Krakow District was SS-Brigadeführer Dr. Otto Wächter.[83]

Heading the Police Security apparatus in the General Government was Higher SS and Police Leader SS-Obergruppenführer Frederick Wilhelm Krüger.[84] The RSHA, now under their new security umbrella, worked out of 2 Pomorska Street, Krakow. SS Chief of Operations was SS-Oberführer Scherna; and SD Chief of Operation was SS-Obersturmführer Ralph Czurda. The Abwehr's local commander was Lieutenant Martin Plathe. SS security services were very much their own masters working out of their offices in Katowice, Oprava, and Breslau. The old rivalries among the SS, SD, Gestapo, and the Abwehr continued despite the act of agreement of the Ten Commandments. The Mayor of Krakow currently was SS-Obersturmbannführer Pavlu and his deputy, Sepp Rohrl.

We arrive at a very important juncture that I would call the "where loyalties lie" point. The questions I would like to pose are these: Was Schindler still an agent of the Abwehr in 1939-40, and if he was, what was he doing buying up the Emalia factory? Why hadn't Schindler been transferred to other duties once Krakow was secured? To find the answers to these questions I think we must look back over the role that Canaris was playing within the German High Command. All the evidence shows that there was a certain faction of the German High Command that was against Hitler. To the likes of Canaris the SS, SD, and Gestapo were an anathema. Despite the patching up of their differences in the past, the personal rivalry between Heydrich and Canaris festered again without respite, each more suspicious of the other. The patching over of old disagreements had now collapsed into open warfare.

Since 1938, Heydrich kept a secret file on Canaris, named "Schwarze Kapelle" (Black Orchestra).[85] This file contained incriminating evidence against Canaris regarding his suspected disloyalty to the State. Heydrich had been reluctant to use the material, fearing a collapse in confidence within the armed services. The file gathered weight over the years and was eventually used to bring down Canaris in 1944 after the attempt on Hitler's life and as we shall see later, Canaris was executed and the Abwehr dissolved. The residue of the Abwehr was swallowed up in the elephantine structure of the RSHA.

To answer my own questions about Schindler, I am inclined to agree with Keneally: Schindler was deliberately placed in Krakow by Canaris as a "spy on the wall," to watch over the SS, SD, and Gestapo, and to filter reports back to Canaris' headquarters. Canaris was a very powerful man, and this would explain how Schindler was able extricate himself from the various situations he found himself in when the Gestapo arrested him on no less than three occasions. Schindler had a trusted procedure that went into effect the moment danger loomed.[86] Within hours of a cry for help, Schindler would benefit from the full force of his backers. The local SS chiefs were unable to resist the commanding orders.

What of the Jews in Krakow at the End of 1939?

A decree dated November 11, 1939, concerning the Judenrat in the General Government, was issued by the governor, Dr. Hans Frank. It set out the regulations for the formulation of the Judenrat and the appointment of an Elder of the Jews. There followed an explosion of edicts under the pen of Dr. Wächter, which amounted to the strangulation of civil rights in the ghettos of Poland.

The Judenrat, or Jewish Council,[87] comprised of 24 members, was set up by the edict of December 1939. On the face of it, the Judenrat was supposed to fulfill the pre-war functions of the Jewish community; but, in fact, its main occupation was to serve the Germans. It was very convenient for the Germans to have their orders carried out by the Jews. From its very inception, the Judenrat was controlled by the Gestapo. All inquiries and prosecutions were administered by Department 111, Room No. 302, Pomorska Street.

The Judenrat's duties included general administration, compiling statistical data and lists of residents, registering stores, distributing food, and providing fuel for the Jewish inhabitants of Krakow and later for the ghetto. In addition to these duties, the Judenrat had its own publishing house to print the many regulations of the occupying authorities. The Jews welcomed this last vestige of control over their beleaguered people.

As the German occupation tightened its control and the implementation of forced labor squads began, the Judenrat met to soften the ferocity of the German demands. To avoid arbitrary abductions or dragnets, several Jewish leaders suggested the establishment of quasi-autonomous Jewish councils to fill the quota of workers fixed by the Germans. The Krakow Judenrat suggested that to prevent Germans from seizing Jews off the streets for labor, it would set up a labor registry available to the Germans when needed. The Police Chief, Wilhelm Krüger, liked this idea and issued a decree on December 2, 1939, empowering all the Judenraten to organize forced labor columns. Apparently, the Warsaw Jews had a similar idea.[88]

During the period of forced expulsion from the city, as the chairman of the Judenrat, Mark Bieberstein, and his council tried to obtain permission for more Jews to remain in Krakow, they began bribing officials. The bribes were discovered by the Gestapo with tragic results.[89] The Krakow Judenrat allocated 200,000 zloty for this purpose. Bieberstein and Housing Secretary Chaim Goldfluss approached contacts within the German administration. In return for money, the administration was to permit 10,000 Jews of Krakow to remain unmolested. Too many people knew about this proposed deal with the result that Bieberstein and Goldfluss were arrested on bribery charges. Bieberstein was sentenced to a two-year imprisonment in the Montelupich prison, Goldfluss to six months in Auschwitz, and the German intermediary, a Volksdeutsch named Reichert, to an eight-year imprisonment. After his release from prison, Bieberstein was sent to the Plaszow camp, where he later died.

The Judenrat policy became one of institutional compliance and the Judenraten became "implements of the German will," moving Jews through the various phases of what was to become the destruction process. Each Judenrat in the occupied territories had its own way of doing things, and its relationship with its Jewish community varied from one to the other. Many of the Krakow Judenrat officials were accused of abusing their authority by favoring relatives, tampering with labor lists, and generally enjoying a far higher standard of living than that of their own community. In the Krakow German newspaper *Krakower Zeitung* of March 13, 1940, a Dr. Dietrich Redecker reported that on a visit to the Judenrat office he was struck by the contrast between its carpet and plush furnishings and the squalor of the Jewish quarters in Kazimierz.[90]

With the end of military government on October 25, 1939, the civil administration, pervaded by the SS, fell upon the Jews. Measures already in place in Germany and Austria were now applied to the annexed and occupied zones of Poland. Dr. Otto Wächter was now issuing decrees from the Wawel Castle.

November 18, special signs to be carried by Jews in the entire district were ordered: "All Jews over twelve years of age should carry visible signs, namely a white band with a blue Star of David on the right arm of their outer garments."

This instruction also contained a definition of the term Jew as the Nazis understood it: "He is a Jew who either is an adherent of the Judaic faith and everyone whose father or mother are or were of Judaic faith." The Germans cut through this definition when it suited them: "You were a Jew if you went to the synagogue." The problem posed by those Jews from mixed marriages, "Mischlings," was never adequately solved.

In December, obligatory work for Jews was enlarged by the decision that every Jew aged 12 to 60 had to work for two years in a compulsory labor camp. The successive orders obliged Jews to hand over their automobiles and motorcycles (December 4), forbade them to change their residence (December 11), and forbade travel by train in the General Government (January 26, 1940).

The workers at Bucheister's continued as usual and awaited the next turn of events. On the morning of December 3, 1939, Schindler made a further visit to see Stern. On this occasion, there was a clear message to all those present. In a raised voice he addressed Stern, "Now it's starting; Jews will be surrounded and murdered. The Jewish quarter of Kazimierz, Josefa, and Izaaka Streets, are going to know all about it."[91]

Schindler Gets to Work

Oskar Schindler, as we know, was a highly placed espionage agent within the Third Reich. It was a Canaris directive that his top agents who had taken advantage of industrial opportunities to make money in the occupied areas, were also a camouflage for their main responsibility: to keep an eye on the SS/SD, whom the Canaris clique considered the real enemy of the new order. Schindler had no experience of industrial management, but in the turmoil of the war, he used his initiative and guile to make money…with Jewish labor.

Upon arriving in Krakow, Schindler and his team went directly to his apartment on Straszewskiego Street,[92] not far from the Wawel Castle. Schindler had bought the apartment from some wealthy Jews, and its luxurious furnishings included porcelain vases, Persian carpets, and heavy velvet curtains. The windows opened to the Planty: a series of parks which followed the contours of the old walls near the Wawel fortress. This was the apartment to which Schindler would take his women friends, particularly Amelia (or Ingrid, in Keneally's book), and a Polish girl called Viktoria Klonowska. Amelia was with the Abwehr, while Klonowska improved Schindler's relationship with the Gestapo.[93] When Emilie visited the Krakow apartment, Schindler's lovers disappeared. Emilie knew the situation and chose to ignore it.

During one of Mrs. Schindler's initial visits to Krakow, she was overcome with serious back pain which nearly paralyzed her. Polish doctors were unable to help her, but her husband, with his contacts, had her referred to specialists in Berlin at the Auguste Hospital, to which only the aristocracy and high-ranking German officers had access. Her personal doctor was Professor Kurt Enger, who diagnosed a serious problem with her spine. Emilie spent several months in the hospital and later in convalescence in Austria. During this long period, her husband never wrote or visited her. When Emilie returned to Krakow, Oskar met her, holding a bouquet of flowers. He apologized, giving the weak excuse of problems with traveling documents. He showed no interest in her medical condition.[94]

Josef Aue stayed with Schindler in the Krakow apartment for about three months during which time Schindler took him to the offices of the Treuhänder,[95] who were supervising the takeover of Jewish premises. Schindler introduced Aue to Walter Muschka, an agent of the Abwehr as well as the head of the Trust Office. Schindler told Muschka that Aue was an administrator from Moravska Ostrava and should be placed in a suitable business. Aue, who had now been given the name Sepp Aue, was handed over to another agent and trust administrator, Ervin Kobiela. Kobiela suggested to Aue that he take over the import/export business of the Jew, Salomon Bucheister at 15 Straddon Street, Krakow.

Ervin Kobiela took Aue to the Straddon Street location, where he was introduced as the new administrator. Kobiela ordered the owner, the Jew, Salomon Bucheister, off the premises. The remainder of the staff was all Jews who helped Aue understand the running of the business. The chief accountant at the firm was Itzhak Stern (69518), who had worked for Salomon Bucheister since 1924. On Stern's advice, Aue immediately re-engaged Salomon Bucheister, who became just another worker; however, he was treated respectfully by Aue.[96]

Aue's behavior immediately aroused Stern's curiosity. Although he had begun Aryanizing the firm and firing some of the Jewish workers as he was instructed to do, at the same time Aue left the discharged Jews' names on the social insurance registry, enabling them to maintain their all-important worker's identity card. He secretly gave these hungry men money as well.[97] Such exemplary behavior could only impress the Jews and astonish the wary and cautious Stern. Only at the end of the war was Stern to learn that Aue was Jewish, that his own father had been murdered in Auschwitz in 1942,[98] and that the Polish he pretended to speak so poorly was actually his native tongue. Aue had already taken on the guise of a double agent.

Not knowing all this, Stern had no reason to trust Aue. Certainly, he could not understand the man's presumption when, only a few days after having taken charge of the import/export firm, on November 19, 1939, Aue brought an old friend, who had just arrived in Krakow, to see Stern. Aue said quite casually, "You know, Stern, you can have confidence in my friend Schindler." Stern said nothing but exchanged courtesies with the visitor and answered his questions with care.[99]

There was an interesting development in the relationship between Aue and Stern. Aue gave Stern a document which he had received from the Reich Secretary of State, Eberhard Von Jagwitz of the Economic Ministry. This document set out the policies to be adopted in the Aryanizing of Jewish businesses. It contained confidential information concerning issues about the Jews and the intentions for all Jewish businesses, including Bucheister's.[100]

Some days later, Schindler returned to Bucheister's specifically to see Stern. He asked his advice on opening a business. Stern was able to take advantage of the information he had seen in the Ministry document and advised Schindler to lease or, better still, buy, but not become a trustee. Stern realized that, from a Jewish point of view, an owner was not limited to the number of Jews permitted to be employed.[101] Schindler was impressed by Stern's analysis and left to think it over.

At the Schindler apartment it was a continual round of entertaining high-ranking officers of the SS, Wehrmacht, and Abwehr. Although Emilie kept very much in the background, she speaks of endless discussions with these gentlemen on Nazi policy. Major von Kohrab, Chief of the Polish section of the Counterintelligence Service, had become a close friend of Schindler. According to Mrs. Schindler, it was von Kohrab who introduced her husband to Abraham Bankier (69268), the bankrupt owner of Rekord on Lipowa Street. Schindler, after discussions with Bankier and Stern, convinced himself that it was Rekord he had to play for. Again, on Stern's advice, Schindler went ahead and applied to the Polish Commercial Court where he obtained a short lease of the bankrupt Rekord Company, at 4 Lipowa Street. With most of the Krakow Trust Administrators also in the pay of the Abwehr, Schindler had no difficulty in concluding the transaction.[102]

**Figure 21: Abraham and Rega Peller Bankier,
former owners of the Emalia factory**

Photo Credit: Svitavy Museum Collection

Figure 22: Itzhak Stern (69518) 1950 [103]
Photo Credit: Svitavy Museum Collection

Administrators were installed at occupied Jewish businesses in Krakow by the Nazis. Schindler, who arrived in Krakow on October 17, 1939, took advantage of his long acquaintance with Simon Jereth and now Abraham Bankier. In November these individuals helped Schindler acquire the Rekord factory to produce enamelware. Bankier also kept the fictitious company records and helped Schindler gain the necessary orders – he brokered contacts with the black market in Krakow. Schindler's address – Krasińskiego 24a – appeared on the first signed documents.

Later, in 1941, Schindler employed his first 190 Jewish workers. On October 21, 1941, the successful entrepreneur finally became the owner of the entire D.E.F. factory and made plans to expand production. Schindler, an Abwehr agent, kept his door open to the Nazis and managed to "selflessly" compensate these authorities. Always finely dressed, Schindler made sure he never missed any party hosted by the Nazi nobility. The global conflict provided him ample orders, and cheap labor from Jews guaranteed high profits. Employment in the arms industry meant protection for Jewish workers against possible deportation to the camps. Itzhak Stern and Roman Günter, members of the Jewish council, therefore tried to find work for as many people as possible. Like the entrepreneur Julius Madritsch, Schindler understood the opportunity being offered.

Schindler's newly acquired Rekord factory had been founded by Jewish partners in 1937. Even though the bank accounts of Jews were frozen, there was still enough working capital in cash for business operations. Aided by experts from Ostrava, Schindler managed to use these funds to successfully launch production. The name of the factory was changed to Deutsche Emailenwaren Fabrik – D.E.F. The factory hall was located at Lipowa St. No. 4 in the Zablocie quarter.

Figure 23: Construction of the Emalia administration building in 1942

Figure 24: Schindler with his Jewish workers in Emalia

**Figure 25: Schindler (second from left). Abraham Bankier (third from the right)
with their Polish staff in Emalia 1940.   Photos Credits: Svitavy Museum Collection**

Apart from this initial meeting of Schindler and Stern in December 1939, they were not to renew their relationship on a more positive level until March 13, 1943, when the ghetto was liquidated, and Stern was moved to Plaszow concentration camp. It was Schindler's view that the Jews had to be saved and that Itzhak Stern was to be the tool to bring this about.[104]

The Stern/Schindler relationship was founded on this early warning and was the pivotal axis that, in my opinion, was to decide the destinies of both Schindler and the Jews that remained with him. The relationship was bonded by mutual respect, a friendship which lasted until Stern's death in Tel Aviv in 1969. It is said that upon hearing of Stern's death, Schindler collapsed and shed tears like a child.

Chapter Five
The Wiener Affair and
Kazimierz: The Jewish Quarter

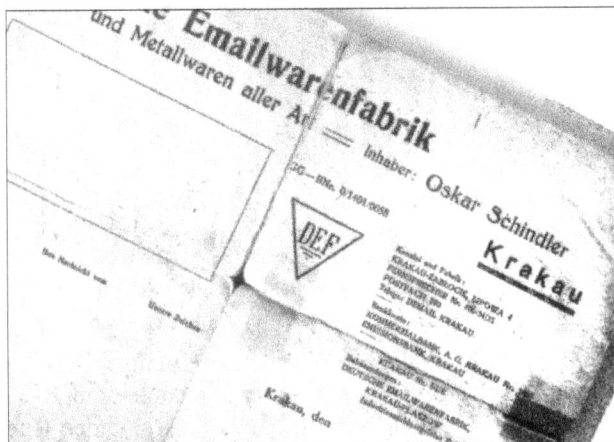

Figure 26: Schindler's correspondence obtained by the author in 1992

Photo Credit: Svitavy Museum Collection

> Schindler called the SS. ... A few SS men came and took
> Wiener to an adjoining office and beat him up. There were
> groans and screaming. When Wiener appeared, he was covered
> in blood and wounds. The SS spoke to Schindler: "We took care
> of him; you get rid of him!"
>
> Natan Wurzel, November 26, 1956

In my introduction, I mentioned that Schindler was a controversial figure.
I think we must call into question at this early stage the darker side of his
character and not rely on the highlighted events that we have come to
know. I want to discuss the part he is alleged to have played in the Wiener
Affair.

In the early part of 1940, the Aryanizing program was gathering
momentum. It was now the practice that if a Jewish company became a
nuisance or an obstruction to some other purpose, the Jewish owner was
thrown into the street. The niceties of the law were conveniently ignored.

Schindler was now in business at 4 Lipowa Street. The Emalia factory was
an imposing building which was fronted by a large arch at the entrance.
Behind the facade was several smaller industrial units owned and used by
independent manufacturers.

Figure 27: Outside Emalia 1942

Photo Credit: Svitavy Museum Collection

The occupier of one of these small industrial units was Natan Wurzel, a Jew, born November 5, 1900, a small-time manufacturer of kitchen units. Schindler had now taken over these premises under the Aryanizing regulations but employed Wurzel on the trade counter in his Emalia factory. By all accounts, although Wurzel had been ousted from business, he was at that time on good terms with Schindler.

Schindler had his eye on another business, in Stradom Street, Krakow: the Chamber of Commerce Wiener, another kitchen wholesale supplier's outlet. This business was owned by a Jewish father and son, Salomon, and Julius Wiener. Schindler had placed his Abwehr woman friend Marta, now a Trust Administrator, into the premises. Marta may have been a proficient Abwehr agent, but she utterly failed to supervise the Wiener business and, according to Schindler, was getting the run-around by the Wieners.

Both the Emalia and Wiener businesses were being used as an outlet of goods to the black market. There was a proviso that all transactions would go via the Schindler works, a position that Marta failed to control. Therefore, she sought the help of Schindler. Instead of working their deals with Schindler, the Wieners were operating separately, to Schindler's disadvantage. There was one subtle difference between the two sites: Emalia was controlled by the Sudetendeutsch Oskar Schindler, who was a party to the occupying power, while the Wiener outlet was being controlled by Jews. To say the least, there was a mighty clash of interests – falling out among thieves – and Schindler was not about to lose the argument, especially to a Jew!

One morning, when Wurzel was at the trade counter in Emalia, Julius Wiener called in to collect merchandise in order to pay off a collecting agent of the SS. According to Wurzel, Schindler was in a furious mood and was threatening to kill the Wieners. The following morning, when Julius Wiener returned to the Emalia factory, working at the trade counter, several SS men entered the reception area, seized Wiener, and took him to another room where he was badly beaten up. On their way out of the factory, one of the SS men said to Schindler, "We took care of him; you get rid of him."

That same day, both Wieners left their premises, leaving the spoils for Schindler.[105]

The Wiener Affair became a *cause célèbre* within the inner circles of Yad Vashem. When Schindler was nominated in 1963 to become a Righteous Gentile, questions were asked about his credentials. This is a point I shall explore later. After the war, Julius Wiener immigrated to Buenos Aires, only to find himself in the same city as the Schindlers. Julius Wiener initiated civil proceedings against Schindler for robbery and seizure of his businesses and assaults by the SS. Wurzel, who had now changed his name to Antoni Korzeniowski, immigrated to Israel. There was an exchange of letters between Wurzel and Wiener to gather the evidence needed by their respective solicitors. After a few years, it was Julius Wiener who was to withdraw litigation due to ill health, and the matter rested. It did, however, open up old sores. It is interesting to note that on the Schindler list the name Julius Wiener (69290), born September 5, 1904, appears. Wiener was in fact saved by Schindler and lived to take vengeance against him. To be saved by the list does not mean that that person agreed with Schindler's actions, as we shall find out later from another Jew, Joachim Kinstlinger (68861).

During Schindler's first year at Emalia, he employed about 70 Polish workers, including only seven Jews.[106] This balance gradually changed, as, with time, he employed more Jews. This was not because he had a love for Jews; quite simply, Jews were cheaper to employ. This was a win-win situation. Employing Jews was financially advantageous for the factory. It was also advantageous to the Jews who received the protection of the Kennkarte (working card), followed very quickly by the Blauschein (blue sticker), an endorsement of the Kennkarte. The changing nature of these working cards was to sift through the work force for the gradual process of elimination.

Life for the Jews in Krakow became increasingly oppressive. SS labor squads roamed the streets, picking up Jews for labor battalions elsewhere. Schindler was in touch with the Jewish labor office to take on more laborers as his business grew. Sometimes he was the recipient of these SS labor squads.

Solomon Urbach (69427):

> "Walking in the street, I was suddenly stopped by the SS. I was taken with a load of kids to the Emalia works. We were lined up for inspection by Director Schindler. He said he would take the men but not the kids. The SS said when we bring you Jews, you keep them. The SS left and we joined Schindler. I survived because of this man."[107]

On some occasions, if Schindler needed a particular skill, he would go into the town and select the man or woman he wanted. This was usually done on the advice of Bankier.

Richard Rechen (69233):

> "It was like falling onto another planet. Director Schindler came into the garage where I was working. He greets me and gives me his hand. He told me not to be afraid. He said he had heard that I was a good mechanic and invited me to come to the Emalia factory where I would never be hungry. I was assured he was not a bluffer."[108]

Figure 28: Schindler's workers at Emalia 1943
Photo Credit: Svitavy Museum Collection

Kazimierz: The Jewish Quarter

Figure 29: Gate of the Krakow Ghetto drawn by Josef Bau (69084)
Photo Credit: Author's Collection

As the Nazis tightened their grip on the Jewish community, word spread that the Schindler works were a good place to be. Three new employees were taken on the direct recommendation of Stern: Magister Leib Salpeter (69282), Samuel Wulkan (69267), and Stern's brother, Natan Stern (69275).

These three were all old ranking members of the Polish Zionist movement. Unknown to Schindler, but organized and arranged by Stern and Abraham Bankier, two other employees were taken on: an engineer named Pawlik, who was an officer in the Polish underground movement, and a man named Hildegeist. Both were non-Jews and were connected to outside underground agencies. Hildegeist had known Schindler before the war. Because of his political views Hildegeist was sent to Buchenwald concentration camp, where he served three years. It was Schindler who personally had him released and brought to Krakow. Although Schindler remained aloof from this intake of dubious employees, he kept himself fully informed of their activities.

On May 18, 1940, the German Mayor announced that Jews could leave the city "of their own free will" and "those who would leave willingly" would be allowed to take baggage of 50 kg per person. The last day for leaving was set for August 15, 1940.[109] Rumors had already spread that the Germans planned to put the Jews into an enclosed area: Judischer Wohnbezirk, or Jewish Quarter.[110]

Governor Dr. Hans Frank had decided on a little evacuation program of his own. His resettlements were to take place within the General Government. Dr. Frank wanted to remove the entire Jewish population from Krakow. Addressing his main divisional chiefs on April 12, 1940, Dr. Frank described conditions in the city as scandalous. German generals were forced to live in apartments occupied by Jews. Frank wanted Krakow free of Jews by November 1, 1940. Only skilled Jews would remain. The Krakow expulsions were divided into two phases: voluntary and involuntary. Up to August 15, 1940, the Jews could move freely, but after this date the Jews would be forced out. However, no sooner had Frank expelled the Jews from the city than the city began filling up again with Jews from incorporated territories. In the first two weeks of August, a third of the Jews of Krakow had been expelled to Warsaw, Radom, Lublin, Czestochova, and other Polish towns. Some Jews made it over to the Russian zone. Expelling Jews in this way enabled the Nazis to make room in the city for the new intake of immigrants that would Germanize the area.

On March 3, 1941, Governor Wächter published an order in the *Karakul Zeitung* for a Jewish residence zone named Gen. Gub 44/91. This order was also posted on walls and announced through loudspeakers from mobile vans. The Jews had to move into this residence zone of Kazimierz by March 21, 1941. Kazimierz, a district of Krakow, was historically associated with the Jews of Krakow for over a thousand years.

Thousands of Jews left the city in order not to be enclosed. The ghetto was set up in the suburb of Podgorze, tucked into the elbow of the Vistula, the east end by the railway line to Lvov, the south side by the hills beyond Rekawka, and the west by Podgorze Place. The face of Kazimierz changed overnight. Its character, built up through the centuries, rapidly disappeared. There was no longer the sight of Jews dressed in long black kapotes and felt hats, skull caps, and fur hats, beards, and long sideburns; gone were the discussions on the street corners with characteristic gesticulations. This was the beginning of the end for one of the finest cultural centers of Eastern Europe.

Figure 30: Gate of the Krakow Ghetto 1942
Photo Credit: Author's Collection

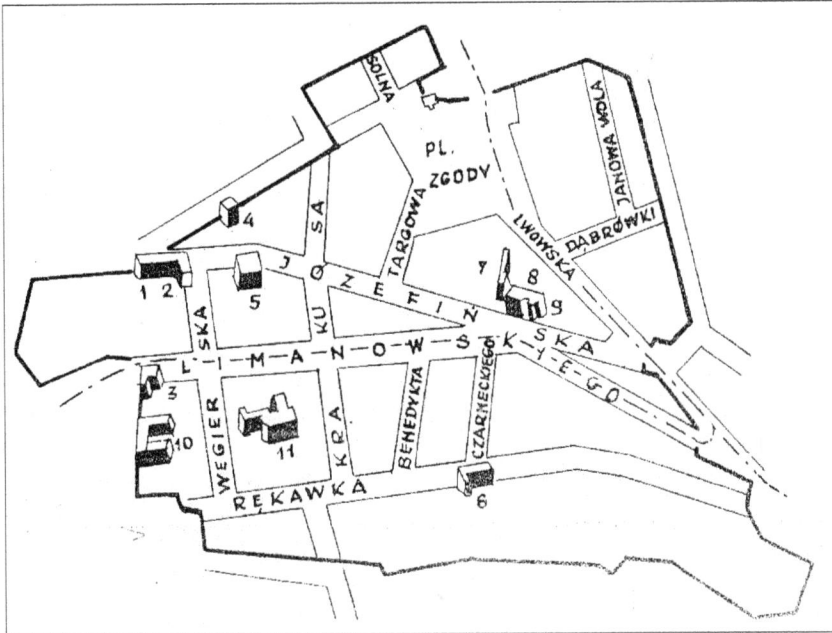

Figure 31: Map of the Krakow Ghetto[111]
Photo Credit: Author's Collection

1. Labor Exchange
2. Hospital
3. Gmina
4. Public Bath
5. Jewish Welfare Community
6. Contagious Disease Hospital
7. Prison
8. Jewish Ghetto Police
9. Boarding School
10. Madritsch Factory
11. Optima

The creation of the Krakow Ghetto

The Nazi administration in Krakow continually tried to strip Jews of all of their rights and remaining privileges. After the closure of Jewish schools in December 1939 Jews were forbidden to have radios and telephones. Jews were required to report all their property, they were banned from using public transport, and on May 18, 1940, a three-month deadline was established for "voluntary departure from the city" with only a small amount of luggage. On August 1 the mass expulsions of Jews began, mainly to the Warsaw and Lublin Ghettos. Of the original 70,000 Jewish residents in Krakow, only 16,000 remained in February 1941. This population was under the direct control of armed SS units. The Podgorze Ghetto was officially created on March 3, 1941, and all Jews were ordered to move there by March 21. Once Jews were concentrated in the ghetto they were under the constant control of the police and SS guards. It often happened that groups of Jewish workers employed in factories in the city would never make it to their jobs. According to their needs, the Nazis used these workers to clean public spaces. Jews in processions were often terrorized by guards.

Using Jewish labor, the Germans erected a wall surrounding the ghetto, set bars in windows of apartments looking out onto the Aryan quarter, installed security posts, and constructed gates, with three providing access to the ghetto. The main gate was at Podgorze Square and above the gate was a large six-pointed Star of David with the inscription in Hebrew: "Jewish Quarter." Located at the main gate were the central post of the German police and the seat of the Judenrat. During the first few weeks of the ghetto's existence, one could gain access with relative ease, usually when it was necessary to reclaim cash from the Jews. On both sides of the gate were dark blue lamps. A trolley ran through this gate along the streets of Limanowska and Lwowska, right through the ghetto, connecting with the Aryan quarter of the city. It sometimes served as an intermittent link between Poles and Jews; many packages were delivered without the knowledge of the ghetto police.[112] The second gate was at the end of Limanowska Street, and the third was in Plac Zgody (Peace Square) opening onto a bridge spanning the Vistula. All three gates were guarded by the Polish, blue-uniformed police and by the Jewish Police, the OD (Ordnungsdient).[113]

About 15,000 Jews were transferred from the city into the ghetto, and an additional 2,500 remained outside, living either in the orphanage, a residential home for the elderly, or huts at the Optima factory.[114] Once a chocolate factory but now used for producing German military uniforms, Optima was the target of frequent attacks by the Jewish fighting organizations that seized large quantities of warm clothing and distributed them to Jewish fighting units around Lublin and Biala-Podlaska.

From early morning until late at night on March 21, the scene was one of pitiful dejection. Families with their possessions were in utter confusion, criss-crossing the streets with their bundles and carts laden with furniture and other worldly possessions, in their haste to beat the deadline. The scramble for the best accommodation was frantic. At the end of the day, several families found themselves sharing one apartment, there being no place else to go.

Figure 32: The Krakow Chemist Tadeusz Pankiewicz with his staff 1942
Photo Credit: Author's Collection

No Aryan was permitted to live in the ghetto; only the staff and guard of the court and jail were allowed to remain within, with one exception – the pharmacist Tadeusz Pankiewicz, who lived in the pharmacy accommodation in Plac Zgody, the heart and pulse of the Podgorze ghetto.[115] From the moment of the creation of the Jewish Quarter, Pankiewicz was the owner of the pharmacy Under the Eagle on Plac Zgody. This was the only one of the four pharmacies in Podgorze that was located in the ghetto. He was the only Pole who lived and worked there without interruption (for two and a half years) until its ultimate liquidation. From a window in the pharmacy, he could look out onto Plac Zgody, viewing the most horrendous crimes committed against the Jewish population by the occupier.

In March 1941, Schindler returned to Svitavy to see his father, who was now in poor health. Oskar intended to patch up past differences. To some degree, he was successful, and when he left, they mutually agreed to bury the past and look to the future.

Schindler returned to Krakow and went via Moravska Ostrava to see his wife, who was still occupying their Abwehr apartment. According to the Ball-Kaduri documents, Schindler gave Emilie an update on his business activities, but made no mention of his relationships with his secretary, Klonowska, or his German mistress. Mrs. Schindler had long accepted that her husband could not hold to their marriage vows. When interviewed on this point by the film Director Jon Blair, she replied:

> "He was a man who loved life. He liked all women. You can fight against one, but not against ten or a hundred. So, you'd better swim with the current ... isn't that true? But it didn't bother me at all; you can't change a man who is like that. He loved women, he loved parties. That was Oskar, and I knew I would never change him – I didn't want to change him."[116]

In Krakow, Schindler was visited by representatives of the Armaments Inspectorate. Emalia was to take on necessary armaments work. Another blow to Schindler was that all wages to his Jewish workers would now be terminated and alternative pro-rated payments would now be paid directly to the SS. The dues he would pay to the police chiefs were the standard SS Main Administrative and Economic Office fees: seven and a half Reichmarks per day for a skilled worker, five Reichmarks for unskilled men and women. These changes took effect immediately and affected all the Aryan factory owners in the General Government. This was a crucial turning point in Schindler's relations with his Jewish workers. They were literally dependent on him for life and subsistence. Schindler bought food for them on the black market at very high prices. He got money on the black market for food – for equally outrageous prices – by selling large quantities of the enamelware that his Jewish workers produced. There is an irony in this, for it means that Schindler paid his workers with the profits of their own labor.[117]

On the western side of the ghetto, a kilometer from Emalia, were two clothing factories of an Austrian member of the Nazi Party: Julius Madritsch, and his manager, Raymond Titsch. On the ghetto gate at Podgorze Square was the name of another member of the Nazi Party: The Austrian Police Sergeant Oswald Bousco. Including Schindler, these four members of the Nazi Party were to be at the center of events in the plight and later rescue of the Krakow Jews.

Chapter Six
Julius Madritsch: Partial Liquidation of the Ghetto

Figure 33: SS guards whipping prisoner (Josef Bau)
Photo Credit: Author's collection

"Save us! Abandon us not in our hour of need!"

Julius Madritsch

It is thus that Julius Madritsch opens his volume of memoirs, *People in Distress*. Madritsch was born on August 4, 1906, in Vienna, the center of the Austro-Hungarian monarchy of Franz Josef.[118]

A pacifist by nature, Madritsch was drafted into the Wehrmacht in 1940, but did his utmost to be discharged. Madritsch was against the Nazi racial policies, which he witnessed in the streets of Vienna. He saw his opportunity to escape the Wehrmacht when his organizational talents were recognized. He was invited by the war recruiting board to move to the General Government and become a purchasing agent for the Wehrmacht. He was subsequently appointed a Trust Administrator of two textile plants in Krakow.[119]

One of Madritsch's eager and ardent accomplices was Raymond Titsch, who was to become the lynchpin between many of the anti-Nazi conspirators in Krakow. As the traveling manager for Madritsch, he visited Bochnia and Tarnow to ensure that their Jewish workers were cared for. He kept diaries and took photographs of the Nazi oppression, which were important evidence after the war.[120]

New edicts were announced with monotonous regularity. Jews were only allowed to work in armament industries and even this was to be short term. The Jews were to be replaced by Aryan workers shortly thereafter. It was this edict that brought together Schindler and Madritsch at a conference with the Judenrat labor office to discuss the implications.[121]

Unknown to both Madritsch and Schindler, another conference had taken place. This conference lasted only 90 minutes, but those 90 minutes sealed the fate of European Jewry! Reinhardt Heydrich, chief of the Gestapo, invited 15 German officials representing various government departments to meet for lunch in a pleasant lakeside suburb of Berlin. What was to become known as the Wannsee Conference took place on January 20, 1942. Its purpose was to coordinate solutions for the various problems related to the Final Solution of the Jewish question. Dr. Hans Frank had sent two representatives to the conference: Under-Secretary Dr. Buhler and Commanding Officer of the Security Police, SS-Standartenführer Dr. Karl Schongarth.[122]

By 1942, the drain on German manpower became so acute and the need for armaments so great that second thoughts had to be given to the ongoing wholesale slaughter of the Jews. In February, Himmler presented a plan to Hitler and to Albert Speer, the newly appointed minister for armaments and munitions. Himmler's proposal was to build armament plants inside the concentration camps and put able-bodied inmates to work on armament production. Propaganda Minister Goebbels recorded the following in his diary for March 27, 1942:

> "The Jews in the General Government are now being evacuated eastward. The procedure is a pretty barbaric one as not much will remain of the Jews. On the whole it can be said that about 60 percent of them will have to be liquidated whereas only about 40 percent can be used for forced labor."[123]

A new department was created, the Wirtschafts und Verwaltungshauptamt (Economic and Administrative Main Office), or WVHA, to deal with economic problems of the Reich.[124] At the same time, all the camp commanders were told that this employment must be in the true meaning of the word "exhaustive," in order to obtain the greatest measure of performance.[125]

Himmler had an obsession about being fiddled with by his SS camp commanders. In response to a memorandum from General von Ginant, dated October 9, 1942, he points out in Paragraph One:

> "I have issued instructions, however, that ruthless steps are taken against all those who consider they should oppose this move in the alleged interest of armament needs, but who, in reality, only seek to support the Jews and their own businesses."

From around the beginning of 1942, the demand for manpower from any source was now overwhelming. No German establishment had to be coerced into taking labor. On the contrary, the firms had to use their influence and persuasion to get all the help possible. The private companies poured millions of Marks into the coffers of the SS for the privilege of using camp prisoners. An elaborate accounting system was set up to be sure that the companies paid the SS for every hour of skilled or unskilled labor and that deductions for the food provided by the companies did not exceed the maximum allowed. The inmates, of course, received nothing. They remained under the control of the SS but also under the immediate supervision of the companies that used them. The companies were required to see to it that adequate security arrangements, such as auxiliary guards and barbed wire enclosures, eliminated all possibility of escape. These new regulations, of course, were mainly directed at the Farbens, Krupps, and Siemens, etc. The likes of the Schindlers and Madritsches were insignificant by comparison, but no less supervised by the SS.

The effects of what had been decided at Wannsee were soon being felt in the Krakow ghetto. The OD was being reshaped, re-equipped with new-style uniforms, and strengthened with collaborating Jews of the ghetto. One appointment was that of Symche Spira, who had been a glazier before the war, but was now the head of the Jewish police. Spira, a much-despised individual, seemed to relish his close association with the Nazis. Spira took his orders not from the Judenrat but from Untersturmführer Brand and the Gestapo.[126] He even organized his own political section, which was used with devastating effects to the advantage of the SS.[127]

Figure 34: Jewish Police in the Krakow Ghetto 1942: Second from right Symche Spira[128]
Photo Credit: Author's collection

In June and October 1942, the Nazis carried out the partial liquidation of the ghetto, an event that cannot be passed over without some detailed comment. During the last days of May 1942, the ghetto was surrounded and sealed at night by a strong cordon of Sonderdienst (Special Police). The Gestapo and officials of the labor office met in the building of the ZSS (Jewish social self-help). A selection began. The Jews lined up, and rapid decisions were made on who was to go and who was to remain in the ghetto. Within two days the selection was complete.

On the morning of June 2, 1942, the deportations started. From then on, a familiar scene in the ghetto was the sight of the Jewish policemen, led by SS storm-troopers, bringing the Jews from their homes to the gathering point in the Optima yard, and from there to the freight train station at Prokocim. The first to be expelled were the old people, women, and young children. Most of them were sent to Belzec and gassed, but hundreds were murdered on the way.[129]

To give some idea of the catastrophe which was engulfing the European Jews, I made an in-depth survey of the numbers deported to the Belzec death camp for the period of its operation: March through December 1942: Table 1 for June 1942, shown below, includes the 10,000 Jews deported from Schindler's Krakow ghetto and 11,500 Jews deported from Madritsch's Tarnow ghetto [130] The numbers for the month of June were low because the first prototype experimental gas chambers were demolished and replaced with a building twice the size, doubling the capacity to six gas chambers capable of killing 3,000 Jews in just one operation. See a similar chart for October 1942 in Chapter Seven of the murderous activity occurring in the name of National Socialism.

Town	Deported	Numbers
13 Czortkow	June 6	1100
14 Kolomyja	June 21	3000
15 Gwozdziec	June 1-4	
16 Kosow		
17 Kuty		
18 Obertyn		
19 Zablotow		
20 Kopyczynce		1100
21 **Krakow**	June 1-8	**10000**[131]
22 Lviv	June 24-26	5000[132]
23 Niemirow	June 19	500
24 Olkusz	June 11-19	3000
25 **Tarnow**	June 11-18	**11500**[133]
26 Dabrowa Tarnowska	June 11	450

Table 1: Deportations to Belzec 1942

The Germans were not satisfied with the number deported. They calculated that many who did not have stamps on their passes did not report. During the nights of June 3-4, 1942, the Gestapo and OD men made surprise raids into the ghetto – inspecting papers, stopping and searching people in the streets, and entering hospitals, apartments, and houses. This time, several thousand Jews were marched to the Plac Zgody. The roundup was brutal and many of the Jews – the old, sick, and the children – were shot in the streets. This scene is vividly portrayed in the Spielberg film and in the recollections of Tadeusz Pankiewicz.

The president of the Judenrat, Dr. Arter Ahron Rosenzweig, was summoned to Plac Zgody, where the SS dismissed him from his position. Rosenzweig and his family were immediately deported to Belzec. They did not survive.[134]

From his pharmacy in Plac Zgody, Tadeusz Pankiewicz watched the partial liquidation of the ghetto. He gives an eyewitness account of events on the evening of June 4, 1942:

> "By the following morning, seven thousand had been assembled. There they were kept throughout the hot summer morning, then driven to the railway station, and sent off to an unknown destination. The roundup was repeated the following day, the sixth of June. The scorching sun was merciless; the heat makes for unbearable thirst, dries out the throats. The crowd was standing and sitting; all waiting, frozen with fright and uncertainty. Armed Germans arrived, shooting at random into the crowd. The deportees were driven out of the square, amid constant screaming of the Germans, mercilessly."[135]

The ghetto now had a new commissioner appointed by the Germans – David Gutter. Gutter, formerly a traveling salesman who sold magazines, was now the "supreme" in the ghetto and behaved like a megalomaniac in the execution of his duties on behalf of the Germans. Gutter created a web of Jewish spies and informants within the ghetto.[136]

Both Schindler and Madritsch met with the Judenrat in the ghetto to discuss ways of relieving the employment situation. One of the solutions, thought up by Madritsch, was to employ more Jews per sewing machine, and to open other factories in the towns of Bochnia and Tarnow, giving hope to an additional 2,000 Jews under the cover of essential armaments contracts. Madritsch's first priority was to change the status of his factories to armaments factories, and thus receive the protection, like Schindler, of the Armament Inspectorate. The Madritsch enterprises in Krakow-Podgorze had a capacity of 300 sewing machines and about 800 workers, most of whom were Jews. His companies in Bochnia and Tarnow had a similar capacity. In Krakow, two shifts of Jewish workers marched daily from the ghetto to their workplace in the Madritsch and Schindler factories. For the time being, if the Jews held their work cards, they were safe.[137]

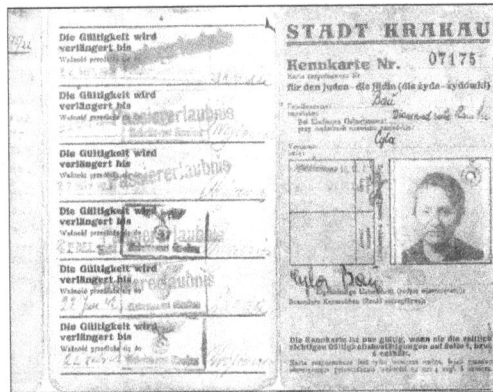

Figure 35: Cyla Bau's (wife of Josef Bau) 'Kennkarte' 1942
Photo Credit: Author's collection

Shortly after the June deportations, a Kinderheim (children's home) was opened by order of the Germans. At the opening ceremonies, Gutter and Spira were present. It was quite an occasion: new lies, new swindles, again designed to discourage vigilance. Parents going to work could bring their children, up to the age of 14. Cared for by experienced personnel, the children would be busy with all kinds of tasks, such as sealing envelopes and weaving baskets. The Kinderheim was filled every day with scores of children who entered willingly and innocently. Imagine that all this was done just a few weeks before the pre-set date for the murder of all these children who attended the Kinderheim.[138]

According to Itzhak Stern, the killing of the children in the Kinderheim was the crucial incident that unsettled Schindler's mind. Schindler changed overnight and was never the same.[139]

At Emalia, production was continuing, but elsewhere in Krakow there was turmoil and panic. The seizure of Jews on the streets continued, and transports were leaving daily for the death camp Belzec. Mrs. Edith Kerner, who worked in the offices of Emalia, was beside herself, having seen 14 Emalia workers seized by the SS in the street and arbitrarily added to an annihilation transport leaving the ghetto for the Prokocim railway station. Among those seized was Abraham Bankier, Schindler's trusted factory manager.[140] Spielberg depicts this incorrectly because he shows Stern as the person taken off the transport. I was disappointed with Spielberg's portrayal of this occurrence, as there are relatives of Abraham Bankier still living who must have been aghast at this inaccuracy. For me, the Spielberg film lost much historical accuracy as a result.

Mrs. Kerner tried to contact Schindler at all his known haunts. After some hours, she managed to speak to him. Schindler drove directly to the railway station. He patrolled the platform, shouting for Bankier. The wagons had been in the sidings all day, the occupants sealed in with no food or water. The SS officer in charge relented under pressure from Schindler and released Bankier and the other workers from the transport with a receipt for their bodies. The Emalia workers had simply forgotten to go to the Jewish labor office to obtain their new blue work permits. Three of the 14 were Szulim Lesser (68938), Jerzy Reich (69010), and Bankier (69268).[141] In the three stages of the first June deportations from the ghetto, 7,000 people were expelled. It was learned later that all the transports were routed to the extermination camp at Belzec. There were no survivors.[142]

To combat further seizures of this nature, both Schindler and Madritsch made use of their contacts with the SS, the Jewish labor office, and the ghetto police. Repeatedly, when receiving information that a roundup and transport were to take place, they kept their workers at the factory under some obscure pretext, so as not to expose them to the SS Action squads.[143]

On October 28, 1942, another 5,000 Jews were expelled from the ghetto, leaving 14,000 inside. In December 1942 the Germans ordered the ghetto to be divided into two parts: one for the working Jews and the other for the unemployed. At the same time, scores of Jewish settlements near Krakow were wiped out, and refugees who succeeded in escaping to Krakow enlarged the population of the ghetto. Also arriving daily were the labor units that were to work on the extension of the Plaszow 1 labor camp.[144] The Bejski family, three boys and parents, were all transported to Belzec. By a quirk of fate, the Nazis urgently wanted laborers for the building at Plaszow. The Bejski brothers were taken to Plaszow, but their parents were gassed in Belzec. The brothers – Moszek (69387) (the Judge), Urysz (69384), and Izrael (69385) – survived with Schindler. One lady who did not survive was Fransica Dortheimer, the mother of Viktor Dortheimer. To escape the turmoil in the city, Mrs. Dortheimer moved to the small town of Skawina, 30 miles from Krakow. Fransica did not escape. In August 1942, a deportation train coming from Zakopane stopped at Skawina to pick up the Jews (including Fransica) who had been rounded up the previous night. The transport continued on via Krakow, Tarnow, and Bochnia to Belzec. There were no survivors.

The Armaments Inspectorate visited the Emalia factory and told Schindler that he was to switch production from enamelware to armaments. The alternative was closure. The factory was re-tooled to manufacture shell casings for bazookas.

Figure 36: Fransica and Viktor Dortheimer
Photo Credit: Author's Collection

Chapter Seven
Krakow's Jews Deported to Belzec

Figure 37: SS Guards in Belzec 1942
Photo Credit: Author's Collection

Final Solution: Number of Victims

Of the estimated six million Jews murdered in the Holocaust, the death camps account for about 1.7 million. This reassessment focuses on the Jews deported from within the General Government, incorporating the Districts of Galicia and the environs of Lublin, from which the Jews were transported to Belzec, Sobibor, and Treblinka between March 1942 and October 1943.

One of the most fundamental and controversial issues in the history of the death camps is the imprecise number of its victims. The exact numbers of Jews who were killed in Belzec will never be fully established because decisions and facts relating to the extermination were rarely committed to paper. History has not been helped by the obliteration of all traces of the Belzec camp in 1943 and, in addition, standing orders for destruction of evidence from the Reichsführor SS.[145]

The catchment area for deportations to Belzec was extensive. Deportation trains to the camp arrived from the towns and villages of Chrzanow and Zywiec in the west, to Tarnopol in the east; from Schindler's Krakow and Madritsch's Tarnow and Bochnia in the west; to Kolomyja and Stanislawow in the south; from the environs of Lublin to cities of Western Europe. Belzec engulfed entire communities and was the commencement of the final chapter in the 1,000 years of Jewish history in Europe.

Table 2: October 1942 was at the height of the deportations to the death camp at Belzec. The decision had been made by the Reichsführer SS to exterminate every living Jew within their grasp. A respite was granted to those Jews (14 - 30 years) who would be utilized for labor, and they would be held in concentration camps. I remind the reader that similar deportations were subjected to a similar fate at the death camps of Sobibor and Treblinka…and elsewhere.

	Town	Deported	Numbers
1	Annopol	Oct 1-14	2000
2	Belzyce	Oct 1-14	3000
3	Bilgoraj	Oct 15-31	500
4	Bolechow	Oct 15-31	400
5	Bolszowce	Oct 26-30	1000
6	Brzezany	Oct 10	4000
7	Buczacz	Oct 12	1500
8	Bukaczowice	Oct 26	300
9	Bursztyn	Oct 10	4000
10	Bychawa	Oct 11	3000
11	Chodorow	Oct 18	350
12	Chorostkow	Oct 19	2200
13	Czortkow	Oct 3-5	2800
14	Drohobycz	Oct 23-29	2300
15	Boryslaw	Oct 10	1500
16	Sambor	Oct 17-22	4000
17	Dzierkowice	Oct 1-14	146
18	Firlej	Oct 1-14	317
19	Grodek Jagiellons.	Oct 14	450
20	Grzymalow	Oct 14	200
21	Jablonow	Oct 3-13	Hundreds
22	Kamionka Strumil.	Oct 28	500
23	Kolomyja	Oct 3-13	4500
24	Konskowola	Oct 1-14	2000
25	Koropce	Oct 8	1000
26	Kosow	Oct 2-13	Hundreds
27	**Krakow**	Oct 28	6000
28	Krasnik	Oct 15	Hundreds
29	Krasnystaw	Oct 16	Thousands
30	Krowica	Oct 15-31	10000
31	Kuty	Oct 10	Hundreds
32	Leczna	Oct 3-13	Hundreds
33	Lopatyn	Oct 23	1000
34	Lubaczow	Oct 22-23	400
35	Lubartow	Oct 10	2000
36	Lubycza Krolewsk	Oct 1-14	4500
37	Modliborzyce	Oct 10	1000
38	Mosciska	Oct 1-14	2500
39	Opole Lubelskie	Oct 10	2000
40	Mosty Wielkie	Oct 14	3000
41	Oleszyce	Oct 22-24	1000
42	Pistyn	Oct 10	Hundreds

43	Podhajce	Oct 3-13	Hundreds
44	Podwoloczyska	Oct 30	1500
45	Pomorszany	Oct 22-24	1000
46	Radomysl nad San.	Oct 22-24	Hundreds
47	Radziechow	Oct 29	Hundreds
48	Sadowa Wisnia	Oct 22-24	1000
49	Sandomierz	Oct 10	500
50	Skalat	Oct 29	3230
51	Sniatyn	Oct 21-22	3000
52	Sokal	Oct 3-13	Hundreds
53	Stryj	Oct 22-28	2500
54	Szczebrzeszyn	Oct 18	2000
55	Tarnopol	Oct 20-21	1000
56	Tartakow	Oct 5-7	750
57	Tluste	Oct 22-24	900
58	Turek	Oct 5	1000
59	Ulhnow	Oct	Hundreds
60	Urzedow	Oct 15-31	1500
61	Witkow Nowy	Oct 1-14	500
62	Zablotow	Oct 22-24	1000
63	Zakrzowek	Oct 3-13	Hundreds
64	Zamosc	Oct 1-14	1176
65	Zawichost	Oct 15-30	4000
66	Zbaraz	Oct 15-31	5000
67	Zwierzyniec	Oct 21	1000

Table 2: October 1942

By treating the resettlement transports from the Galician District to Belzec individually, we can establish a clear pattern of deportations throughout the General Government. The calculation method is, as stated, inhibited by the lack of documentation relating to transports of Jews deported to the camp. The only evidence of non-Jews murdered at Belzec mentions approximately 1,500 non-Jewish Poles sent to the camp for execution because of anti-Nazi activity or assisting/hiding Jews. In Lvov, a special "operation" was directed against non-Jewish Poles who were seized in the streets, stores and public places. A transport consisting entirely of non-Jewish Poles was sent to Belzec, where they shared the same fate as their Jewish compatriots. This occurred on just **one** occasion.[146]

An overview of the deportations for Belzec shows that during a matter of selected days, complete geographical pockets of the Jewish community were targeted and transported. For example, we see Zakopane is followed by Skarwina, Krakow, Tarnow and Bochnia. Office-bound bureaucrats had devised a coordinated, systematic method of destruction. There is one incontrovertible fact: although we may never know the exact numbers, the tragedy of the genocide is not in dispute.

Schindler Learns about Belzec

Only a handful of Jews escaped from Belzec but one of this small number was a young pharmacist from Krakow, named Bachner. In June 1942,

Bachner was part of a large transport of several thousand Jews from Krakow destined for the nearby death camp at Belzec. Against all the odds, Bachner made good his escape and returned to Krakow to tell his tale.

No one knew how he had got back inside the ghetto, or the mystery of why he returned to a place from which the SS would simply send him off on another journey. But it was, of course, the pull of the known that brought Bachner home. All the way down Lwowska Street and into the streets behind Plac Zgody he carried his story. He had seen the final horror and was now mad-eyed and his hair had silvered in his brief absence. All the Krakow Jews who had been rounded up in early June had been taken to Belzec, a camp situated on the Russian border. His account continued: When the trains arrived at the railway station the people were driven out by Ukrainians with clubs. There was a frightful stench about the place, but an SS man had kindly told people that it was due to the use of disinfectant. The people were lined up in front of two large warehouses, one marked "Cloak Room" and the other "Valuables." The new arrivals were made to undress, and a small Jewish boy passed among the crowd handing out lengths of string with which to tie their shoes together. Spectacles and rings were removed. So, naked, the prisoners had their heads shaved, an SS NCO telling them that their hair was needed to make something special for U-boat crews. They were assured that it would grow again, maintaining the myth of their continued usefulness.

At last, the victims were driven down a barbed-wire corridor to bunkers with a Star of David on the roof which was labeled "Baths and inhalation." SS men reassured them all the way, telling them to breathe deeply as it was an excellent means of disinfection. Bachner saw a little girl drop a bracelet on the ground, and a boy of three picked it up and went into the bunker playing with it. They were all gassed. Afterwards, the camp work Jews were sent in to disentangle the pyramid of corpses and take the bodies away for burial.

While waiting in a great enclosure for his turn Bachner had become alarmed by the tone of the reassurances issuing from the SS. He lowered himself into the latrine pit where he slept standing for three days, the human waste up to his neck. His face a hive of flies, he remained standing, wedged in the hole for fear of drowning. fInally, he crawled out at night and slipped away under the wire, following the railway line back to Krakow.[147] Bachner was the only survivor of a transport that had contained several thousand Krakow Jews.

There is no record of what happened to Bachner after his return, but one of the indictments against Goeth, the commandant of Plaszow camp, was the shooting of a Bachner family in Plaszow in 1943.[148]

Oskar Schindler knew about Belzec. It is inconceivable that he did not know as Belzec was the designated death camp for the environs of Krakow. Also, Amon Goeth (the Mad Dog of Lublin) was part and parcel of Aktion Reinhardt in Lublin. Goeth was the planner and instigator of the modus operandi for clearing the Jewish Ghettos in the Lublin and Galician districts so graphically described in the film *Schindler's List*. Schindler, on hearing

Bachner's story, went to Belzec to verify the details but was turned back by the SS-guards. Schindler had on a number of occasions attempted to penetrate the security cordon around Belzec but was unable to do so, even with his security clearance documents. According to Mrs. Schindler he never got nearer than the small town of Tomaszow-Lubelski, some five kilometers from the camp.

Personally, or using couriers, Schindler sent the Jewish Defense Committee in Budapest information about Belzec and the tragic fate of Jews in the General Government. Schindler distributed secret Hebrew letters concerning the situation and conditions in the Plaszow camp, deportations, and Nazi terror. Oskar Schindler was travelling very close to detection and arrest. It is a fact that any person, high ranking or not, found within the Belzec camp perimeter without authority from the highest level (Odilo Globcnik at Reinhardt headquarters or the Reichsführer SS Himmler) was summarily shot. Schindler would have been no exception.

To this day the residents of Belzec village are still burdened by the former death camp, which was the deadliest and most brutal of all the Nazi killing grounds. Belzec is the forgotten camp of the Holocaust and has not been treated extensively by historians despite being the blueprint and precursor to Sobibor and Treblinka. It was Oskar Schindler who brought news of what was going on in the east and alerted the world.

Between March 15 and December 12, 1942, no less than 600,000 Jewish men, women and children were murdered by gassing in the extermination camp at Belzec.

Chapter Eight
The Mad Dog of Lublin

Figure 38: SS-Hauptsturmführer Amon Leopold Goeth, Plaszow 1943

Photo Credit: Author's Collection

Amon Leopold Goeth was born in Vienna on December 11, 1908. He was married and divorced twice – in 1934 and 1944 – and had two children. He studied agriculture in Vienna until 1928. From 1928 until 1939 he was employed by Verlag für Militar und Fachliteratur, a company in Vienna. In 1930, Goeth joined the NSDAP, and in 1932 he became a member of the SS. On March 5, 1940, he was called up by the Wehrmacht with the rank of Unterfeldwebel. He was promoted in succession to SS-Obersturmführer (1940), Untersturmführer with the letter 'F' [professional officer in war time] (1941), and Hauptsturmführer (1944), and was the holder of the Cross of Merit with Swords.

Goeth joined the staff of SS General Odilo Globocnik as an inspector of concentration camps, serving in Cieszyn, Katowice, and Lublin. In February 1943 he left Lublin after a conflict with SS Major Hermann Hofle and was transferred to Krakow with the rank of SS-Unterscharführer, as the Commandant of the Plaszow labor camp. Goeth's duty in Krakow was from February 11, 1943, until September 13, 1944.

Goeth arrived in Krakow after February 11, 1943, with the commission to liquidate the ghetto and set up a concentration camp in the Krakow suburb of Plaszow. While commander of the camp Goeth became acquainted with Oskar Schindler. The two men shared common interests – a life of luxury, women, and alcohol. Goeth's influence among the Nazi elite was indisputable and Schindler needed additional army contracts. Goeth was the person who provided Schindler with Jewish prisoners from the camp; he arranged everything Schindler required to achieve his goals. Schindler managed to reward Goeth: the corruption prevalent among Nazi administration led to unimaginable opportunities. Oskar Schindler was well aware of this fact and was able to use it to his (and the Abwehr's) own advantage.

It was clear that Goeth had come with a brief to destroy the remaining Jews of Krakow. To do this, the Nazis chose a most symbolic site – the new Jewish cemetery on the outskirts of the city, in the suburbs of Plaszow. Huts were constructed there in desecration of the freshly dug graves and a fraudulent sign was hung up, reading Arbeitslager (labor camp).

When the Jews from all the ghettos within the area fell into the grasp of the SS, the true nature of the sign was revealed: concentration camp. In the beginning, the sparsely wooded camp did not awaken any special misgivings. The first residential huts, the kitchen, bakery, latrines, and workshops geared to local needs did not give rise to any great panic. Fears, however, very quickly returned. It was a prototype of a concentration camp, with all the infamous facilities meeting the exact requirements necessary for the mass extermination of the enslaved population. The camp led off from the cemetery, where the road was paved with tombstones from the desecrated graves. A special detachment of prisoners ground the magnificent tombstones into pebbles and gravel, and a second group of prisoners pressed the pieces into the earth of the cemetery with the aid of sledgehammers and hand rollers.

Slowly and in stages, the camp began to occupy more and more space; it expanded, swallowing up huge chunks of land, homes, and plots until finally its perimeter stretched for about two kilometers. The camp was built to hold about 10,000 Jews who were destined to be the raw material for the new factories at nearby Auschwitz. Towards the end of 1943, the number of prisoners in Plaszow grew to more than 25,000.

Figure 39: Paving slabs (Josef Bau)
Photo Credit: Author's collection

SS-Hauptsturmführer Amon Goeth is described here by Josef Bau (69084) as:

> "... a hideous and terrible monster who reached the height of more than two meters. He set the fear of death in people, terrified masses, and accounted for much chattering of teeth. He ran the camp through extremes of cruelty that are beyond the comprehension of a compassionate mind, employing tortures which dispatched his victims to hell.
>
> For even the slightest infraction of the 'rules' he would rain blow after blow upon the face of the helpless offender, and would observe, with satisfaction born of sadism, how the cheek of his victim would swell and turn blue, how the teeth would fall out and the eyes would fill with tears.
>
> Anyone who was being whipped by him was forced to count – in a loud voice – each stroke of the whip and if he made a mistake was forced to start counting over again. During interrogations, which were conducted in his office, he would set the dog on the accused that was strung by his legs from a specially placed hook in the ceiling. In the event of an escape from the camp, he would order the entire group from which the escapee had come to form a row, would give the order to count ten, and would, himself, kill every tenth person. At one morning parade, in the presence of all the prisoners, he shot a Jew because, as he complained, the man was too tall. Then, as the man lay dying, he urinated on him. Once he caught a boy who was sick with diarrhea and was unable to restrain himself. Goeth forced him to eat all the excrement and then shot him."[149]

Women prisoners were not exempted, as Gena Turgel describes:

> "My sister Hela was in a group of women sitting, breaking tombstones into tiny pieces for building roads. Another older woman was working with Hela, when Goeth appeared and told the older woman she was not doing it right. Goeth showed her how to do it. When the older woman returned to her work, Goeth shot her.
>
> The first thing in the morning was that Goeth would walk over to the men's side. It was so quiet; you could have heard a fly buzzing. The atmosphere was tense and full of fear. I could hear the echo of Goeth's shouting, and the growling of dogs. Goeth would appear with his bodyguard. Goeth walked slowly staring at each man in turn. He would say, "You haven't shaved today," and shoot the man down; or to another, "you look too clever" and shoot him down.[150]

To emphasize the brutality of Goeth, outlined below are many of the incidents that formed the basis of the indictments against him when he was finally arraigned before the military court in Krakow shortly after the war.

The record also shows his complicity within the corruption of the Plaszow camp. The archived material on Goeth is substantial, and the selection is based on record cards which contain factual accounts of incidents relating to Goeth while he was Commandant of the Plaszow concentration camp. All the incidents are supported by evidence obtained during Goeth's interrogation – first, by the SS during the war, and second, by post-war investigations into his conduct. This evidence formed the basis of the indictments against Goeth in the Polish courts after the war:

1. In February 1943, he shot four Jews in KL Plaszow. (1/106)
2. He shot the Jew Szab in the camp. (1/219)
3. Goeth did not obtain a receipt from the Jewish gravedigger, Ladner, for gold found on the corpses, which was contrary to regulations. (39/298) [Ladner was on special duty for the Commandant. Whether the gold came from a Jew or not, he handed property to Goeth, who should have signed for it. The SS accountants were ruthless about non-compliance. Goeth just pocketed the goods. In Nazi Germany you could kill Jews, but stealing their property, which was the property of the Reich, meant a death sentence. Many SS officers were shot, not for abusing or killing Jews, but for stealing their property, an offense against the Party.]
4. On March 14, 1942, he was present at the execution of 300 Jews in KL Plaszow. (774/84)
5. On March 13, 1943, he supervised the extermination of the Krakow ghetto, and, to acknowledge his contribution, he was promoted two ranks (from SS-Untersturmführer to SS-Hauptsturmführer). Goeth claimed that he was not present in the ghetto on March 13, 1943. (2586/52)
6. Goeth organized a range of workshops in the camp to use prisoners as slave laborers. He started full-blood horse breeding and a stock farm; he gave pompous parties for high-ranking SS officials; he organized a brothel for the camp guards and personally selected good-looking Polish girls from the assembly ground. (968/3)
7. He organized a brothel in the SS barrack 173. (843/248).
8. He claimed that the camp in Plaszow was self-sufficient, had its own farm with vegetables, cows, and pigs. (2586/50)
9. In the summer of 1944, in his presence, 70 parachutists and nine Jewesses were shot. (774/156)
10. On September 3, 1943, he took small children with mothers on a transport from Plaszow to the Tarnow ghetto and shot them. (774/)
11. In February 1943, he shot Sonnenschein, Spielmann, and Schwed in the Plaszow camp. (954/1)
12. In February 1943, he shot four people from the Balsam family in Plaszow: Dr. Shtermer and three people from the Bachner family. (967/6)

13. Goeth shot all the sick, the doctors, and the workers from the Jewish hospital; he shot Schoenfeld, Fleiss, Sonnenschein, and Ferber. (971/1) [151]

14. Goeth personally chose dates of selections and supervised them. (774/162)

15. Without authorization, he extended the imprisonment of prisoners in the camp. (774/125)

16. In September 1943, he shot Inberg for slow progress of building work supervised by him. (774/109)

17. Inberg (proxy of Bonarek's brick yard) was shot for errors during the allocation of labor. (2586/30)

18. From September 1943 to February 1944, he supervised the liquidation of the Szebnie camp. On September 2, 1943, he personally selected people in the Tarnow ghetto for transport. (774/134)

19. On September 13, 1943, he supervised the liquidation of the Tarnow ghetto. He misappropriated property of the Tarnow Jews. On September 13, 1944, he was arrested by the SS and Polizeigericht V1 in Krakow for large scale fraud. (2586/32-980/3)

20. Goeth was also interrogated by the Sicherheitspolizei for giving information to the engineer Grunberg about the liquidation of the Krakow ghetto. (2586/119)

21. Grunberg, a German Aryan, was sympathetic to the Jews and was closely associated with Stern, Pemper, and Schindler. He passed the information on to Schindler who, in turn, warned the ghetto leaders. Goeth arranged the escape of the collaborating Jews Chilowicz and his wife. He informed Koppe about a planned riot in the camp and received approval for the liquidation of Chilowicz and his wife as leaders of the planned riot. They knew too much about Goeth. (2586/32)

22. He beat the prisoner Olmer with a riding whip, then shot him.

23. During the liquidation of the Krakow ghetto, he shot about 50 children.

24. He shot his Jewish maidservant in order to destroy evidence of "racial disgrace."

25. He shot his orderly because he gave him the wrong horse to ride.

26. On March 14, 1942, he was a participant in the execution of 300 people in the camp's limestone quarry. (774/84)

27. On August 3, 1943, on his order, a 16-year-old boy named Haubenstock was hanged for singing a Russian song.

28. The engineer Krautwirth was hanged for making comments about camp guards. (2586/33)

29. According to Goeth, both Haubenstock and Krautwirth were hanged because they incited mutiny amongst the Ukrainian guards. (2586/53) [152]

30. On March 29, 1943, Goeth interrogated and tortured Frankl and Lieberman after their attempt to meet their families in Julag. (774/158)

31. There was a similar incident with a German Jew. (1044/4)

32. In 1942, Goeth was a participant in the extermination of the Rzeszow ghetto. (972/6)

33. During the liquidation of the Tarnow Ghetto, he shot a girl who asked him for a transfer to a different working group to be together with her fiancé. (774/134)

34. In March 1943, Goeth murdered Kapo Hirschberg. In November 1943, he murdered Kapos Penner and Scheinfeld. He also ordered the killing of Odeman Bloch and ten prisoners.

35. In May 1943, he ordered the killing of Kapo Beim.

36. In the summer of the same year, he ordered the killing of 16 people working in the firm Kabel. (2586/33)

37. Under the leadership of Hässe, he prepared the plans for the extermination of ghettos in Tarnow, Bochnia, Rzeszow, and Przemysl. (2586/29)

38. On September 3, 1943, during the liquidation of the Tarnow ghetto, he shot the wife of Chaski Klappholz and a number of other people, including all the children. (2586/35)[153]

39. On September 13, 1944, after his arrest by the SS, he was accused of allowing prisoners of Jewish nationality (Mietek Pemper) to inspect personal records of camp officers. (2586/71)[154]

Viktor Dortheimer:

"It was May 1943; there were about 50 of us in the painters' barracks in Plaszow. Goeth arrived and asked how many prisoners were present. Ferber replied 50 or 51. Goeth shouted, 'Are there 50 or 51?' Kapo Ferber said that maybe one had gone to the toilet. Goeth pulled his pistol and shot Ferber in front of me. He was dead before he hit the ground."

Figure 40: Viktor Dortheimer (left) and Josef Bau, Israel 1995
Photo Credit: Author's collection

At the rear of the women's barracks was the death pit – a vast open grave measuring 20 meters long, 6 meters wide, and 3 meters deep. All those who were executed by the SS or who died by other means were dumped unceremoniously into the pit and left to rot. Those prisoners brought to the pit by the SS for execution were shot at the edge of the pit and, with the momentum of a bullet in the nape, would tumble in, to be covered by a shovelful of lime.

Schindler and Goeth

Schindler met Amon Goeth at the newly constructed Commandant's villa, *Rotes Haus* (Red Villa), occupied by Goeth and his mistress, Ruth Kalder. This informal dinner party was attended by all the bosses of the establishment, the armaments and supply factories, security, and police chiefs – the establishment of the New Order. Schindler was there because of his persona and reputation for giving charitable gifts. He was also there doing his duty for Canaris.[155]

Emilie Schindler remembers her first meeting with Goeth:

> "He was the most despicable person I ever met, a schizophrenic: one side was that of a refined Viennese gentleman, and the other was dedicated to terrorizing the Jews under his jurisdiction. He was two meters tall, with feminine hips, dark hair, and fleshy lips. I remember him as being thin, not overweight as in the film. Whilst we ate, Goeth drank incessantly, and Oskar began to

follow the rhythm. Before knowing the Nazi society, he hardly drank (contrary to all the evidence), but now I was afraid he would become an alcoholic. During the day, he [Goeth] would kill for the sake of killing. In the evening he could criticize the pitch of any one note in a piece of classical music."[156]

In early January 1943, Schindler astutely read the situation that the Jews were destined for disaster. Many of his workers had been taken to the Plaszow labor camp, which entailed a daily march from the camp to the Emalia works, escorted by the Ukrainian guards. Schindler bought a plot of land adjacent to his factory from a young Polish couple. Through his contacts with the Armaments Inspectorate, he acquired the necessary permission to build barracks within the Emalia complex. He then applied to the SS offices at 2 Pomorska Street, Krakow, for planning permission to construct the barracks in accordance with the known regulations. Site meetings were called and final approval came from the SS bureaucracy and from Amon Goeth for the release of the Plaszow prisoners to the Schindler factory barracks.

Approximately 900 Jews worked for Schindler in 1943. These workers came to Emalia from the Plaszow camp without the typical prisoner convoys under SS guard. Schindler was able to convince Goeth to allow him to set up a sub-camp next to his factory in Zablocie. The camp was established on May 8, 1943, under the command of Albert Hujar, Eberhard Behr and Edmund Zdrojewski. By May 22, 1942, a total of 66 Jews were living in the camp; three days later this number had risen to 558. A total of 11 quarters were located in the camp – seven for prisoners, the camp kitchen, infirmary, and quarters for SS guards and the Jewish police units.

The Emalia factory grew continuously, as did the number of workers employed. In 1942 a total of 550 people worked at Emalia; this figure was by no means the final count. Upon request from Jews themselves, Schindler set up a "rest area" for workers adjacent to the workshops in 1942. Guard services in the sub-camp were performed by Ukrainians and "Werkschutz" – factory guards. Peretz Selinger became the head of the camp. Order units were charged with registering prisoners when they arrived for work and for inspections on their return.[157]

A distinct advantage to the SS was that they would no longer have to supply daily escorts for the prisoners who were traveling some three kilometers daily from the Plaszow camp. Instead, the Jewish labor force would be within 50 meters of Schindler's armament production factory. Goeth supported Schindler's plans and facilitated the project by supplying experts from the Plaszow camp to work on the construction of the barracks. Adam Guard (69515), a young engineer, was transferred by Goeth from Plaszow to the new building project at the Schindler works.[158] In the new Schindler barracks, kitchens, a laundry and even showers were installed. These new facilities were questioned by the SS, but Schindler just mentioned the control of typhus and lice to end any argument.

It cannot be repeated too often that his factory became a haven for Jews, a haven in which Schindler sheltered many who were old and weak, and, therefore, inefficient workers. It is important to keep this fact in mind when one hears the charge that Schindler's self-interest was most important when he built his sub-camp. Without a doubt, there is some truth in this. By saving his workers from daily harassment and torture, he increased their efficiency and the output of his factory and profits. But it is equally evident that his compassion often outweighed his profit motive. Schindler took advantage of the rivalries between the Armaments Inspectorate, the Gestapo, and the SS, since he knew the Armaments, Inspectorate was likely to support any scheme that would add to the difficulties of the SS. It is not hard to imagine the pleasure and sense of power he got from playing various Nazi institutions and officials against each other. Schindler made good use of his contacts within the Armaments Inspectorate throughout the war, thereby acquiring the reputation of an industrialist interested in producing weapons required by the army. The result of this reputation was that he was able to increase the leeway he needed to pursue other purposes. Similarly, the more invaluable his reputation made him, the more help and protection he could offer his workers and other Jews outside the camp.

This episode did not come cheaply to Schindler. Emilie Schindler recalled:

> "My husband built the barracks under SS supervision. Goeth, of course, arranged the transfer of labor from Plaszow, but it was all based on my husband paying him. That was done with diamonds, presents, and other things, as money had no value."[159]

From a report Schindler wrote in July 1945 to Dr. Ball-Kaduri, we are able to grasp the turmoil confronting him:

> "Because of the persecution of the Jews in the whole of Poland, the elimination of their earning capacity, the liquidation of the ghettos, and the opening of concentration camps in 1942, I had to make a decision – either do without my Jewish workforce or leave them to their fate, as did 99 percent of Krakow businesses who employed Jews; or to build a private, respectable company facility and encamp all my Jewish workers there. My attitude towards the Jewish workforce helped me overcome the threatening difficulties that confronted me. In only a few days we were able to erect and build our new camp. This saved hundreds of Jews from deportation. I, myself, resided near the camp. Jews came from neighboring camps, i.e. NKF, a cooling and air parts factory called Hodermann, the Krakow crate company Renst Kuhnpast, and the barracks of the army garrison administration, also the engineering works, Chmielevski. Thus, I saved another 450 Jews from deportation. I am proud to say that it was through my initiative that these Jews remained in my work camp. With no fear on my behalf, I conducted all the negotiations regarding the Jews directly with the governing

body of the SS. The establishment of my work camp had to be
financed entirely out of my own funds. It was enough for the SS
if their safety regulations were adhered to."[160]

At one time I was dubious about the credibility of his statements. I am
becoming persuaded that they must receive due credit as the Schindler
story has now unfolded. Corroboration of his activities comes from
independent sources, by Estera Pinkas (76399) and Leopold Dagen
(69434), whose accounts of the new barracks were reported to the French
Military Police on their flight to the Allies after the war. Affidavits from
these two witnesses plus a number of others are in the archives at Yad
Vashem. Estera Pinkas (the wife of Richard Rechen) was interviewed in
Haifa in 1995. The Dagen affidavit not only corroborates Pincas but refers
to Schindler offering the same protection to his 600 free Polish workers
who were in constant danger of labor transports. Dagen refers to Schindler
having to go to the SS to rescue his Polish workers who had been seized
off the streets. This is significant when assessing the motives of Schindler.

Figure 41: Plaszow Camp as drawn by Josef Bau
Photo Credit: Author's collection

Z.......Women's Barracks
N.......Men's Barracks
W.......Workshops
M.......Houses for Germans
+.......Hospitals
L.......Latrines
K.......Crematorium
E.......Pools
T.......Watch Towers
S.......Quarries

Hospital..........................20,21,22	Rabbits................................139
Epidemic Hospital......................1,4	Chicken Run............................140
Quarantine...........................18,19	Latrine for Quarantine..................20
Jewish Police...........................14	Laundry................................23
Central Latrine......................27,32	Meat Storeroom.........................30
Food Storeroom..........................31	Kitchen................................37
Bakery..................................38	Clothing Store.........................48
Bath House..............................49	Delicing Center........................50
Brush Manufacturer......................95	Hairs for Brushes......................77
Blacksmith..............................84	Central Store....................85,88,105
Cobbler.................................82	Watchmaker.............................83
Electrician.............................87	Potato Store...........................81
Paper Utilisation.......................90	Carpentry...........................91,94
Printing Shop...........................92	
Barracks for Watchman..................163	(Wachkaserne)
Morgue.................................164	(Leichenhalle)
Telephone Exchange.....................155	
The Grey House.........................171	(Graues Haus)
Administration.........................172	(Verwaltung)
Brothel................................173	Dog Kennels............................180
Officers Villas.........177,181,179,182,183	The Red House..........................176
Hospital for SS........................200	
Commander..............................201	(Kommandatur)
Railway Station....................202,203	Main Gate..............................294
Women's Camp Gate......................205	Hujowa Gorka...........................206
Mass Grave.............................207	Tailors.............117,118,124,107,108,113
Madritsch..........127,126,125,111,115,121	Upholsterers...........................120
Furmakers...........................114,119	Chemical Laboratory................130,131
Pig Stye...............................137	Car Repair.............................132
Bookstores..........................133,134	Horses and Carts.......................138

Figure 42: Legend: Plaszow Camp
Photo Credit: Author's collection

Chapter Nine
Destruction of the Ghetto

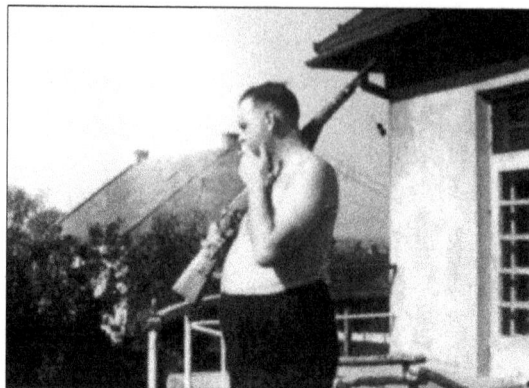

Figure 43: Amon Goeth, Plaszow 1943
Photo Credit: Author's collection

The ghetto in Podgorze existed until March 13, 1943.[161] In the final "Action," the SS, with the help of Ukrainian volunteers, brought to an end the Jewish community of Krakow, known also as "Kehila Kedosha Kruke" – the holy community of Krakow. Only its famous synagogues, the Alte Schul, the Remu synagogue, the synagogue of Rabbi Isaac and others, are preserved to this day.

The population of the ghetto decreased each day. Almost daily, transports were sent to the camp in Plaszow. They started billeting people who worked on the barracks in Plaszow and also those who were employed in many other shops, offices, and factories beyond the ghetto area – such as Schindler's Emalia, the airport and cable workshops at Montelupich, the clothing manufacturing firm of Madritsch (Podgorze's Main Square 2), Deutsche Rustungsfabrik in Zablocie, and the brick factory in Bonarka. Jews were billeted in only a few places. The others were brought to work under close guard from the camp and were returned to the camp in Plaszow after completing their work. Long columns of people could be seen, wretched and abused physically and mentally, filing slowly through the streets of the former ghetto.

The first doctor from the Krakow ghetto who was sent to the Plaszow camp was Dr. Leon Gross. He later became chief camp doctor, elevated to that position because he was the first one who came to Plaszow,[162] and he was used by the Nazis for selections in the camp. Dr. Gross and his stepson were on the Schindler list that left Plaszow for Brünnlitz via Gross-Rosen. All fathers and children were later transferred from Brünnlitz to Auschwitz in late 1944. Much against his will, Dr. Gross was again used by the Nazis for selections. Dr. Gross and his stepson survived the war. On direct orders from the Reichsführer SS, the destruction of the ghetto was carried out under the command of SS-Obergruppenführer Friedrich Wilhelm Krüger,

Commander of the Police and SS Forces in the General Government. Krüger was assisted by Amon Goeth and SS-Sturmbannführer Willy Hasse.[163]

The Nazis had prepared the ground beforehand. In November 1942, Jewish work details[164] were employed, building barracks for the new extension to Julag 1. The area to be extended was between Abraham and Jerozolimska streets, where two Jewish cemeteries belonging to the Krakow and Podgorze communities were situated. Both cemeteries were completely destroyed during the course of leveling the ground. The newer cemetery on Miodowa Street was devastated. Here the tombs and tombstones were overturned and broken, granite and marble monuments were torn out. Large black marble slabs were prepared for export, because they were needed for paving the walks leading to the villas of German dignitaries; two more remote cemeteries were destroyed. Only one solitary headstone remains standing on the site, the headstone of Chaim Jacob Abrahamer, who died on May 25, 1932.[165]

At the beginning of 1943, the ghetto was divided by a wooden fence and barbed wire into two parts: Ghetto A for those who were working and Ghetto B for those who were not working. In Plaszow there were now three camps fully equipped for the intended intake of prisoners: Julag I in Plaszow, Julag II in Prokocim, and Julag III in Biezanow. Julag I, the main camp under the command of Amon Goeth, was to be used exclusively for Jews. The Jews who lived in Ghetto A were rounded up and paraded on Plac Zgody, where the selections began. The men were separated from the women and children. The children were separated from the women, with the assurance from the SS that they would be taken to a special barracks in the Plaszow Kinderheim. Many of these mothers did not trust the SS and were unwilling to leave their children alone. Taking their children, they would cross from Ghetto A to Ghetto B. Their survival was not calculated to last 24 hours. Transfer from the good to the bad was allowed – i.e., from A to B, but movement from B to A was forbidden. Spielberg gives us a graphic account (I believe taken from the Pankiewicz documentation) of the liquidation of the Krakow ghetto, the brutality and the fear, the hopelessness and despair, the surrender of the weak against the full might of the battle-tested SS.

Under the directions of SS-Obergruppenführer Schermer, the gates of Ghetto A were opened, and in columns of four-abreast, the Jews designated for Plaszow were marched out of the ghetto and headed to the Plaszow camp. The preliminaries were completed. Late in the afternoon, the last inhabitants of Ghetto A departed, with the exception of the OD, Gutter, and a few members of the Judenrat, who were ordered to stay until the liquidation of the ghetto was complete.

During the evacuation of Ghetto, A, many people tried to escape, but were shot on the spot and left lying in the road. Others had devised clever escape methods by lifting off the covers to the main sewers that crossed under the streets of Podgorze and disappearing into the stinking waste and crawling to the outlet on the Vistula. This was how Dr. Julian Aleksandrowicz escaped with his wife and small son.[166] There were two main escapes into the sewers: one at the junction of Jozefinska and Krakusa streets, and the other at the crossing of Jozefinska and Wegierska streets. Many escaped this way until the SS discovered this route, waited at the outlets, and shot the escapees.

Now it was the turn of Ghetto B. At dawn on March 14, the Sonderdienst (auxiliary police units) composed of Lithuanians, Latvians, Ukrainians, and the Blue Police, surrounded the ghetto. People in the ghetto were running in all directions in absolute panic. Shouting, crying people were loaded down with possessions looking for a sanctuary where there was none. Then, there was utter silence and all those in the area froze, their eyes turned towards Targowa Street. Dressed in a black leather coat, holding a riding crop in one hand and a short automatic rifle in the other, accompanied by two large dogs (Rolph and Ralph), and surrounded by his personal bodyguards, stood Amon Goeth. Other dignitaries arrived and selected their favorites, their informants, and selected personnel who were not to be subjected to the upcoming liquidation.[167]

Figure 44: Jews marching five abreast in Plaszow 1943
Photo Credit: Author's collection

Following are contemporary accounts of this day. Tadeusz Pankiewicz notes from his observation post only meters from the Action:

> "Ghetto A had been completely liquidated; all close and distant friends were gone. People were moving like lunatics in corridors, cellars, and attics of the buildings in Plac Zgody. There were the old, carrying religious books and ritual attire under their arms. Children were wandering on their own, holding one another's hands. They sat down on asphalt in utmost composure. They were laughing. And the throng was swelling; the square was getting more and more crowded. And now the SS and Sonderdienst units enter the gate on Plac Zgody. Helmeted, fully armed, the sons of Herrenvolk (master race)

draw up in a double line. And again, the scenes in front of our windows are similar to those already seen; but now the butchery expands in ever widening circles. It looks as if the Germans wanted to choke with blood to satisfy their hunger for it. Everyone is shooting; everyone who wants, everyone who is willing.

I saw how the OD man Immerglück led his own mother. As a token of recognition for his dedicated service in the OD, he was permitted to accompany his mother. He covered her with a blanket, gave her last directions for the journey, embraced her, and smoothed her hair. The farewell – a long, suffering, unending kiss, the son's tearful eyes and the infinite terror in his mother's face. When he left the square walking slowly, she stood with her arms outstretched. The Germans stood nearby, but somehow this time; they did not laugh. Several hours later, the son was stripping off his mother's clothes and carried her still warm corpse to the platform where the murdered were collected. Thus, she was saved from deportation.

Deathlike silence lies heavily on the empty streets and houses of the ghetto. Emptiness breathes from every corner, every street, and every threshold. The ghetto ceased to exist..." [168]

Victor Dortheimer (69124):

"On March 13, 1943, when the ghetto was liquidated, I was selected for labor and taken to the Plaszow labor camp. I was ordered to join a detail to dig mass graves. The next day, at 10 a.m., flat topped wagons loaded with corpses and covered with tree branches started to arrive. We buried thousands that day. All the Jews left in the ghetto had been shot. My father joined me in Plaszow, and he was put to work in the stables."[169]

Victor was 24 years old.

Solomon Urbach (69427):

"On the night of March 12/13, 1943, I was working in the Emalia factory. Schindler told us not to return to the ghetto. He told us that there was trouble in the ghetto. The ghetto was liquidated, together with my family, my parents, two sisters, and two brothers. One brother was shot down as he crossed from one line to another. The rest of the family's fate is unknown to me, but I suspect they went to Auschwitz."[170]

Solomon was 17 years old.

Moshe Pantirer (69040):

"Goeth himself, together with the SS, were in charge. Children and sick people were shot on the spot and the bodies were brought up in flat trucks into our camp in Plaszow. I myself, with a group of other boys, had to unload the corpses. In one case we asked a German to give a 'kindness' shot to a young kid who was still alive. The German told us it was a shame to waste a bullet on a Jew. We had to pour gasoline over the bodies and keep burning them. My father and mother, my younger sister and youngest brother were all split up. The Germans put the men to one side and the women and children to another side. My father decided not to be separated. My mother was holding a child in her hand and my father was holding a child by the hand, and the SS shot him on the spot. I know that for a fact. A few days later people who witnessed this told me and said that my father was a hero, and that's the insanity of it. That we, the innocent, felt guilty for what the murderers did to us."[171]

Moshe was 17 years old.

Young children were led by the hand by the SS around a corner and lined up, one in front of the other. With a single rifle shot several children were killed with the one shot – a scene that was graphically displayed in Spielberg's film.

Elsewhere in the ghetto on that morning, 3,000 Jews were rounded up for deportation. Even before the trains could leave for Birkenau, several hundred small children were shot in the entrance to one of the houses, and several hundred old people were shot in the streets. The sick were also killed. When the Gestapo entered the hospital, an officer ordered Dr. Zygmunt Fischer to abandon his patients. He refused to do so and was shot, together with his wife and child. The patients were then killed in the wards. Also murdered were doctors Blau, Bruno, and Palin. Dr. Wladislaw Sztencel was murdered in Plaszow and Dr. Stanislaw Eibeschutz had been deported in one of the transports to Belzec. Two women doctors, well-known in Krakow, were transferred to the camp in Szebniach: Dr. Paulina Wasserberger and her sister, Dr. Door. They were both killed in the liquidation of that camp. Dr. R. Glassner perished in the camp at the airport.

From his observation post, the ghetto pharmacist Tadeusz Pankiewicz saw other SS officers personally known to him: W. Kunde, K. Olde, Heinrich, K. Heinemayer (chief of the political division of the Gestapo and his deputy, specialist SIPO Koener), and, of course, Goeth's personal bodyguard, Oberscharführer Albert Hujar, who was personally responsible for shooting all the patients in the main hospital at Jozefinska Street. Pankiewicz noted, "Hujar was running amok like a rabid animal through the entire building, leaving a trail of blood and corpses; he shot the guard at the gate and the dog cowering in the doghouse."

Many of the Jews committed suicide, mostly with cyanide. At first, getting a supply of the poison was difficult. Later, a source was found: the lamp factory of Wachs on Lwowska Street used cyanide in the manufacture of their products. People were able to obtain the poison there which was coveted as a priceless treasure. Entire families always carried it with them in small bottles just, as the saying goes, in case.[172]

For three days it was carnage on the streets of the ghetto. There were sad hearts and an air of depression everywhere. There was not one person who was not affected by the events in the ghetto. Schindler had witnessed the carnage from the vantage point of Krzemionki Hill overlooking the ghetto.

In another incident during the liquidation of the ghetto, Julius Madritsch was hard at work in his clothing factory within the ghetto. As an SS subsidiary factory manager, he was obliged to issue his workers with identity papers. While finalizing these papers, he received terrible news. All the small Jewish children were to be resettled. Madritsch frantically wrestled with himself. How could he at least save the children of his workers?[173]

Oswald Bousco,[174] a German-Czech, had joined the SS when in Vienna, but he was now Lieutenant Bousco, assistant to the German police commander in Podgorze. He was well-known and respected by the Jews in the ghetto. Bousco came to Madritsch in his greatest hour of need. Bousco, Madritsch, Schindler, and Titsch smuggled men, women, and children out of the ghetto, to the safety of the Madritsch factory. To do this, Bousco had to dope some of the smaller children with luminal and codeine which he had obtained from Pankiewicz, the Podgorze chemist, and put the small children into rucksacks. With the help of the other conspirators, he smuggled them out of the ghetto to safety on the Aryan side. Many Poles came forward to help in this rescue. Olek Rosner, the six-year-old son of Henry Rosner (69261) [Goeth's music maker] was one of these children.[175]

Even soldiers of the Wehrmacht were appalled at the brutality of the ghetto liquidation. Some of these Wehrmacht soldiers assisted in spiriting away women and children to the Tarnow ghetto, away from the danger.[176] The full might of the Third Reich bore down on an unarmed and defenseless people with no sign or suggestion of retaliation by force of arms. These were the heroes of National Socialism, the SS. It was a massacre.

"How much longer will we go as sheep to the slaughter? Why do we keep quiet? Why is there no call for escape to the forests?"[177] asked Emanuel Ringelblum in a speech he gave in mid-June 1942, to the head of the Jewish Social Relief Organization in Warsaw. This is the one central question that has been intensely on the minds of many. Pankiewicz was no exception and gives us his simple and logical explanation:

> "I was frequently asked, in the company of my Polish acquaintances, whether the Jews were so oblivious that they could not realize what was in store for them. Why, knowing that they were to be deported and would be killed, did they take these things with them? [Pankiewicz was referring to the bundles, packages, bedding, and household items which the Jews took with them on the transports, knowing they were going to their deaths.] Why didn't they resist in self-defense? Why did they let themselves be led docilely like sheep to the slaughter? Such questions could only be asked by people who eyewitnesses to these events were not, whose information was received obliquely and not quite completely.

Anyone who did not see first-hand the awesome horror could not understand or grasp the dire circumstances that plagued these people. They could not fathom the perfidious lies which misled them the day before their death. If my questioners could spend even a few hours in the funereal atmosphere in which these "Actions" took place they would understand. Every few steps someone was killed, beaten, humiliated, and tortured. If one could look behind the scenes of these crimes and see the perpetrators, observe the means they used to instill fear and terror, cruelly shooting, and deceiving the 'resettled' with a hope that they would live; if the inquirers knew about the threats of revenge on the entire family for even thinking about escape, for sabotage, and for any self-defense act – he would no longer ask "why." Besides, unlike the Warsaw ghetto, for instance, the Krakow ghetto could not use resistance because of its geographical location. After all, deep in the heart of all glimmered the hope of survival that was a wonderful word in those days; this was my impression arrived at in those fateful days as a result of my experiences in the ghetto."[178]

Within a few hours, the Germans had killed approximately 1,500 persons and a further 3,000 were transported to Auschwitz. The Sauberungskolonne (cleaning up teams) worked in the ghetto until December 1943, selecting and storing objects, furniture, equipment, etc., left behind. The ghetto enclosure was then taken down and the area reverted to dwellings for the Polish inhabitants of Podgorze.

Julius Madritsch, who had a previous warning of the impending massacre, had been able to hold on to his workers but there were still hundreds of Jewish families evading and fleeing selection. Madritsch transported scores of them at night to the cellars of his workshops and then over a period removed them to his other factories in Bochnia and Tarnow, and even later, to sanctuary through Slovakia to Hungary.

Jacob Sternberg (68882) writes:

"Madritsch was entirely aware of the acts of rescue being carried out through his workshops, and, obviously, he thereby exposed himself to great risk. Nevertheless, he did not interfere, and so, greatly imperiled his own life. I was a witness to these acts of mercy and to Madritsch's involvement and sense of responsibility, as I was, at the time, in charge of the kitchen in the cellars, which was a focal point of the operations."

Stern and Schindler Cement Their Relationship

A very special relationship had now developed between Schindler and Stern, the compassionate helper and altruist. Two charismatic men of diverse personalities had come together in the Jews' greatest hour of need. Contrary to popular belief, Stern and Schindler had been leading quite independent lives in Krakow. Apart from their initial meeting in November 1939, they were not to realize their true friendship until after the liquidation of the Krakow Ghetto. Stern, working independently, had proved himself to be essential to the Ghetto Jews. An articulate report writer, he satisfied all needs. He was respected by both the Judenrat and the German administrators. In lieu of payment from the Joint Distribution Committee, he accepted luxuries such as milk, cocoa and cheese, which he distributed to the children and to the main hospital. Although the Stern / Schindler activities were quite independent of each other, Schindler ensured that Stern's funds were adequate by topping up the coffers at the most unexpected times and places.

In addition to his charity work, Stern sought security working on a part-time basis for a previous employer, Unkelbach. Unkelbach was from Bavaria. He was a product of the Hitler Youth, the NSDAP, and a former member of the Einsatzgruppen in Russia and had boasted of killing thousands of Jews. Wounded, he sought the quiet life of an administrator in Krakow.[179] Schindler knew all about Unkelbach and had warned Stern to be very careful in any dealings he might have with him. Schindler was privy to this information through his past and recent contact with SS-Standartenführer Dr Karl Eberhardt Schoengarth in the drinking establishments of the officer's clubs in Krakow.[180]

Stern was now at the very center of the turmoil engulfing the Jews. He was privy to some of the most sensitive intelligence concerning impending operations by the SS, which had been imparted to him by Schindler. He was clever enough to glean information from Unkelbach and balance this information with his loyalties to Schindler, the Judenrat and his fellow Jews. With the liquidation of the Ghetto, Stern found himself in the melting pot of Plazow labor camp, and he knew that they were on the last stages of "resettlement." His and his fellow Jews' last hope now was with Schindler.

It was not long before Unkelbach's workers brought trouble to the "Progress" factory. Shortly after the concession from Goeth, three employees from "Progress" disappeared, provoking a scandal. An inquiry was held, and it was established that, once delivered by the guards, the workers were allowed to wander around unguarded and unsupervised in the factory grounds. They were able to walk into Krakow to taste life's freedom. Because of this scandal, the factory was closed, and all workers returned to Plaszow. The disappearance of the three Jews was, at first, not followed up. Maybe Goeth wanted to protect Unkelbach? They were both friends.

The Jews, when in the ghetto, had been under the jurisdiction of the Gestapo, who benefited economically from them. As soon as the Jews were put into camps, they were placed under the jurisdiction of the SS, who then rented them out to various companies. The friction between the Gestapo and the SS affected the Jews. Some members of the Jewish Council and the Jewish Security Police worked with the Gestapo to track down hidden Jews. The Jews believed that by their cooperation they might survive the war.

For whatever reason, the missing Jews from factory "Progress" were reported to the Gestapo, who lost no time in accusing Goeth of negligence. Goeth issued an ultimatum to the whole camp: *"Give me their whereabouts or you will all be shot..."* Goeth seized Stern as a hostage. Within hours an address was forthcoming. An armed posse of SS went to the address in Krakow. It proved to be correct and there was a bloodbath. Stern was saved.

Unkelbach had lost the confidence of Goeth and was arrested. He was accused of taking bribes from Jews to allow Jewish children to be smuggled into the camp. Despite Unkelbach's utterance of wanting to kill all the Jewish children, he was disarmed and arrested. According to Stern he was never seen in the camp again.

An insight into Stern's character was given to the author by Menahem Halberthal, who worked closely with Stern after the war. Reflecting on their special relationship Menahem recalled:

> "Stern was not religious, but he retained a close interest in religious matters. His knowledge of Judaica was immense. He was a man of compromise, a negotiator, a man of understanding. He was always philosophizing and had a quotation or anecdote for every occasion and always tinged with humor. He never argued but persuaded by gentle coaxing. This was his strength and the strength that supported all those around him, even Schindler."[181]

Stern's attitude, even under pressure from the SS, did not fail him. Dr. A. Lilienfeld, a doctor at the Gestapo prison in Lvov, was interviewed after the war by Ball-Kaduri and stated that in his experience, "...sadistic instincts are less aroused when not showing fear."[182]

In the Plaszow camp, various small workshops were sprouting up. Every extension to these workshops meant more work for the Jews and, therefore, greater security. It was apparent that there were four stages in carrying out the "Final Solution": concentration, segregation according to the fitness and exploitation through physical labor, extermination, and finally physical destruction of the habitat. This plan had held up well in the ghettos and camps of Eastern Europe with characteristic German efficiency, though, as will be noted, some unforeseen developments altered both the timetable and the course of the operation.

The chief architect of Plaszow camp was a Pole, a man named Zygmunt Gruenberg, a particular friend of Stern. Gruenberg suggested to Goeth that he put Stern to work in the "works" office as he had vast knowledge of managing small industries and was a professional bookkeeper. Goeth agreed and Stern joined a team of outstanding Jewish workers in the administration offices of the camp. Among them were the Jews Joseph Bau (69084), Moshe Bejski (69387) and the man who was to hold the key to essential intelligence of the forthcoming events, Mieczyslaw Pemper (69514).

Stern was to make two personal interventions and seek the help of Schindler. The first was in respect of Peltzmann, of South African birth, who was living as an Aryan on forged South African papers. Her parents, Gusta Peltzmann (76392) and Hersch Peltzmann (68967), were suffering physically in Plaszow. Mania Peltzmann made a direct approach to Schindler and requested help in getting her parents into Emalia. The second intervention was in respect of Rabbi Jacob Lewertow (68872). Rabbi Lewertow was being harassed by Goeth and it was only a matter of time before Goeth would deal with him. In both cases, the three fugitives found their way into the temporary safety of Schindler's factory.[183]

Julius Madritsch had been able to hold on to his workers. Although they were now in the Plaszow camp, they left the camp daily for his factory and in the evening would return to the gates to be searched before entry. There were still hundreds of Jewish families evading selection. Madritsch continued to transport scores of them, at night, to the cellars of his workshops and then over a period of time remove them to his other factories. Jacob Sternberg (68882) writes:

> "Madritsch was entirely aware of the acts of rescue being carried out through his workshops, and obviously he thereby exposed himself to great risk. Nevertheless, he did not interfere, and so, greatly imperiled his own life. I was a witness to these acts of mercy and to Madritsch's involvement and sense of responsibility, as I was, at the time, in charge of the kitchen in the cellars, which was a focal point of the operations."[184]

The final act in the destruction of the ghetto was on December 14 and 15, 1943. In the early evening, truckloads of helmeted and armed SS, under the direct command of Amon Goeth, surrounded the OD building. All members of the OD, with their families, were loaded onto trucks, driven away and executed in Plaszow. For some reason a Mrs. Katz and her children and Dr. Kessler with his wife and children escaped execution. It became known at a later date that these survivors of the OD executions were as the direct result of the intervention by Tadeusz Pankiewicz.

Chapter Ten
Emalia, Plaszow and Jewish Resistance

**Figure 45: Celebrations for the fourth anniversary of the founding of D.E.F (Emalia)
were held in 1944: Polish workers with Oskar Schindler
Photo Credit: Author's collection**

The liquidation of the ghetto left a lasting impression on Schindler. Months, even years later, he still had difficulty believing what he had seen. As he put it, he knew that he saw what he saw, but it remained beyond belief.[185] The liquidation of the ghetto signaled, as in other Polish cities, the end of even the last shreds of hope for the Jews. Thousands were massacred and thousands were deported to labor camps and to the death camps, where the Final Solution was in full swing. In Krakow, miraculously, one-half of the Jewish population survived the liquidation of the ghetto.

The newly erected barracks at Emalia were a great success. No longer did the Schindler Jews have to march the three kilometers from the Plaszow camp to the Emalia factory and endure the harshness of the discipline in Plaszow. The punishments of 25 lashes disappeared; the persistent parading and the fear of the evil-eye of Goeth descending upon them were now in the past. Whenever the SS visited the barracks, Schindler forewarned them, allowing for the hasty disappearance of unauthorized artifacts. Even when Goeth made an impromptu visit to see Schindler, the shutters of the barrack windows were closed. No SS man ever walked into the barracks without Schindler's personal agreement.[186]

Approximately 900 Jews worked for Schindler in 1943. These workers came to Emalia from the Plaszow camp without the typical prisoner convoys under SS guard. Schindler was able to convince Goeth to allow him to set up a sub-camp next to his factory in Zablocie. The camp was established on May 8, 1943 under the command of Albert Hujar, Eberhard Behr, and Edmund Zdrojewski. By May 22, a total of 66 Jews were living in the camp; three days later this number had risen to 558. A total of 11 quarters were located in the camp – seven for prisoners, the camp kitchen, infirmary, and quarters for SS guards and the Jewish police units. The Emalia factory grew continuously, as did the number of workers employed. In 1942 a total of 550 people worked at Emalia; this figure was by no means the final count. Upon request from Jews themselves, Schindler set up a "rest area" for workers adjacent to the workshops in 1942.

In accordance with requirements, his sub-camp had guard towers and an electrified fence, like any forced labor camp. A small SS garrison was assigned to it. But Schindler's talents to fool the official world by displaying a Nazi facade when his purpose required it made it possible for him to forbid the SS to enter his factory or barracks. When he had his sub-camp, it was, of course, easier for him to perform acts of kindness for his workers. He took to visiting the factory daily, where he spoke to small groups of workers, reassuring them and giving them hope. How important his reassuring words were was brought to my attention by many of those interviewed.

In the Wundheiler documentation (see Bibliography), she refers to the individual concern Schindler expressed for his workers:

> "Among them was a 14-year-old girl, an orphan; Schindler gave her a weekly allowance for her personal necessities. He never gave the allowance personally but asked someone else to deliver it to her. The girl, now of course an elderly woman, never doubted the reason. 'He did not want to embarrass me – he was always very considerate of other people's feelings.'"[187]

The financing of the new barracks came out of Schindler's own pocket; the funds were procured by the various black market deals he operated. He was selling 80 percent of all goods produced on the black market. Food for the works kitchen was the result of more black-market sales and the bartering of rationed goods. Medicine and clothing were also acquired in this way.

A considerable expense was incurred by Schindler in paying enormous bribes to influential Party members, SS leaders, police and camp commanders, and other parasites in order to continue his activities. Schindler bought diamonds, famous paintings on the black market, anything that had value[188] at that time or would have in the future. Only in this way could he afford to bribe those people that he needed for his particular purpose. Three shifts were working 24/7. Throughout the duration of the Emalia, Schindler was paying five zloty per day per worker to the box office of the SS and the police. This was in addition to the usual bribes and favors.

Although the Emalia barracks were becoming overcrowded, he tried to keep families together. There were often conflicts of loyalty among the workers because their overwhelming desire was to keep their kinfolk safe. Schindler employed disabled and capable workers, the old and infirm as machine operators and the children as metal polishers. He falsified factory records; an act that can only be described as extremely reckless. Old people were listed as being 20 years younger; children were listed as adults; lawyers, doctors, and engineers were registered as metal workers, mechanics, and draftsmen – all trades essential to the war effort.

One of Schindler's habits was that upon entering the workshops he would light up a cigarette and then immediately stub it out and drop it on the floor, knowing that it would be picked up and used for barter. His workers accepted that they would receive harsh treatment from him in the presence of the SS. The workers would be sworn at, cuffed around the head – all actions appreciated by the SS. Goeth had given notice that an inspection of the Emalia factory would take place. Accompanied by a full retinue of high-ranking officials, Goeth walked with Schindler on a tour of the factory. Goeth noticed a poor Jewish wretch pushing a cart very slowly across the factory yard. Consistent with his erratic behavior he ordered his bodyguard, SS-Unterscharführer Franz Grunn, to shoot him! The unfortunate Lamus was taken and positioned against a wall, awaiting his fate. Schindler intervened with Grunn, pointing out that Lamus was an essential worker, the usual Schindler protestations. Schindler's promise of brandy made Grunn relent and Lamus was dismissed. A witness to this extraordinary incident with Lamus was Benzion Florenz (69362): "Grunn was aiming his pistol at Lamus when Schindler said, 'Why waste a bullet, he will die anyway. I have some real Martell in my office, let's have a drink.'"[189]

On another occasion, the SS visited Emalia with orders to arrest the Wohlfeiler family for falsifying and possessing Polish (Aryan) personal documents. This family of five had been betrayed by an SS informant. Incriminating documents were produced to Schindler, implicating the family. Schindler produced some of his best brandy. Three hours later, the two drunken SS investigators left empty-handed. Another prayer had been answered.[190]

Jews themselves had different names for Schindler's factory and the camp. The most common terms to describe these places during and after the war were: an oasis of hope and humanity, Oskar Schindler's ark, a safe harbor, paradise in comparison to the hell of Plaszow, a synonym for salvation, a sanctuary of freedom, life insurance, Noah's Ark, an oasis of humanity in the desert of moral apathy, an island of survival in the sea of mass murder. Despite Schindler's friendship with Goeth, the persecutions continued. On a Friday shortly after the Wohlfeiler affair, two Orthodox Jews, the Danziger brothers, accidentally broke an old press in the factory. Again, they were reported by an informant. Schindler was away at the time and had no influence over the consequences that were to follow. The brothers were arrested and taken to the Plaszow camp. Goeth issued orders that the brothers were to be executed by hanging. The gallows were already erected, and 25,000 Jewish prisoners were paraded to witness the event.

Schindler, who had now returned to Krakow, heard the news and went directly to Plaszow to see Goeth, taking with him various offerings of inducement, probably diamonds. He remonstrated with Goeth, telling him that the press was old, and it was only a matter of time before it would break down completely. Goeth listened and accepted Schindler's protestations.

Whatever the reasons, the Danziger brothers were released and were taken back to Emalia. This is another example of Schindler conceiving of and initiating his own actions and behaving totally spontaneously.[191] The Danziger incident was witnessed by many of the Schindler survivors including Bejski, Bau, and Pemper. The three women of the Wohlfeiler family – numbered on the Madritsch list as Roza (8022), Halina (8020), and Rena (8021) – all worked for Julius Madritsch when Emalia closed. The men of the Wohlfeiler family all remained with Schindler – Henryk (69330), Ignazy (68842), and Roman (69414). All six of the Wohlfeiler family survived because of Schindler.

Resistance

It is not possible in this assessment of Schindler to ignore the Jewish resistance. Within and outside the Plaszow camp, in the wake of the great wave of killings and deportations, the youth of the Jewish political movements began to organize armed resistance to the Germans. Deprived of family, they gained their individual freedom and no longer felt inhibited. The knowledge of the death camps and sense of death's inevitability pushed caution aside and they prepared themselves for the final test.

The idea of self-defense had never been extinguished in the ghettos of Poland, and despite the destruction of the Krakow ghetto, and many like it in other parts of Poland, the Jewish youth maintained the idea of survival. The young and inexperienced, as well as the experienced, had realized in the early ghetto days that they were no match for the heavily armed SS. In addition, there was the knowledge of reprisals should there be any active offensive against their jailers. The cost of human life and misery under occupation for such actions would surpass any benefit. However, when it became clear to the underground that no option, but death existed, the idea of resistance took on another aspect.

Again, they realized that resistance would not save the remaining Jews under occupation, but at least they would redeem their honor. The resistance likened itself to the suicidal stand of the zealots of Masada against Rome's imperial legions. Fatalism and the surrender to death haunted many young people. "We are going on the road to death, remember that" said Aaron Liebeskind, Akiva activist in Krakow. "Whoever desires still to live should not search for life here among us. We are at an end."

At the head of the organization stood a united command: Heshek Bauminger and Benek Halbreich from Hashomer Hatza'ir; Dolek Lieberskind and Shimshon Dranger from Akiva; Golda Meir from Akiva and associate splinter groups; Abraham Laban-Leibowitz from Dror, and Elimelech Eisenstein from Akiva Beth (splinter group from Akiva). Each group continued to act separately, but important decisions were made jointly.[192]

The organization's accomplishments included many acts of sabotage and decisive tactics against the Germans. In October 1942, an attempt to assassinate the Gestapo informer Marcel Gruner and his wife occurred. Another warranted exploit of the resistance was the execution of Adams, of the Department of Press and Propaganda of the General Government. In September 1942, the ZOB (Jewish Fighting Organization) started to publish a Polish language journal, *Democrat's Voice*. In October 1942, the assault division GL, to which the Iskra (spark) of the ZOB belonged, under the command of Jakub Halbreich, set fire to a garage on Wloczkow Street where three cars and barrels of gasoline were stored.

On December 24, 1942, Iskra, headed by Idek Liber, bombed the coffee house Cyganeria on Szpitalna Street in Krakow. Eleven Germans died in this attack and 13 were seriously wounded. Perhaps these attacks were futile, but they lifted the morale of the Jews to heights not experienced before.

In Krakow, the Jewish underground was able to penetrate to the heart of their people. The Akiva newspaper, *Hechalutz Halochem*, which published about 250 copies every Friday, included about ten typewritten pages and was distributed by pairs of fighters in Krakow. The paper, written in Polish, called for help and military intervention against the Germans and their collaborators by the free nations in the war. A copy even found its way into Schindler's Emalia. Victor Dortheimer and Roman Wohlfeiler (69414), both working in the factory, were reading the newspaper when Schindler suddenly walked into their workshop. Wohlfeiler hurriedly hid the newspaper behind a cupboard. Schindler, by some sixth sense, went directly to the cupboard and removed the paper, saying, "You are stupid, do you know what would happen if you are caught?"[193]

Resistance took on a more urgent guise. It was imperative that the information known by many in Krakow had to be got out to the outside world. Towards the end of 1943, Stern was called to Schindler's factory. A ghetto policeman had orders to escort Stern from Plaszow to Emalia. On entering Schindler's office Stern was confronted by Schindler and two strangers. The strangers immediately asked Stern what was going on inside Plaszow camp. Stern took Schindler aside and questioned the wisdom of talking to these people. As it turned out, one of the gentlemen was Dr. Sedlacek working for the "Joint" (Joint Distribution Committee) and the other was from a dubious source but as Stern recollects, he was an agent from the Canaris office (Franz von Kohrab). Schindler had stated that the men had recently come from Hungary and Turkey. Stern gave them a run-down of the situation and suggested they visit the camp to see the mass graves. Schindler agreed to this and contacted Goeth to inform him that he had some special armament visitors and that that night he would be giving a party to which Goeth was invited.[194]

This was an amazing front by Schindler, but it worked. That night during the festivities Goeth invited the armament contractors to visit the workshops in the camp. Schindler received authority to speak to Stern and have him accompany the inspection. Stern was instructed to stop near the site of the mass graves and attend to his shoelaces. Photographs of the scene taken with a concealed camera were later smuggled out to Budapest to his old contacts Kastner and Springman and then on to Palestine.[195]

German Resistance

The doves of past liberal and democratic Germany were circling Hitler's clique. Headed by Admiral Canaris and his compatriots, including Oskar Schindler, they were just waiting to strike. Only three groups succeeded in mounting a positive resistance. There was the conservative circle around Carl Goerdeler, a former Mayor of Leipzig, and Ludwig Beck, a retired army chief of staff; the Kreisau Circle, led by Count Helmuth von Moltke and dominated by a Christian and socialist philosophy; and the regime's opponents within the military, including Canaris and the likes of Schindler.[196] Admiral Canaris was later to be implicated and executed for his support of ridding Germany of the Fuhrer. On July 20,1944, the attempt on Hitler's life was broadcast on the radio. Schindler shared this moment of history, listening in the company of Adam Garde (69515). Both were to be disappointed when, later in the night, they heard the Führer's voice on the radio.[197]

Chapter Eleven
Schindler in Budapest

Rudi Kastner

Joel Brand

Oskar Schindler

Adolf Eichmann

Figure 46: The Hungarian Quartet
Photo Credit: Author's collection

By his actions, it is conceivable that Stern altered the fate of many Jews. Through his work, he gained an extraordinary insight into the day-to-day activities, the confusion, and the confrontations within the German administration. He distributed money and medicines to the needy on behalf of the Joint Distribution Committee. Itzhak Stern was a loner and had previously occupied a small room in the ghetto where he carried on his welfare work in the Krakow district.[198] Before the enforcement of the ghetto residence regulations, there had been a serious outbreak of typhoid in the shtetlech on the outskirts of Krakow. Stern bought vaccines with the allotted zloty from the Joint and singlehandedly organized a mass vaccination program. Within two days, all the Jews had been vaccinated. TOZ (the Joint Distribution Committee) received a thank-you letter from the German Health Authority.[199]

In her psychological analysis of Schindler, Dr. Wundheiler makes the following interesting comments:

> "As stated before, it is one of my purposes to show that Schindler underwent a development from a person whose concerns were limited to people he knew, to someone whose concerns included many human beings he did not know at all. Firstly, one needs to consider that he employed many at Stern's request. He not only knew Stern, but a very special relationship

between him and Stern had already begun to develop. From early on, Schindler seemed eager to please Stern."

Dr. Wundheiler's analysis of Schindler is, in my opinion, correct. We must remember that the Schindler/Stern relationship went back to November 1939, and that Stern, the Zionist, was working for the Joint and was very influential in securing employment for selective activists in Emalia. Above all, the relationship between the two men was symbiotic. Stern may have been the first and only human being to recognize Schindler's deepest motives and bring out his greatest talents. Stern admired his intelligence and inventiveness, his courage and love of taking risks, and he called on and developed Schindler's compassion. He brought out the best in him and Schindler thanked Stern by loving him. We are dealing with an exceptional relationship between these two men – indeed, so exceptional that it may have altered the course of survival for the Jews of Krakow.[200]

Working conditions for the Jews in the ghetto were becoming critical. Many of the Jews sought security by working for the Wehrmacht as they felt that this afforded them a certain protection. Stern also considered this action prudent and procured for himself a job at the Broadcasting Equipment store in Krakow. In addition to this job and his voluntary work, Stern worked for the Trust Administrator Unkelbach, referred to earlier. Stern audited the books for Unkelbach once a month. He wrote the accounts for the Treuhändstelle, which had to be written on special forms and done with typical German thoroughness. For these jobs, Stern was allowed out of the ghetto, giving him some freedom of movement and useful opportunities to further his charity work and report on the day-to-day situation.

In October 1942, Stern was taken ill with suspected appendicitis and was taken to a hospital in the ghetto. He was due to have an appendectomy the following day. Unkelbach, a well-known SS murderer, came to the hospital. Unkelbach confronted Dr. Hilfstein (68895) and ordered him to abandon the proposed operation on Stern and to send him home immediately. Failure to comply would result in the shooting of all the doctors. Nobody knew why Unkelbach had issued this ultimatum, but Stern went home immediately. Three days later the reason became apparent.

The Jews of the ghetto braced themselves, trembled, and again prayed to the Almighty. The SS were more thorough than in the June Action. Selections, deportations, and killings proceeded in an orderly way. Hospitals in the ghetto were surrounded and raked with gunfire. Doctors, patients, and orderlies were shot on the spot. Stern's life had been saved.[201] In an interview with the author, Mrs. Stern confirmed this incident and stated that her husband was only running a high temperature and, therefore, an operation had not been necessary. Later it was learned that Stern's sudden removal from hospital had been instigated by Schindler, who used Unkelbach to repay an old debt.[202]

It may have been that Unkelbach had double-crossed Schindler. A few days after Stern's release from hospital, Schindler was arrested by the Gestapo and taken to Pomorska Street, where he was interrogated over alleged black-market deals. His company's books had been seized and inspected for irregularities. The exigency plan was activated by Schindler's secretary. Wherever the phone calls came from is not known, but within hours Schindler was released without charge. The pressure from above was too much for the Gestapo and the SS.

It was not long before Unkelbach's workers brought trouble to the factory Progress. Shortly after the concession from Amon Goeth to allow selected prisoners to move freely about the town, three employees from Progress disappeared. There was a huge scandal. An inquiry established that, after being delivered by the guards, the workers were allowed to wander around unguarded and unsupervised in the factory grounds. They were able to walk into Krakow and taste life's freedom. Because of this scandal, the factory was closed and all workers returned to Plaszow. The disappearance of the three Jews was at first not followed up. Perhaps Goeth wanted to protect Unkelbach, his friend.

In the ghetto, the Jews were under the jurisdiction of the Gestapo who benefited economically from this labor. As soon as the Jews were put into camps, they were placed under the jurisdiction of the SS, who rented them out to various companies. The friction between the Gestapo and the SS affected the Jews. Some members of the Jewish Council and the Jewish Security Police worked with the Gestapo to track down hidden Jews. The Jews believed that by their cooperation they might survive the war.

For whatever reasons, the missing Jews from factory Progress were reported to the Gestapo, who lost no time in accusing Goeth of negligence. Goeth issued an ultimatum to the whole camp: "Give me their whereabouts or you will all be shot." Goeth seized Stern as a hostage. Within hours an address was forthcoming. An armed posse of SS went to the address in Krakow. It proved to be correct and there was a bloodbath. Stern was saved. Unkelbach had lost the confidence of Goeth and was arrested. He was accused of taking bribes from Jews to allow Jewish children to be smuggled into the camp. Despite Unkelbach's claim of wanting to kill all the Jewish children, he was disarmed and arrested. According to Stern he was never seen in the camp again.

An insight into Stern's character was given by Menachem Halberthal, who worked closely with Stern after the war. He reflected on their special relationship:

> "Stern was not religious, but he retained a close interest in religious matters. His knowledge of Judaica was immense. He was a man of compromise – a negotiator, a man of understanding. He was always philosophizing and had a quotation or anecdote for every occasion and always tinged with humor. He never argued but persuaded by gentle coaxing. This was his strength and the strength that supported all those around him, even Schindler." [203]

The Chief Architect of the Plaszow camp was a Pole, Zygmunt Gruenberg, and a particular friend of Stern. Gruenberg suggested to Goeth that he put Stern to work in the works office, as he had vast knowledge of managing small industries and was a professional bookkeeper. Goeth agreed and Stern joined a team of outstanding Jewish workers in the administration offices of the camp. Among them were the Jews Josef Bau (69084), Moshe Bejski (69387), and the man who was to hold the key to essential intelligence of the forthcoming events, Mieczyslaw Pemper (69514).[204]

Figure 47: Mietek Pemper
Photo Credit: Author's collection

Shortly after, Schindler was smuggled out of Krakow in the back of a newspaper van to Budapest to meet his Jewish contacts.

Many of us know of the infamous "blood for trucks" deal proposed by Adolf Eichmann when things began to go against the Nazi war machine. Under the macabre offer, thousands of Jewish lives would be bartered by the Germans in exchange for 10,000 military trucks to be turned over to the Nazis. How seriously the West considered the offer came to light in the report of a disclosure by Schindler. Jewish authorities in Budapest wanted desperately to know as early as 1942 whether the Eichmann offer could be trusted. Schindler had given personal testimonies to the death factories and to the terror being unleashed upon the Jewish people. Having delivered his message, he was taken back by the same route. From Schindler, the West had confirmed the facts of German murder. This singular exploit brings into focus the true man.

At an informal select gathering, Schindler was introduced to Dr. Sedlacek by his old boss in Krakow, Major von Kohrab. It was suggested that he should make a trip to Budapest[205] to meet with the Jewish Relief Organization and pass on the true nature of the extermination of the Jews in Poland. Firsthand knowledge was essential as the information coming out of Poland was unbelievable to the Jewish agencies and more importantly, elsewhere. Schindler, in his position as an agent of the Abwehr, was the holder of a special security passport that enabled him to travel within and outside of the Reich. Usually, he would drive his Hawk motorcar across borders but, on this occasion, he was smuggled across the borders in the back of a newspaper van.

In Budapest, he was to meet with Samuel Springman and Rudy Kastner, members of the Zionist rescue organization and leading figures in the Jewish Relief Organization. After the war Samuel Springman recounted his meeting with Schindler at a reception held in Jerusalem in Schindler's honor:

> "I am not of Schindler's men. My acquaintance with him started during meetings in Budapest. The first meeting was in a Budapest hotel. Schindler looked around to see if we were not followed – and he gave us a report of what was going on in the camps. The information given by him was forwarded to the Jewish rescue committee. I was happy I had the opportunity to meet him again."[206]

To Springman and his associates he handed evidence of the Jewish transports to the death camps and the cruelty inflicted on the Jews of Poland. He gave his listeners hard numbers: 80 percent of the Jews of Warsaw had already been murdered as well as 66 percent of the Jews of the Lodz ghetto and 50 percent of the population of the Krakow ghetto. Those who were still alive after the ghetto liquidations rapidly disappeared into forced labor camps. After his report, the Zionists in Budapest trusted Schindler enough to ask him to transmit rescue money to the Zionists in Krakow and to enlist his long-term cooperation in rescue acts. On Schindler's return to Krakow, he handed a large number of zloty to the Jewish Defense Committee in the ghetto. Schindler also had a list of important Jewish Zionist activists who were working undercover, both in the ghetto and on the Aryan side. He was requested to get them into Emalia as one of the few havens in Krakow. Over a period of a few months, Schindler had traced 18 persons on the list and had taken them into his factory.[207]

Dr. Wundheiler's observation on the Budapest Action is interesting:

> "His long-range cooperation with the Zionists is possibly the most important evidence of development that I am trying to sketch. Certainly, this cooperation was risky, and one might argue that Schindler did what he did because he enjoyed taking risks. Perhaps that is true, but so what? Is an action less high-minded and admirable because the actor enjoys it? Besides, one should keep in mind that the typical hazarder likes to take risks because any victory in a life full of risks adds to the risk-taker's glory in his eyes as well as in the eyes of others."[208]

Since Schindler's activities had to be entirely clandestine, there was not even the reward of temporary glory. There was no monetary reward either, since unlike some others who transmitted money to Zionists in various Eastern European cities, Schindler never kept a percentage of the money for himself.[209] Whether or not his cooperation with the Zionists appealed to the gambler in him, it drew on his compassion and altruistic feelings in that it required selfless actions on behalf of people who were strangers to him and about whom he knew nothing except that they were in terrible danger. In summary, during this period he continued to shelter Jews he knew, and, in addition, he took many under his wing – those whom he did not know, but who needed his protection.

It is difficult to imagine what state of mind Schindler was in at this time. In his report to Ball-Kaduri he writes of coming near to a nervous breakdown and of being at his lowest ebb. Well after the war, Moshe Bejski (69387) asked Schindler why he had gone to all the trouble to help the Jews and at the same time lay himself open to detection by the SS. Schindler simply stated:

> "I knew the people who worked for me. When you know people, you have to behave towards them like human beings. If I'm walking in the street and I see a dog in danger of being crushed by a car, wouldn't I try to help?"[210]

I have already referred to Schindler's utter depression when the children of the Kinderheim were transported. Because of its importance, I will refer again to the Wundheiler notes relating to Schindler's love and compassion for children. During some of the worst excesses of the SS, Schindler, with the help of Bousco and Madritsch, smuggled a few children out of the ghetto by delivering them into the caring hands of Polish nuns. Exact data concerning the number and ages of the children is hard to come by. According to Wundheiler, a German doctor named Stroder, who was a pediatrician at the hospital in Krakow, stated that many of the children he attended were Jewish and he believed that most of them came to the hospital with the aid of Schindler.[211]

This was an act of compassion, deepened and enhanced by Schindler's identification with the children as well as with their parents. These parents surrendered their children to strangers, in the anxious and uncertain hope of saving them and seeing them again. Schindler recognized that the greatest need of these parents was to have their children saved, that the pain of the temporary loss with the hope, however slim, of seeing them again at some time, is infinitely more bearable than total loss through death. It is noteworthy that this was probably Schindler's main motive behind all his rescue actions during this period. Furthermore, we must remind ourselves that Schindler was still an active agent of the Abwehr, albeit directed against the enemy within.

Chapter Twelve
Hungarian Deportations

Figure 48: Women in Plaszow May 7, 1944
Photo Credit: Author's collection

"Everything else was a game. This was the true contest. With your stomach turning and breath thin, you ran – beneath the throb of the lying music – for your golden life."

"To the inexperienced children, it would be complete panic; they would stand in the open and believe themselves invisible."

Another indication of the desperate situation now confronting the Plaszow Jews was the arrival of thousands of items of blood-stained clothing that had been sent to Plaszow for laundering and repair. Stern was told by a Ukrainian police officer that he should escape or else he would be like those in Tarnow.[212]

When the Krakow ghetto was liquidated, Julius Madritsch transferred 232 men, women, and children from Krakow to Tarnow on March 25 and 26, 1943. On September 1, 1943, the Tarnow ghetto came to a brutal and violent end. The day before the liquidation, Madritsch and Titsch were invited to a ceremonial dinner for Commandant Goeth and other high SS officials. When Madritsch requested to leave, SS-Obergruppenführer Schermer ordered him to stay until dawn and left him with two SS officers to keep him company.[213] At 5 a.m. the following morning, Madritsch and Titsch were released. They drove directly to Tarnow where they saw Goeth, who informed them that the ghetto had been liquidated and was no more. Goeth assured Madritsch that his workers were safe for the time being. Large bribes weren't offered but were demanded by Goeth and Schermer. Madritsch later noted that there had been a fierce resistance in the ghetto and that many Jews had been shot. All Jews who survived the onslaught were transported to Birkenau and gassed. Only the Madritsch Jews survived.[214]

Like Schindler, Madritsch was taking dangerous chances to protect his Jewish workers. Never did a week go by when these two entrepreneurs didn't risk their luck for the sake of their workers. Madritsch refers to many instances of help he received from the Wehrmacht and from a sympathetic German officer named Lt. Col. Mathisen, who assisted in evacuating Jewish families to safe areas.[215]

It seems that the bigger the lie you tell the greater chance you have of getting away with it. Stern, Pemper, and Schindler decided on an audacious ploy. Mietek Pemper (69514), who worked in Goeth's office, had seen the report from Oranienburg requesting that an immediate list of inventories of machinery and prisoners be made. In his position as administrator of the workshops, Stern compiled a highly inflated projection of production in the camp. All this information was printed neatly in book form, with many graphs and drawings. Pemper submitted the material to Goeth, who immediately checked it. He found the information was incorrect and raved over the fraud. Then, according to Pemper, he laughed and said nothing. In an odd way, Goeth, Schindler, Bejski, Stern, Bau, and Pemper got on well; accepting the status quo was in everyone's interest. Goeth knew that this was an effort to save the camp and obtain concentration camp status. As it was also in his interest, Goeth signed the account, which was sent on to Berlin.[216]

Some days later, the camp was visited by a team of statisticians from the main office in Oranienburg to check the projected productivity of the workshops. The team was headed by SS-Obersturmführer Mohvinkel and his assistant, a German Huguenot named LaClerc. The books and plans were scrutinized, while Stern and Pemper could only wait and hope. The inspection was short and sharp. Stern was at the beck and call of the inspection team that kept him busy bringing books and plans. Stern did not flinch; he was respectful, direct, and cool. Stern knew that he had the responsibility on his shoulders to ensure the safety of the camp.

At the end of 1943, no decision had yet been made; now, everything depended on receiving orders from the Wehrmacht. Plaszow's output was mainly through its tailoring shops, but to survive they needed to transform the workshops into metal stamping and press machinery. Goeth sought the help of Schindler; after all, it was in everyone's interest that the camp's status be upgraded. Frantic work went on in Plaszow to be ready for an inspection that was soon to take place. On the last Sunday in December 1943, a high-powered inspection team, led by SS-Obergruppenführer Krüger, arrived at the camp. The inspection team toured the camp with Goeth. In the workshops, which Schindler had realized would not stand scrutiny, he made a special arrangement. As the tour commenced, there was a sudden blackout in the workshop. The inspection went ahead in the gloom so that everything appeared enhanced. Whatever the assumptions, it appeared to have worked. In fact, Schindler had arranged for the electricity to be cut during the early stages of the inspection.[217] In January 1944, Plaszow was designated Konzentrationslager under the central authority of SS-Obergruppenführer Oswald Pohl's SS Main Economic and Administrative Office in Oranienburg, in the outskirts of Berlin.

Plaszow's change of status brought a slight relief to the prisoners. No longer were there to be summary executions. Everything had to be sent to Berlin in triplicate, and hearings and sentences had to be confirmed by the new head of Department D, SS-Obergruppenführer Gluecks.

Mieczyslaw Pemper[218] had a photographic memory, and for many months he was memorizing the highly classified documentation that went through Goeth's office. Over a period of some weeks, Pemper had pieced together secret information transmitted from Gerhard Maurer, Hitler's Chief of Concentration Camps, to the Commandant of Plaszow. The information was depressing. Several thousand Hungarian Jews would be arriving at KL Plaszow, and room was to be made for them. Goeth was frantic as Plaszow was already overcrowded.[219] Goeth asked permission to cull the camp to make room for the necessary space.[220] Gluecks authorized this course of action in another memorandum, which Pemper just happened to memorize. KL Plaszow was to disperse its labor in all directions and to give its excess to Auschwitz-Birkenau.

Pemper's contribution in this war of information cannot be underestimated. Goeth's personal secretary was a young Polish girl (Keneally refers to her as German – Frau Kochmann), who was very efficient in her general work but who, because she had problems when inserting multiple sheets of paper and carbons in the typewriter, always asked Pemper to help. On many occasions, he would slip in an additional piece of carbon paper and retrieve it after the typing was done. By holding the carbon to a mirror, Pemper was able to clearly read the most secret information. This extra carbon would be spirited out of the camp via Stern and Schindler. Schindler then passed this vital information – which was central to the West's grasp of the Hungarian transports – to the Jewish agencies in Budapest.

Amon Goeth was busy. Under the code name *Die Gesundheitaktion* (the Health Action), he set about the partial liquidation of KL Plaszow. Space for 10,000 had to be made in the camp. Auschwitz was working over capacity but would be able to take these Hungarian prisoners in a matter of weeks when the pressure on the crematoria had subsided. The selections at KL Plaszow began on the morning of May 7, 1944. On the Appellplatz, row upon row of prisoners in barrack formation, stood silent. They knew it was their last chance. Block by block they were marched to the reception area. Ordered to strip naked, as each name was called out the prisoner presented him or herself to the examining teams of doctors headed by the SS Dr. Blancke. Also assisting in this selection was Dr. Leon Gross. The women had to line up and walk forward, one by one, and jump over a series of large holes that had been especially dug to test their level of fitness and, consequently, their right to survival. Prisoners were made to run up and down in front of the examiners. Some women who were suffering from chronic diarrhea rubbed red cabbage leaves into their faces to give them color.[221] During the course of the SS Aktion, Goeth turned his eye to the 280 children housed in a separate compound (the Kinderheim), where working parents could bring their children up to age 14. Cared for by experienced personnel, the children were kept busy and safe. Now was time to deal with the children. Sensing trouble, Goeth sought reinforcements from Krakow. Parents seeing their children separated and confined without the opportunity of proving their worth began to wail and scream for their loved ones. There was panic and pandemonium everywhere. Whole families were separated in the selection, some to the left, and some to the right. No one knew for sure whether they were on the good or the bad side. To the experienced prisoner it was not difficult to guess; looking at the group which contained the elderly, the sick, and the disabled was a sad realization.

Some children, the urchins of the camp, had their hiding places already prepared. Even so, when they dived for cover they would find that their space had been taken by someone else, and they ran in frantic search of another sanctuary. To the inexperienced children, it would be complete panic; they would stand in the open and believe themselves invisible.[222]

Figure 49: The Appellplatz drawn by Josef Bau
Photo Credit: Author's collection

On May 14, all became clear. That day, everyone standing at attention on the Appellplatz knew their fate. There was an air of sad resignation around those selected for transport. Those Jews not selected for deportation were distressed and saddened seeing their parents, grandparents, children, and friends marched off to the waiting wagons destined for Auschwitz. It wasn't uncommon for mothers, in order to protect their teenage daughters, to change coats and join the column marching out to the transports. The individual camp number sewn in the breast of their coats was sufficient identity when being checked by the guards.[223] During the course of the Action, dance tunes and lively music were broadcast over the loudspeakers, providing a musical background for the sick and the young children who were being sent to the ovens of Auschwitz. As the Jews marched to the train, the radio technicians, with their sense of German humor, could be heard singing the German lullaby, "Goodnight, Mommy."[224]

Schindler visited the camp a few days after the main transports had left. He was dismayed to see another transport of several wagons in the siding, guarded closely by the SS. This transport was destined for Mauthausen. On this very hot day, with the heat shimmering off the roofs of the wagons, the wailing and shouts for water could clearly be heard. Outraged and in the presence of Goeth and his posse of SS officers, Schindler persuaded the Commandant to allow hoses to be directed onto the wagons. [225]

A shimmer of steam from the locomotive broke into the air. Schindler played probably one of his final cards by imploring Goeth to allow this indulgence, much to the mockery of the SS present. As in the Spielberg film, Schindler brought in additional watering appliances to quell the heat of the wagons. He gave the guards on the transport baskets full of liquors and cigarettes and requested that at each stop the prisoners should be given water and the doors opened. Well after the war, two survivors of that transport, doctors Rubenstein and Feldstein, confirmed to Schindler that this was done.[226]

The selections and transports made in May to make way for the 10,000 Hungarian Jews were the most difficult accounts to relate for many of those that I interviewed. The late Dr. Moshe Bejski had to have several breaks in the interview before he could bring himself to complete his account.

Figure 50: Author with Dr. and Mrs. Bejski, Tel Aviv 1996
Photo Credit: Author's collection

The End of the Plaszow Camp

The Red Army's great offensive in 1944 resulted in the hasty retreat of German forces. Transports began to leave the Plaszow camp for extermination camps as early as February. Defense inspectors began to visit Plaszow as well as Schindler's Emalia. Both Goeth and Schindler made efforts to ensure that the camp and factory were deemed essential for the needs of the military. The Plaszow camp was completely overcrowded with 30,000 prisoners. A special SS commando unit arrived at Plaszow with the task of obliterating all traces of Nazi operations. A work force comprised of Jews exhumed mass graves, burned the remains, and created ,new graves at execution sites.

After the outbreak of the Warsaw Uprising on August 1, 1944, a total of 7,000 Polish men were taken to the Plaszow camp. Schindler intervened on behalf of his Polish workers and helped some of them leave Krakow.

Chapter Thirteen
Schindler's Lists

"To me, Schindler was still a German, a Nazi. I'm never going to believe he was a Jew lover. To me, he represents the German system – Nazi – and he was a guy who made money."

Joachim Kinstlinger (68861)

Figure 51: The Davar List, the original "Schindler List":
the list of Emalia employees (with dates of birth) that was published
in the newspaper *Davar* in Palestine on September 1, 1944
Photo Credit: Author's collection

There have been two major revelations concerning the list by the author: (1) the original Madritsch list of Jews selected to join the Schindler group in late 1944: the list was drawn up by Raymond Titsch, and (2) the Davar list of September 1944. These documents came into the author's possession from outside sources. The Madritsch list is perhaps the only authentic list to have survived the war. The Davar list relates to clandestine internal movements of Jews within the Krakow factory complex. The importance of all other lists purporting to be the Schindler list is, in the author's opinion, exaggerated. In 1996, the author corresponded with Genia and Nachum Manor (Monderer 69439). Nachum kindly read the author's MA dissertation on Schindler and suggested several corrections and possible additions which should be considered when discussing the lists of Oskar Schindler.

The *Davar* newspaper was a very important and popular newspaper in Palestine. The issue of August-September 1944 contained lists of names of the Jews that Oskar Schindler saved from going to the Plaszow camp. It is believed that these lists were given to the Jewish Rescue Committee in Istanbul by Schindler. If this is so, then during the war years, the lists in the *Davar*, as well as the Madritsch list, take precedence as genuine original lists that were compiled many months before the so-called Brünnlitz lists.

There are five Davar lists numbered 1-5: List 1, dated August 31, 1944; List 2, dated September 1, 1944; List 3, dated September 3, 1944; List 4, dated September 4, 1944; and List 5, dated September 5, 1944. Lists 1- 4 were primarily details of Jews in the Plaszow camp. List 5 is our Schindler's list. This list contains some 200 names that were selected by Schindler for transfer to the Newe Kuhler Fabrik – NKF, a factory where refrigerators and aircraft parts were manufactured. The original list was published in Hebrew in the newspaper *Davar* and was taken by Schindler to Hungary when he made a clandestine visit to meet influential Zionist sympathizers and inform the world of the destructive events in Poland at that time. Schindler's employees stopped being anonymous – their names became known all over the world!

The veracity of the lists is complicated and to assist in untangling the different versions, read the Introduction to the JewishGen database "Schindler's Lists" at the link below. The searchable database contains 1980 names from two lists:

http://www.jewishgen.org/databases/Holocaust/0126_Schindlers-lists.html

The Madritsch and Davar lists will be examined in the context of the information available. In August 1944, the order came from the Director of Armaments for the disbandment of Schindler's factory and for all Jewish workers to be taken to KL Plaszow. There were now about a thousand Jews working in Emalia. Three hundred were to remain to dismantle the factory; the rest were sent to KL Plaszow and/or KL Gross-Rosen.[227]

The 700 Schindler Jews marched out of Emalia for the last time to the unknown of KL Plaszow. The 300 that remained were bona-fide technicians who stayed in Emalia to carry out their work. Solomon Urbach (69427) was one of the lucky 700. As the main body of people was lined up and ready for the orders to march, Urbach mentioned to Schindler that there was no carpenter left in the camp. Schindler took him at his word and physically put him with the group that was to remain.[228]

On August 17, 1944, Emalia awoke to a mighty explosion. Barracks were on fire and secondary explosions were erupting all over the area. An allied Liberator bomber had crashed on the Emalia sub-camp. The aircraft was part of 205 Group, Royal Air Force (one of 178 Squadron Liberators)

supplying the Jewish insurgents in Warsaw from their bases in Italy. The Australian navigator of this aircraft, Squadron Leader Liverside, was killed. Another Australian, Flight Lieutenant A.H. Hammet, although wounded, parachuted to safety and was hidden by a partisan group until January 1945, when Russian troops occupied the area. The remainder of the crew died in the crash: F/Lt. Pilot William D. Wright, RAF, and F/Sgt. A/G John D. Clarke. A commemorative plaque to the memory of these officers is affixed to the wall at the Emalia factory at 4 Lipowa Street, Krakow.[229] The graves register states that Liverside died in action over Poland on August 17, 1944, and was buried in the Krakow Military Cemetery, Plot 1, Row C, and Collective Grave 6-8.[230]

In August 1944, the operations from Italy were mainly aimed at the Ploesti oil fields. There does not appear to have been operations against Polish targets.[231] According to several of the Schindler Jews who were present at the time, the Germans accorded full military honors to the dead airman in the crashed Liberator aircraft.[232] In 1997, I visited the Krakow Military Cemetery and laid a wreath on collective grave 6-8.

It was at this time that Schindler visited Plaszow to see Stern and to bring him the news of the death of Oswald Bousco. Bousco, the police commissioner in the ghetto, was held in high esteem. His kindness to and consideration of the oppressed in the Krakow ghetto had not been forgotten. Without the power, position, and panache of Schindler and Madritsch, Bousco had carved a very special niche in the hearts of the Jews of Krakow.[233]

Schindler was now looking for new territories where he could transfer his machinery. He went to Berlin seeking the assistance of Colonel Erich Lange, Chief of Staff of the Armaments Inspectorate at Army Headquarters. He was passed from department to department but eventually acquired the authority to transfer his factory.[234]

We have arrived at what I would term "the crucial period" of Schindler's activities. Schindler had amassed great personal wealth, which afforded him a guarantee of his personal safety out of the Reich to Switzerland. He thought long and hard of his circumstances, his wife, and the people that looked to him as their only chance – their last chance. This was not a game; this was not now a money-making venture where he could see the profits mounting up. This was reality, the reality of life and death, not only to those who were with him, but to those who languished in rotten Plaszow. The stuffing had been knocked out of him and he was on the brink of a very serious mental disorder, living on the edge of madness.[235] After the war, Moshe Bejski asked the question, "Why didn't you go when you had the chance? Were we that important?" Schindler replied, "Yes, you were that important. If I had run, I could never have lived with myself. I am not proud of myself; I have a lot to answer for. I knew that I had no choice; I just had to see it through."[236] This was Schindler, the altruistic and compassionate helper. His common sense of right had overridden all possibilities.

The Brünnlitz venture made Amon Goeth appear like a good friend, despite his cruelty and murderous ways. At least he knew with whom he was dealing. In the environs of this Judenfrei district of Moravia, the battle to bring his factory and Jewish workers was only beginning. Schindler even pondered Berlin's offer to remove his factory from the Rhineland to a village near Semmering, but without his Jewish workers.

The new factory back in the Sudetenland was between his hometown of Svitavy and the industrial city of Brno; but, to be more precise, it rested between the villages of Brezova-Brnenec and Moravska Chrastova. The factory nestled in a valley, surrounded by mountains, and was chosen because it would be difficult to bomb from the air.

As soon as it was clear that Schindler's efforts to gain permission to move his factory to the safer interior would be successful, preparations for the transfer began at a feverish pace. The commander of the Plaszow camp, Amon Goeth, was arrested by the Gestapo on corruption charges and replaced by SS-Obersturmführer Arnold Büscher. Schindler obtained the consent of authorities to move a thousand Jews to the newly established camp at Brünnlitz near Schindler's hometown.

Schindler was to occupy part of the Brueder Hoffmann spinning mill. Herr Hoffmann, a former trustee of this mill and well-decorated with Party protectionism, made the move very difficult for Schindler. Hoffmann was a typical Nazi bureaucrat. In former years he had been a dairy salesman from Vienna. Now he would hinder all moves to establish Schindler's new armaments factory. Hoffmann had considerable influence with the District Magistrate, the Gestapo, and the Kreisleiter. A typical remark by officialdom was, "Do not allow this Schindler to poison our area with Jews. He will bring typhoid and other diseases along with his Schindler gang." Chaos and bureaucracy, jealousy and spite – these were some of the hurdles Schindler had to overcome. The opposition continued but the decisions of the SS-Reichführung were final.

Schindler resorted to inviting high-ranking SS officers to Brünnlitz to impress the local dignitaries of his influence within the Establishment: Heinz Bignall, adviser to the SS and Polish leaders in Krakow; and SS-Standartenführer Ernst Hahn and his adjutant, SS-Obergruppenführer Heissmeier. These high officers of considerable power and influence had nothing to do with the employment of Jews, but thanks to their pompous uniforms, the visit was a great success. The locals were impressed, and Schindler was able to proceed.

Schindler's initiative, which had established a principle at the very highest authority, had penetrated the anti-Semitic bureaucracy of Moravia. Through this action alone, the Armaments Inspectorate was to release 3,000 mainly Polish Jewish women into other camps in the previously Judenfrei area. These women prisoners, in groups of 300, were allocated to small textile factories: Trautenau, Freudenthal, Jagerndorf, Liebau, and Grulich. This was a major accomplishment which has been overshadowed by events in Emalia.

The considerable funds needed to move from Krakow to Brünnlitz made a heavy dent in Schindler's accumulated fortune. Then there were the usual inducements to the bureaucrats. He personally delivered luxuries to keep the "SS-gentlemen" in a cooperative mood. There were gifts to Berlin and for the SS leaders in Krakow, the little officials of the Eastern Railway, the Armaments Inspectorate, and the Commandant of Gross-Rosen, SS-Standartenführer Hässebroek, who would be supervising Brünnlitz. Schindler estimated that these gifts alone cost him 100,000 Reichmarks in addition to the 200,000 Reichmarks set aside for the move to Brünnlitz.[237]

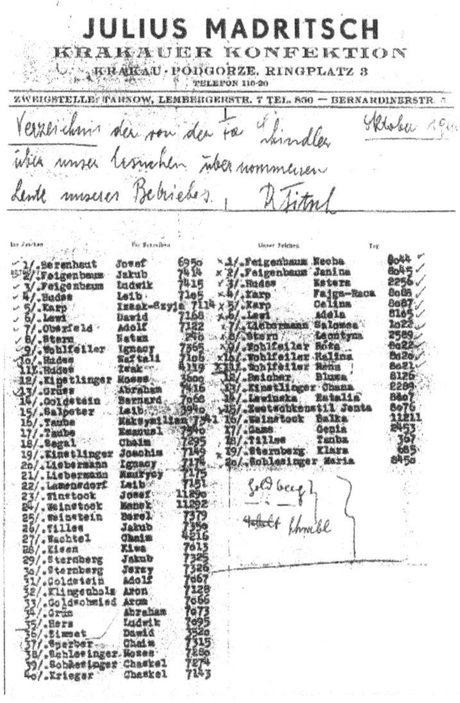

JULIUS MADRITSCH
KRAKAUER KONFEKTION
KRAKAU-PODGORZE, RINGPLATZ 3
TELEFON 110-20
ZWEIGSTELLE: TARNOW, LEMBERGERSTR. 7 TEL. 850 — BERNARDINERSTR.

Verzeichnis der von der Fa Schindler über unser Ersuchen übernommenen Leute unseres Betriebes. R Titsch

Ihr Zeichen — Ihr Schreiben — Unser Zeichen — Tag

1/.	Berenhaut	Josef	6950	1/.	Feigenbaum	Necha	8044
2/.	Feigenbaum	Jakub	7414	2/.	Feigenbaum	Janina	8045
3/.	Feigenbaum	Ludwik	7415	3/.	Hudes	Estera	2256
4/.	Hudes	Leib	7165	4/.	Karp	Fajga-Raca	8086
5/.	Karp	Izaak-Szyja	7114	5/.	Karp	Celina	8087
6/.	Lewi	Dawid	7168	6/.	Lewi	Adela	8165
7/.	Oberfeld	Adolf	7122	7/.	Liebermann	Salomea	1022
8/.	Stern	Natan	246	8/.	Stern	Leontyna	2589
9/.	Wohlfeiler	Ignacy	7365	9/.	Wohlfeiler	Rota	8022
10/.	Hudes	Naftali	7106	10/.	Wohlfeiler	Halina	8020
11/.	Hudes	Izak	4119	11/.	Wohlfeiler	Rena	8021
12/.	Kigstlinger	Moses	3600	12/.	Reicher	Bluma	8126
13/.	Grüss	Abraham	7416	13/.	Kinstlinger	Chana	2289
14/.	Goldstein	Bernard	7068	14/.	Lewinska	Natalia	8407
15/.	Salpeter	Leib	3940	15/.	Zwetschkenstil	Jenta	8076
16/.	Taube	Maksymilian	7341	16/.	Weinstock	Balka	11211
17/.	Taube	Emanuel	7340	17/.	Gams	Genia	2453
18/.	Segal	Chaim	7295	18/.	Tilles	Tauba	307
19/.	Kinstlinger	Joachim	7149	19/.	Sternberg	Klara	685
20/.	Liebermann	Ignacy	7174	20/.	Schlesinger	Maria	8450
21/.	Liebermann	Maurycy	7175				
22/.	Lamensdorf	Leib	7151				
23/.	Tinstock	Josef	11290				
24/.	Weinstock	Manek	11292				
25/.	Weinstein	Berel	7379				
26/.	Tilles	Jakub	7356				
27/.	Wachtel	Chaim	4216				
28/.	Eisen	Kiwa	7613				
29/.	Sternberg	Jakub	7325				
30/.	Sternberg	Jerzy	7326				
31/.	Goldstein	Adolf	7067				
32/.	Klingenholz	Aron	7128				
33/.	Goldschmied	Aron	7066				
34/.	Grün	Abraham	7073				
35/.	Herz	Ludwik	7095				
36/.	Zimmet	Dawid	3520				
37/.	Sperber	Chaim	7315				
38/.	Schlesinger	Mozes	7280				
39/.	Schlesinger	Chaskel	7274				
40/.	Krieger	Chaskel	7143				

Goldberg

Figure 52: Madritsch List: Handwriting at the top of page reads, "Inventory about people of our company who were taken over by the Schindler Company at our request." R. Titsch.

The signature below is of Marcel Goldberg.
Photo Credit: Author's collection

Rumors were spreading in KL Plaszow that Schindler had acquired a new factory in Czechoslovakia and was selecting workers to go with him. Schindler had conferred with Stern, Bankier, Madritsch, and Titsch over the decisions about the personnel to go on the list. First to be chosen were the 300 Jews presently engaged in the decommissioning of the Emalia factory. Schindler's plan was to join forces with Madritsch and transfer their labor collectively. Madritsch supplied only 60 names – 40 men and 20 women. When Schindler inspected the Madritsch list he noticed that between the last name on the list and the signature of authorization there was a large space. Schindler engineered a further 20 names and, on his own account, added a further 30 names. Thus, 50 more workers won the lottery of life.[238]

Jacob Sternberg:

> "Schindler gave the commander of Plaszow concentration camp the list of his employees in his enamel factory, including the names of other metal workers who he was allowed to transfer to Brünnlitz in order to employ them in the munitions plant which he erected there. Due to the pressure on Raymond Titsch, Schindler got permission to add a further twenty workers to the Madritsch list, in spite of the fact that they were not metal workers. Schindler then, in tiny handwriting, added a further thirty names (50 in all)."[239]

Acrimony suddenly surfaced between Madritsch and Schindler. Schindler felt that Madritsch, although having looked after his workers up until 1944, was not now fully committed to the cause. From the Madritsch personal papers there are indications that Madritsch did not fully approve of Schindler's ethics, not specifically because of what he did to the list. To be fair to both men, there was turmoil in KL Plaszow at this stage and everyone was under suspicion for one thing or another.[240] And, of course, these were two very different men from different backgrounds.

The Madritsch and Davar lists, as I have suggested, are perhaps the only genuine Schindler lists to survive the Holocaust. The Madritsch list came into my possession in 2000. The handwritten name of Goldberg will be noted. Every one of the 60 Jews selected by Madritsch and Titsch for the Schindler transport has a story to tell. Over the years, the author interviewed many of them, and some interesting facts emerged. I believe that the name Goldberg shown on this original list corroborates the view that he (Goldberg) was at the very center of the Brünnlitz list compilation. Although the list was sent from Madritsch to Schindler, it was Goldberg who handled selections ... for reward.

With Schindler's commitment to the new factory in Brünnlitz, he handed over the compilation of the list to the Jewish labor office in KL Plaszow, which at that time (in the absence of Amon Goeth) was being administered by SS-Unterscharführer Franz Müller, who controlled the office of work distribution. Also working in this office was the Jew Marcel Goldberg (69510).[241]

Both Simon Jereth and his wife Chaja (76316) were placed on Schindler's list despite Goldberg's efforts to remove them: Jereth was a very religious man. Oskar got tefillin for him (two small leather boxes in the shape of a cube with a wad of parchment with hand-written texts from the biblical Exodus. During the Morning Prayer service, the men over 13 years old fix tefillin with the leather thongs to the forehead and the left forearm). Jereth lent his tefillin to anyone who wanted to pray with him. Every morning there was a queue and he called, "Who is next?" When Schindler was about to leave Brünnlitz in his bid to get to the west, Jereth sacrificed his golden bridge put in by a dentist in Krakow before the war. He had the bridge taken out by the dentist, Hirsch Licht (68987), and it was converted into a ring with the text written in Hebrew: *"Whoever saves one life saves the world entire."*

Amon Goeth had taken leave and visited his father, Amon Franz Goeth, a publisher in Vienna. During his absence from the camp, officers of the SS Bureau V RSMO (Reich Security Main Office) descended on the camp and began a full-scale investigation and audit of Goeth's affairs. Just prior to going on leave, Goeth had been covering up his criminal activities. He had the well-known informers and collaborators who had been assisting him, the Jewish families of Chilowicz and Finkelstein, shot. Bureau V of the SS consisted of professionals who systematically worked through every aspect of Goeth's activities. There was no shortage of informers among other SS officers of the camp. To the relief of everyone, Goeth was not to return to the camp. He was arrested by the SS investigators at his father's address in Vienna and taken to the SS prison in Breslau, where he remained in custody.

A new Commandant was appointed to KL Plaszow, SS-Hauptsturmführer Buscher, who was aware of the impending closing of the camp. Buscher wanted a disciplined rundown and cooperated with Schindler's transfer activities.

Meanwhile, the list had permanently passed into the hands of Marcel Goldberg, who was now the sole arbiter and chose to use his authority and power to make himself a very rich man indeed. Dr. Alexander Biberstein (68913), who had been one of the most influential persons in the ghetto and privy to all of Schindler's dealings with the Jewish Resistance, was to find that he and his family had been removed from the list at Goldberg's intervention. The list was subtly changing its format to reveal that most people on the list were now wealthy camp functionaries. To make room for the wealthy, Goldberg even had some nominees evacuated to Auschwitz. Schindler was in Brünnlitz and too preoccupied with setting up his new camp and saving his own neck now that Goeth was in custody.[242]

To be saved by Schindler and the list did not mean that that person agreed with Schindler's actions:

Joachim Kinstlinger (68861) remarked: "To me, Schindler was still a German, a Nazi. I'm never going to believe he was a Jew lover. To me, he represents the German system – Nazi – and he was a guy who made money."

Julius Wiener (69290). Although protected and saved by the list, he sought litigation to expose Schindler as a criminal, as shown in the Wiener Affair.

Ruth Kalder, mistress of Amon Goeth, said: "You think Schindler liked Jews? He loved them. Oh, no, no. He was a loveable opportunist and he needed them – so he worked with them. But he didn't take them to his heart."

The doctors nominated would, at first glance, draw no special inference. The fact was that these doctors were all contributors to and associates of Goldberg. Many doctors who Schindler specifically requested did not make it onto the list. The following doctors are shown on the list for Brünnlitz: Chaim Hilfstein (69295), Mirko Koniowitsch (77192), Matilda

Low (76354), and Leon Gross.[243] In spite of urgent pleas by Mietek Pemper, Itzhak Stern, and Jerzy Schek (68836), Dr. Biberstein and his family were not reinstated. Another unfortunate was Dr. Idek Schindel, who had come up against the unscrupulous Goldberg. Dr. Schindel had requested inclusion on the list along with his two young brothers, but Goldberg insisted on diamonds. This was a well-known fact with many of those I interviewed.[244]

On October 15, 1944, at 5 a.m. on the Appellplatz, the list of workers going to Brünnlitz was read out. The Bibersteins and the Schindels, although not called, joined the group anyway, only to be removed by the SS at the last moment of boarding the transport.[245] According to Biberstein's account after the war, the seven wagons were for the men on Schindler's list to Brünnlitz via concentration camp Gross-Rosen. Something underhanded was going on as the properly listed personnel were being refused. It wasn't until later, when the transport arrived at the intermediary camp, that the reasons became clear.

Transport of Men from Plaszow to Gross-Rosen:[246]

After being lined up and registered, the men were undressed and inspected. They received prisoner uniforms from the camp warehouse, wooden clogs, and wax paper prisoner clothing. After being deloused and disinfected the prisoners were herded into camp quarters. The commander of the camp was SS-Sturmbannführer Johannes Hassebroek. Schindler struck up a "business" relationship with the commander and Hassebroek became a customer of goods in short supply: kilograms of tea, sardines, a porcelain service, and liters of alcohol. On October 15, 1944, 700 of Schindler's men departed, crammed into eight wagons without food, water or toilets; they arrived at the Gross-Rosen marshalling yard one day later where they were stripped and all personal property was confiscated.

On the following morning, seven wagons were sent straight to Brünnlitz; the eighth wagon contained Jews who were to remain at Gross-Rosen or be sent elsewhere. Goldberg was still active: he crossed off the names of 24 prisoners and wrote in the names of prisoners from the eighth wagon in the free spaces. Goldberg also changed the occupations of several prisoners. The final version of the official transport list arrived from Plaszow on October 20, 1944, when the discrepancies were found but too late to retrieve the prisoners.

Having arrived at Gross-Rosen, the men were processed and camp numbers beginning with 68821 were recorded. It is these numbers allocated at Gross-Rosen that remained with the male Jews until the war collapsed. It is these lists showing these names and numbers which have been mistaken for a "Schindler list" when, in fact, these lists were just a record for the purposes of supplying the prisoners with food in the Brünnlitz sub-camp. It was at Gross-Rosen that Goldberg's ploy collapsed. Goldberg had given Gross-Rosen his own list of worthies, using official forms taken from the labor office. The official list from KL Plaszow had now arrived at Gross-Rosen, and, of course, did not correspond with Goldberg's. There was a frantic flurry of activity by the SS administrators, but it was too late for many of the original nominees who could not be found. Dr. Biberstein was reinstated on the Brünnlitz list but it was too late for Dr. Biberstein's family, Dr. Schindel, and many others who had been left behind.[247]

According to Dr. Biberstein and many other Jews, the conditions at Gross-Rosen were horrendous. Treated like cattle, the men were forced into a small square where they were ordered to undress and leave everything they had in a pile.[248] They were then herded to the bathhouse where they were shaven, and after a cold shower, wet and naked, they were prodded like cattle for two kilometers to a store where they received a shirt, clogs, trousers, and a beret. All their personal possessions were taken. Forced into a barrack built to accommodate 40, these 100 prisoners had to sit between each other's legs as there was no room to stand.

Kept in the barracks for three days, unable to see to their natural needs, people became dirty, and the barracks stank. The camp administrators clarified the official KL Plaszow list and the prisoners were sent on their 24-hour journey to Brünnlitz. Without water or use of private facilities, they arrived at the station Brezova nad Svitavou, where Schindler was waiting for them. In batches of five abreast the men were marched to Schindler's camp, some two kilometers from the station.[249] The men had arrived at Brünnlitz, but where were the women? [250]

Josef Bau gives us an indication of Schindler's concern and thoughtfulness:

> "At Gross-Rosen all our personal property was taken. Amongst my property was a book of poems and memoirs I had managed to keep throughout the war. We had been in Brünnlitz for a few days when Schindler entered the factory and asked for Josef Bau. He handed me my book of poems and said, "I believe this is yours." What kind of man would do that? I didn't know him."

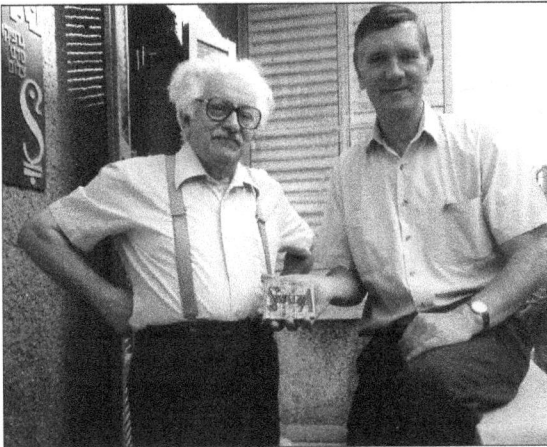

Figure 53: Josef Bau with the author, who is holding the book of poems which Schindler recovered from Gross Rosen. Tel Aviv 1995
Photo Credit: Author's collection

Schindler performed a similar kindness for Leon Rosner by returning his violin. The evidence shows that Schindler was never in Gross-Rosen but somehow, he had arranged these kind deeds for people he didn't really know. It says much about his character.

The 300 Schindler women left KL Plaszow for Schindler's Brünnlitz. Unknown to them, their transport took another direction – Auschwitz.

After October 21, 1942, only 600 prisoners from the liquidation work force remained at Plaszow; on January 14, 1945, these individuals were shipped to Auschwitz. The Red Army liberated the Plaszow camp on January 18, 1945.

Chapter Fourteen
Brünnlitz Camp

Figure 54: Oskar Schindler's office in Brünnlitz
Photo Credit: Author's collection

The port to which "Schindler's Ark" was to set sail became the village of Brünnlitz. The village in the Sudetenland near Schindler's native Svitavy was to become the setting for the next chapter in the Schindler story.

The village of Brünnlitz in the Svitavy River Valley was predestined for industrial development. The first cloth mills have been documented to the 17th century and at the beginning of the 19th century the first cloth factory and paper factory were founded. The paper factory was bought in 1854 by Izák Löw Beer from Svitávka, who then converted it into a wool spinning factory that employed 1,600 workers at the height of its fame. Daubek's steam mill near the wool factory also played a role in Schindler's story. Having been taken over by the Nazis and under the administration of the Hoffmann brothers of Vienna since 1940, Löw Beer's factory was turned into a branch of the Gross-Rosen concentration camp – the Brünnlitz labor camp, the destination for Schindler's Jews in 1944.

The Brünnlitz camp, a sub-camp of Gross-Rosen, was now under the command of SS-Obersturmbannführer Josef Leipold, assisted by about 30 guards considered unfit by the Wehrmacht for front line duties. Leipold, a hairdresser before the war, was a stereotypical Nazi who tried to run the camp with a rod of steel, only to be frustrated at every turn by Schindler, who constantly challenged his authority. Commandant Leipold was becoming exasperated with Schindler's apparent personal consideration of the welfare of his Jewish workers.

The construction of the Brünnlitz labor camp was likely launched in April 1944. At the beginning of 1944 the forced labor camps in the Sudetenland were annexed to the Gross-Rosen camp. Gross-Rosen oversaw 16 branch camps in northeastern Bohemia, Moravia, and Silesia. The Nazi-controlled Löw Beer factory was leased out to three firms during the war – the munitions manufacturer MEWA (Metallwaren Fabrik), the truck assembling company SUDETIA, and Schindler's company. The actual grounds of Schindler's company were built to SS specifications. Watchtowers were built and the camp was surrounded by barbed wire. The commander of the camp and its 30 guards was Josef Leipold, with whom Schindler frequently came into conflict.

The Brünnlitz factory was far from being finished when Schindler's Jews arrived. The equipment and machines shipped from Krakow had not been installed and for three weeks after their arrival men were forced to sleep on straw on the floor. A washroom, clothes washing room and a disinfecting room had to be built. Prisoners began to come down with typhoid and scarlet fever. At the beginning the camp doctors Hilfstein and Biberstein were forced to treat patients without the required medication.

Schindler Is Arrested by the SS Corruption Squad

Unknown to the Schindler groups, Oskar had been arrested and was in the custody of the SS for conspiratorial crimes associated with Amon Goeth. The men, who were now in the comparative safety of Brünnlitz, were becoming anxious about their women. Already segregation had commenced: all the male children at Brünnlitz were to be transferred (with their fathers) to Auschwitz. Amongst them were Dr. Gross and his eight-year-old adopted son. Also transferred were Herman Rosner and his son Olek; Eugeniusz Ginter, age 14, (born February 8, 1929) and his father; Richard Horowitz, age 4, (born May 5, 1939) and his father; Richard Nussbaum, age 14 (born March 22, 1930) and his father; Roman Ferber, age 14 (born January 25, 1931) and his father; and Abraham Wisniak, born 1930 (69242) and his father. It seemed that without the authority of Schindler the breakup of this select company was imminent. The SS had decided that this was to be.

Again, Mrs. Schindler made telephone calls to the highest echelons of power in the Abwehr and Armaments Inspectorate. Whatever happened, it worked, as Schindler arrived at Brünnlitz a few days later, disheveled and shaken, but pleased to be back. The news of the boys' transport to Auschwitz shook him badly. This was corroborated by Maurice Finder (76291) in a statement after the war. "I was installing the new machines when Schindler came over to me and asked whether I had any children on the transport. I replied in the negative and he replied – thank God." Maurice Finder had good reason to be thankful to Schindler. His wife had been taken for immediate transportation to the death camp at Belzec. Finder appealed to Schindler, who went directly to the train which was preparing to leave (just as in the Bankier episode). Schindler argued with the SS, stressing once again that this woman was an essential worker for the armaments factory. Schindler not only obtained the release of Mrs. Finder, but also that of her sister.[251]

Mrs. Schindler recalls the early days at Brünnlitz:[252]

"A Miss Kronovsky worked at the factory as a secretary. She was in charge of the lists of workers which had to be presented to the Germans every eight days on the arrival of the food rations. These rations were calculated on the calories which our workers supposedly required.

Miss Kronovsky's work was hard, as the Germans had many deadlines and did not accept mistakes. They examined the lists thoroughly and any mistakes were punished rigorously and with monetary demands, too.

The munitions factory was under the supervision of the German army, which surrounded it with an electric fence and had 250 armed men at their disposal. They were beneath the command of the Obersturmführer Leopold, a short and fat Austrian who had previously commanded a concentration camp at Budzyn, Poland, which produced airplanes.

The Jews were untouchable (safe) while we were at Brünnlitz, but Oskar and I were also prisoners. If we tried to escape, he would be sent to the front and my fate would be unimaginable.

The officer in charge was called Lange, the head of all German munitions factories. He was a total gentleman and visited us in civilian clothing to show us his disapproval of the Nazi regime. He worked for his country, not for any particular government.

He was known for being straight and having a strong sense of justice, and his arrival caused fears that we would be unable to meet the criteria of his strict regime. When he arrived from Berlin, I invited him to lunch so that he could rest before the inspection. Luckily, all went well.

Despite Brünnlitz being milder than Plaszow, terror was still part of our daily lives. Soon after we arrived, a woman was hanged in the square, accused of having fallen in love with an English prisoner. She was brutally interrogated as if her love was an unpardonable crime. Her body remained hung up at the tree for eight days, as a warning to anyone considered an enemy of the Führer and the Third Reich.

We were constantly afraid of the S.S. finding out about how we helped and fed the Jews. Another fear was that of typhus, which was transmitted via lice. We boiled their clothing in the laundry at 120 degrees C to exterminate them, and the pest would have been enough of a reason for the Nazis to close down the camp.

We received a large consignment of irons, to be converted to shell casings. We had troughs of sulphuric acid, furnaces. But nothing was ever produced.

We were surrounded by high fences and alert guards at their posts, from which they could see the river and town, where there were the Skoda and Bota factories.

We slept in a room next to a hall where the machinery was, with only Rex and Karin, our sheepdogs, for company. (Rex had won three medals for his pedigree.) My business at Brünnlitz was to organize the food for the workers. We had our own electric generator, both carbon and gas, so we had heating and hot water for the winter.

As well as the members of the 'list' there were also some Czechs and Poles. Despite our efforts, the provided rations were not always sufficient. Jewish workers received a more substantial amount due to their challenging work. I ensured that they had more bread than regulations stated, and more nutritious soup. They were weighed every time they bathed. The few funerals were carried out in the Catholic cemetery to avoid cremation, and the grave-diggers were paid with an extra kilogram of bread. Despite all this, the sight of starvation made extreme measures necessary.

Near the factory was a mill which belonged to a lady from the aristocracy by the name of Von Doubeck. I had heard she was an open and polite woman, so I asked the director of the mill to arrange a meeting with the owner, and I found myself invited to tea the next day. This surprised me, and I considered the arguments necessary to convince her, but in the end I settled on the truth: the rations would not support our ever-weakening workers.

Oskar had gone to Krakow, so I was alone in my nervous state. Only the image of the starving workers made me walk the footpath to her mansion. Also the refusal to return with empty hands spurred me on, on this beautiful autumn afternoon, as I carried a bouquet of flowers as a gift.

She was awaiting me in an enormous living-room. She stood as I entered, and came to greet me. She was about 50, dressed in a modest fashion, whose manners showed an exquisite education. We served ourselves with each one of the delicacies and with tea (prepared in the English way), and then I explained my proposal. We needed grain from her mill to help feed our starving workers. She listened attentively and gave her consent, telling me to speak to the director of the mill, and with her authority take on whatever I needed. She then stood and excused herself cordially. I returned to the factory with a cargo of grain and semolina.

Oskar once brought back a thousand bottles of vodka and a large box of Polish cigarettes from Krakow to bribe S.S. officers. The night of my interview with Lady Von Dubreck, a Polish Jew called Obereck and I stole a few packets of cigarettes and a few bottles of vodka.

Another Jew called Bejski forged stamps out of rubber for passes so that we could go out looking for petrol, bread, flour, cloth or cigarettes. Oskar had exchanged some diamonds for 1,000 kilograms of bread and I went to the Black Market for similar exchanges. I realized that if I was caught, I would be executed, but God or Fate seemed to be on my side, and nothing went on.

I also had a duty to socialize and associate with the wives of the S.S. officers. I moved from one world to another, from the hunger and desperation of the Jews to the reality of these women, whose husbands took the war all over Europe. A lieutenant-major in command of armaments once sent his wife and child due to fear of the Berlin bombings. We travelled to Mahrisch Ostrav, preceded by Viktorka, who prepared our old apartment for our stay. There, this woman and I had some slight disagreements. First of all, she was an alcoholic and her 12-year-old son had taken a few of my belongings: a pen, a little silver vase (a present from my mother) and another thing, which I have forgotten.

Another incident involving the little thief was the theft of some money from the cashbox. A Polish worker at the factory was accused by the S.S. She was so insistent over her innocence that the Germans investigated further, and blamed a Jewish family, who were immediately executed. Finally, they found out that it was Commandant Hartweg's son who had taken the money. That was how Nazi justice worked.

These social duties were necessary for my security, and that of my husband. I was permanently nervous and I smoked incessantly as a result. I had no favorite brand, and I smoked whatever there was. There were some decent Polish cigarettes, but most seemed to be made of straw. Fifteen years ago the paralysis of my foot made me have to quit it. At the time, I was smoking 40 a day, as it was the only thing which could calm my nerves."

One interesting document that came to notice during the Schindler investigation was a legal contract between Schindler and the family Butchovsky to rent a piece of land for use as an allotment to produce food for his workers. The document refers to the rent of 3,000 square meters, to be surrounded by fencing. Rent would be 47 Reichmarks per year, beginning November 1, 1944, and continuing as long as the war lasted. The rent would be paid in advance or on signing. Both sides of the contract will confirm that they are Aryan.

Figure 55: Men's accommodation Brünnlitz Camp
Photo Credit: Author's collection

Chapter Fifteen
Schindler's Women

Figure 56: Mrs. Anna (Chana) Hofstatter née Laufer
Photo Credit: Author's collection

In the autumn of 1944, the 300 Schindler women, together with the children Bronislaw Horowicz (76307), Celina Carp (76318), Ewa Ratz (76404), and Halina Horowicz (76308), left KL Plaszow in sealed wagons en route to Schindler's factory at Brünnlitz. To their dismay and horror, the transport arrived at Auschwitz-Birkenau.[253]

Figure 57: Auschwitz-Birkenau 1944 where the Schindler women were received
Photo Credit: Author's collection

Three Long Weeks of Fear

A transport with 2,000 women, 300 of whom were from Emalia, left Plaszow on October 22, 1944, in the direction of Auschwitz and Brünnlitz. The women did not leave for Gross-Rosen as the men did because every prisoner had to go through quarantine and an inspection and Gross-Rosen was not equipped to handle women for these purposes. After their arrival at Auschwitz the women were divided and quartered in camp B-IIc.

Dr. Josef Mengele selected 1,765 women from the transport (including Schindler's women). The remaining prisoners were sent to the gas chambers.

The 300 Schindler women were now to experience the terror of Auschwitz as depicted in Spielberg's film: the dramatic scenes in the showers when the women did not know whether poisonous gas was about to be released are based on the testimony of numerous survivors. The stressful life in the camp, Goldberg's manipulation of the transport list, uncertainty and fear all provoked the feeling that Schindler had abandoned the prisoners to their fate.

Figure 58: The main gate at Auschwitz-Birkenau as depicted in the film "Schindler's List"

Unbelievable drama occurred at this location. Immediately upon their arrival the unsuspecting prisoners were herded from the wagons and separated by SS guards into those capable of work and those who were sent straight to the gas chambers. This selection was one of the first things new prisoners encountered. Life frequently depended on the mood of the guards, their commanders and doctors who, with a mere wave of the hand, sent people to instant death or to a slow death by torturous work. The Schindler women were kept isolated as specialist munitions workers.

**Figure 59: Women prisoners in Auschwitz-Birkenau being chosen for the gas chamber
Photo Credit: Author's collection**

Irma Griese is supervising the selection process. The watercolor, entitled *Frauen-Selektion in Birkenau,* was painted by a former prisoner W. Siwek after 1945 and now hangs in the Auschwitz Museum.

Stella Muller (76372)

Today Stella Müller-Madej owes her life to Schindler's list. She was 14 but registered as being two years older and as a metal worker – all so she could survive as essential for the war industry. Both she and her parents would not have survived World War II without it. She captures her recollections of the wartime period in her book, *Through the Eyes of a Child.* [254]

> "In '44 there were around 700 women who were transported from Plaszow, 300 of whom were on Schindler's list, and Schindler fought for us like a lion, because they didn't want to let us out of Auschwitz. He was offered better and healthier 'material' from new transports, unlike us, who had spent several years in the camp. But he got us out … he saved us...."

On leaving Plaszow with her mother, Berta Müller (76371), and the other Schindler women, Stella was sick and when the Schindler transport arrived in Auschwitz-Birkenau she was sent to the Krankenstube (medical room) where she remained until rescued three weeks later by other "Schindler women" to join them on the last part of the journey to Schindler's factory.

Irena Scheck:

"We arrived at Auschwitz at night. The SS guards opened the cattle cars and ordered us to get out. We were separated into groups and walked in absolute silence. We saw chimneys and the dark smoke and fire they emitted. The guards stopped us and ordered us to remove all of our clothes. We were to go to the building with showers. We entered the building, but there were no showers there. The Jews that worked there told us that the next morning we would be sent to the gas chambers. The next morning, we lined up outside. Dr. Mengele, the 'Angel of Death,' was there. We went through the first selection. He sent some people to the right, others to the left. I was lucky to end up in the right line. We went through many selections over the course of those three weeks. I was so thin I didn't know which part of my body to show at the inspections."

Irena Scheck

Estera Pinkas:

"We were lined up in silence as the capo began to read the list of names in alphabetical order. I waited impatiently to hear my name. The capo reading the list didn't notice that several women that were not with us had slipped into our group. And when a name was read several hands went up. When my name was read one of the women that had joined the group said, 'I am Ester Pinkas.' There was great confusion. The line-up was cancelled and we were forced back into the barracks so that the list could be investigated. Only Schindler knew the real names, but he was far away. You can't blame those desperate people. Luckily for me Schindler's group was kept together. Within three days the list had been definitively verified."

Estera Pinkas (Rechen)

After delousing, cold showers, and hair shaves, the Schindler group, who were barracked separately, remained uncertain of their future.[255]

On the following morning the women, all marked with red paint, were marched to the transport en route for KL Brünnlitz. At the point of departure there was an unusual coincidence. Working on the other side of the wire were some of the Schindler men and boys who had been brought on the Brünnlitz-Auschwitz transport. Manci Rosner (76423) and Regina Horowitz (76309) with her daughter Niusia had seen their men-folk working in the men's compound on the other side of the wire. There was a brief encounter between Manci Rosner and Regina Horowitz and their sons.

The women's ordeal was over. Only two women were missing: One of the two was the mother of Itzhak Stern.[256]

Richard Horowitz was later re-united with his mother when she returned to Krakow after the war. She only discovered that her son was still alive when she saw a newsreel of the survivors of Auschwitz on liberation.

Figure 60: Schindler's Women in Auschwitz (Josef Bau)
Photo Credit: Author's collection

The delay in the arrival of the women to Brünnlitz was now of great concern. Stern went to Schindler and begged him to do something. Too late to stop the transport of the boys to Auschwitz, he used all his influence to have the women released. Emilie Schindler takes up the story:

> "Oskar and I were at the office. On the table, the inevitable bottle of cognac. My husband picked up the telephone and called in our engineer, Schoenborn. When he came in, Oskar looked sternly into his eyes, took a small bag out of his pocket, the contents of which were very familiar to me. Oskar said, 'I must entrust you with an important mission. Without the women we cannot go on with the factory. We need their labor, and besides the men are getting very restless asking why their wives have not come yet. They fear something has gone seriously wrong. You are to go to Auschwitz immediately, speak to whomever you have to, pay whatever the price may be, but I want you to get the women here. I have full confidence in you: I know you are an honorable gentleman who can be trusted and will make good on your word.' 'It will be done as you say, Herr Direktor,' Schoenborn answered, taking the bag of diamonds and pressing it to his chest. We have no answer whether Schoenborn completed his task but it was clear it hadn't worked."[257]

Again, there were phone calls to friends in high places. A second emissary was sent to Auschwitz to accomplish this task. This was a young, trusted female associate of Emilie Schindler named Hilde, the daughter of a wealthy industrialist in Svitavy.[258] In the Spielberg film, Schindler is shown making a personal visit to the Commandant and bribing him with diamonds. There is no evidence that Schindler was ever in Auschwitz.

Emilie:

> "Desperate, Oskar drove to Zwittau to speak to an old childhood friend called Hilde, and he asked her to go to Auschwitz and deal with recovering the women personally. I don't know what high Nazi contacts Hilde had, but she succeeded. Days later, the 300 workers arrived at the platform.
>
> She was the daughter of a rich German industrialist, who left one day, quite unexpectedly, for Mexico, never to return. She had an uncommon beauty, thin and svelte, with blonde hair which caught everyone's attention. She was an independent character, who loved freedom above all things. She never told me why or how she did it, but I'm sure her great beauty played a part.
>
> Our long-standing relationship with Hilde came from the time when she was part of our summer group, and shone as an excellent swimmer. Oskar and her had been friends since childhood. I eventually found out that she worked for the Wehrmacht, and soon after freeing the women we lost all trace of her."[259]

Whether Hilde was successful we do not know, but shortly after the women were en route for Brünnlitz. The more acceptable explanation is that the orders and the paperwork had been completed many weeks earlier. It was a question of expediting the transfer orders of these women, who were considered important armament specialists, out of Auschwitz on a special transport to Arbeitslager Brünnlitz.

The release was eventually accomplished with little difficulty but not without incident. The Schindler list of women taken by the courier to Auschwitz did not quite agree with the list (already filed) held in the administration office of Auschwitz. On the official camp list held at Auschwitz were two women with the same name, Helena Dortheimer (76229) and Helena Dortheimer (76230). One was the wife of Viktor Dortheimer (69124), now at Brünnlitz, and the other was the wife of his brother, David Dortheimer, who had been shot by Goeth in KL Plaszow. (In November 1943, 51 prisoners – 50 men and one woman – returning to the camp after work were searched. Potatoes were found in their possession. Goeth was called and ordered all the prisoners to be shot, one of them being David Dortheimer).[260]

The discrepancy on the lists was pointed out to the courier and she was asked which Helena Dortheimer was to be transferred. The quick-thinking courier asked for both and explained that it was an error by the Schindler Armament Works in Brünnlitz. Viktor Dortheimer's wife and sister-in-law were thus safe; either one could have perished in Auschwitz.

Figure 61: Helena Dortheimer (76230), wife of Viktor
Photo Credit: Author's collection

Emilie Schindler:

> "The arrival at Brünnlitz of the train with the female workers caused a great commotion. In the celebration there were tears and laughter, while the German soldiers watched in silence, their sidelong glances still threatening. The women arrived from Auschwitz in a disastrous condition: fragile, emaciated, and weak. I took care myself of handfeeding them semolina porridge and making them take their medications. They improved almost instantly, feeling protected and taken care of, safe at least as they stayed in Brünnlitz."[261]

One of the most extraordinary occurrences at Auschwitz was that the Schindler women were the only known group of women who were brought into the camp for labor or for the gas chamber but who actually left the camp unmolested. Five abreast and all marked with red paint, they were marched to the transport en route to Brünnlitz and Schindler's camp. The transport of women prisoners from Auschwitz to Brünnlitz was to depart on November 10, 1944, but the transport document is stamped with the date November 12. The women had spent three weeks in Auschwitz.

Stella Muller en route to from Auschwitz to Brünnlitz continues:

> "On leaving Auschwitz, after a number of false starts when the train carrying the women broke down within the Auschwitz complex, they feared being returned and that their last chance of escaping the 'gas' had failed. But soon another locomotive was found, and the train again began its journey to Brünnlitz. Hunger and thirst now swept through the cars and some women feared they would starve to death. When the train stopped again, another voice from outside asked whether there was anyone in the cars. In unison, the women shouted, 'We're here. Why have we stopped?' A person outside replied, 'They want to take you back to Auschwitz.' Stella said that everyone 'went crazy.

Anything except that! Let them kill us here.' Despite their fears the train moved on and eventually arrived at Brünnlitz. The arrival of the train caused great celebration, which the soldiers watched with silent menace. The women were in a terrible state; starved to the point of being skeletons.

As the women paraded in line two men appeared: one dressed in an SS uniform, and the other, we later learned, was Oskar Schindler. The SS guards were offended by the women's appearance, and one of them said, 'O, wie die Frauen stinken.' (Oh, how these women stink).

On arrival at the camp, they were met by Schindler who spoke to them in a caring voice:

'I know that you have been through hell on your way here. Your appearance says it all. Here also, for the time being, you will be forced to suffer many discomforts, but you are brave women. We did not have a great deal of hope that it would be possible to bring you here. That is in the past now. I am counting on your discipline and sense of order. I think that the worst has been overcome. The bunks should be here in a few days. Now you must put things in order yourselves. The doctors should report to the head physician and you should elect block supervisors. Dr. Hilfstein and Pemper will show you where you can wash. The sick and those who need bandaging should go with the doctors.'"

Figure 62: Women's accommodation at Brünnlitz
Photo Credit: Author's collection

The suffering of the women continued. Hunger and disease remained a serious problem. They had also been warned to be very careful of the commandant, Josef Leipold, who was dangerous and had to be watched.

Three women died in the camp at various times: Janka Feigenbaum, Elizabeth Chotimer, and Anna Hofstatter (Laufer). Leipold issued orders that the bodies were to be incinerated in the factory furnaces. Schindler openly defied this order and challenged Leipold, who conceded; and instead, the bodies of the three women were placed in wooden coffins and buried at various locations with full rites supervised by Rabbi Jacob Lewertow (68872).

Janka Feigenbaum (Janina), the sister of Lewis Feigenbaum, had been ill for some time before she arrived at Brünnlitz. Mysteriously, she was given an injection by Dr. Hilfstein and died shortly after. After the war, her family exhumed Janka's body and reburied it in the New Jewish Cemetery in Prague.

Mrs. Hofstatter

One of the enduring mysteries of the Schindler story is the true identity of Mrs. Hofstatter. The evidence clearly shows that a Mrs. Hofstatter was part of the Schindler women in Brünnlitz, that she died on Christmas Eve 1944, and that she was buried in a parcel of land purchased by Schindler in the Christian cemetery in the village of Nemecka Bela (now Bela nad Svitavu), a few kilometers from Schindler's Brünnlitz camp. Mrs. Hofstatter clearly existed, as she is referred to by Keneally and Itzhak Stern.

**Figure 63: Judge Bejski far left. Schindler third from right,
"listening to Stern" at the Schindler reception
Photo Credit: Author's collection**

In a survivor's reunion in 1962, at which Schindler was the honored guest, Stern addressed details of the Hofstatter incident directly to Schindler:

> "You remember that Mrs. Hofstatter passed away. Commandant Leipold ordered the body to be cremated. I turned to you and asked you to intervene. You did not hesitate and arranged a Jewish burial. Despite it being a Sunday, you rode to a nearby village where you persuaded a priest to sell a parcel of ground adjacent to the Christian cemetery."

Stern then turned to the guests:

> "He fenced in this parcel of land and founded a Jewish cemetery for one Jewish woman who had died a natural death. That day, a Jewish burial service took place, and Rabbi Levertov [Lewertow] with ten Jews officiated with all the traditional prayers, and this was done specifically on the orders of Schindler. He ordered a coffin to be prepared from the most expensive wood, put a metal board inside it with all her details inscribed on it. Gentlemen, this was the only case in conquered Europe when a Jewish cemetery was formed. One of the SS sergeants from the camp took care of the cemetery, with flowers and plants, for a special fee from Schindler. It is necessary to emphasize that he endangered himself by all of this. And it was a very heroic deed."

Some of the leading archivists, historians, and self-appointed experts on Schindler in the Czech Republic and elsewhere have failed to locate and identify the real Mrs. Hofstatter – that is, until the author, with the help of her granddaughter, Chani Smith – solved this simple mystery.

First, let us look at the facts and background of this woman that have given rise to the ambiguity and mystery surrounding her. Anna (Chana) Hofstatter (née Laufer) was a lady of immense charm and beauty. She was born on December 12, 1878, in Sieniawa, Poland, but lived with her husband Meir in Krakow. Mrs. Hofstatter's husband owned a chemist shop in Krakow and was well-respected in the close-knit Jewish community. During the German occupation and times of the general violence and abuse against the Jewish population (described in these chapters), her husband, son, and daughter-in-law were shot in Plaszow. Because the name Hofstatter was a target for the Gestapo, Anna, fearing for her own life, reverted to her maiden name of Laufer. Anna Hofstatter (Laufer) had two daughters – Ala (Sara Rosenberg [Hofstatter]), born January 7, 1905, (76419) and Mala (Mala Mandelbaum [Hofstatter]), born, July 24, 1903, (76281), who went into hiding after the shootings.

It is a recurring fact that lists and personal details are not all how they appear. Changes of names, dates of birth, occupations, and all manner of personal identification were sometimes manipulated depending on circumstances at the time. This was all part of the survival instinct. On the transport list for October 1944 from KL Plaszow to Brünnlitz via Auschwitz, all three women gave false dates of birth.

Ju.Po 76281	Mandelbaum (Hofstatter) Mala July 24, 1917 (1903)
Ju.Po 76419	Rosenberg (Hofstatter) Sara January 7, 1916 (1905)

139.	"	9	Kurz Tauba	10. 6.1903
140.	"	76340	Kugner-Lewkowicz Renata	6.12.1915
141.	"	1	Laufer Roza	16.10.1924
142.	"	2	Dembitzer Sar	17. 6.1896
143.	"	3	Lampel Anita	26. 5.1928
144.	"	4	Lampel Celina	14. 3.1907
145.	"	5	Landsberger Helene	12. 7.1908
146.	"	6	Laufer Anna	12.12.1898
147.	"	7	Leder Paula	1. 2.1921
148.	"	8	Lejson Chana	15. 6.1900
149.	"	9	Löffel Sabina	22. 2.1913
150.	"	76350	Lejzor Pescha	3. 5.1926

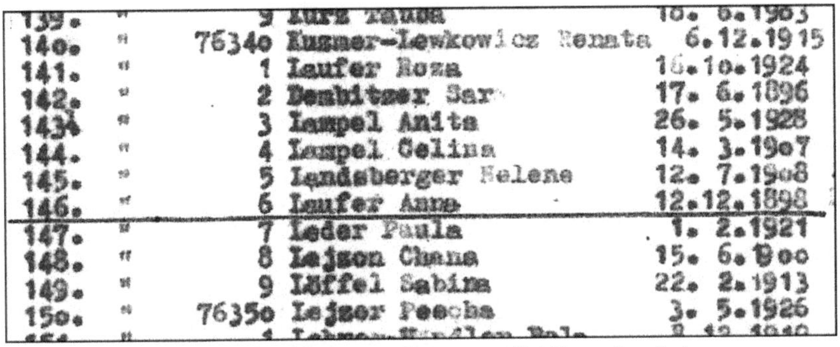

Figure 64: Certified copy of transport list (Anna Laufer)
Photo Credit: Author's collection

Therefore, Anna Laufer (Hofstatter) does not appear on the so-called Schindler's list compiled in April 1945, which has, in my view, been grossly exaggerated as Oskar Schindler's personal "list for life."

The sisters survived the war and later immigrated to Israel. Immediately after the war they returned to Krakow, where they retrieved family treasures that had been buried under a tree just before their forced removal into the ghetto. Quite simply, Mrs. Hofstatter, in a moment of immediate danger, had changed her married name and reverted to her family name – Laufer.

Chapter Sixteen
The Golleschau Tragedy

"The box weighs 35 kg and I only weigh 32 kg. How can I carry the box?"

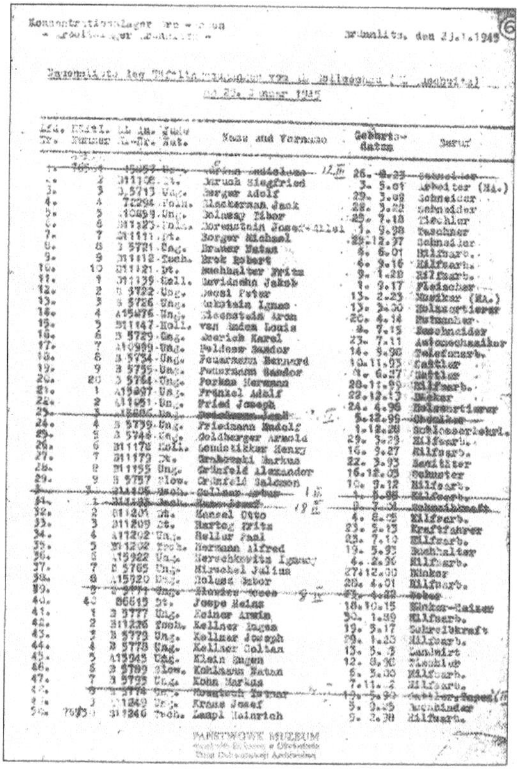

Figure 65: The Golleschau Transport List January 19, 1945: (Namenliste des Häftlingszuganges vom Al Golleschau (KL Auschwitz) am 29. Janur 1945 (List of Names/Roll of the Prisoners from the Work Camp Golleschau on the January 29, 1945 list.[262] Photo Credit: Author's collection

New Prisoners in Brünnlitz

A sub-camp of the Auschwitz complex was located near Těšín in the village of Golleschau. The Red Army launched a great offensive on the Eastern Front on January 12, 1945; as a result, the concentration camps near the front were liquidated and prisoners were sent to the interior, including Golleschau.

The Golleschau camp was located on the Polish-Czech border. In July 1942, the SS-company the Ostdeutsche Baustoffwerke GmbH opened the Golleschau Portland-Zement AG plant in Golleschau and used Jewish slave labor, about 1,000 Jewish workers. Prisoners at Golleschau worked in the cement factory or in the nearby quarries. They also built the railroad tracks and cable car lines in the plant. Conditions were harsh, and prisoners who tried to escape were shot or hanged in public. Prisoners who were exhausted were killed with a lethal injection of phenol.

On January 22, 1945, a transport left to take approximately 100 Jews to work at the company Barthel in Svitavy. However, the company refused to take these people; imprisoned in a sealed train wagon, the Jews faced death by freezing. Though Schindler was not in Brünnlitz at the time, he agreed to receive the new prisoners at the Brünnlitz camp. According to period testimony, the train on January 29, 1945, contained around 100 prisoners, of whom 16 died. However, these figures vary in different sources. The official list of accepted prisoners contains 81 names, 10 of which were crossed out in pencil due to death.

With the onslaught of the Russians who were approaching the Auschwitz district in January 1945, many of the sub-camps of Auschwitz were being disbanded. The Golleschau (January 29, 1945) and Landskrom (February 2, 1945) transports were no exception. In the middle of the month, 120 quarry workers from Golleschau were put into two cattle cars. They traveled for more than ten days without food or drink. The doors were not only locked but frozen shut, for it was bitterly cold. Eventually, the cars were uncoupled and abandoned in the rail yards of Svitavy. Schindler reported (in a letter preserved in the archives at Yad Vashem) that a friend of his called his wife Emilie from the depot and reported hearing moans from inside the cars.

When the critics and doubters of Schindler's motives articulate their views, I would refer them to his actions when dealing with the deaths that occurred in the camp (by natural causes) and in particular from the Golleschau transport. It is of some interest to explore the exact movements of the Golleschau transport and examine the documents that traveled with it: e.g., the Bill of Lading. This document was noticed well after the war when Moshe Bejski escorted Schindler to Yad Vashem. While checking the many files, they found the original Bill of Lading of the Golleschau transport,[263] which carries all the names of those on the transport and the dates when they passed the railway stations. There is an erasure on the document of the station Svitavy, and in Schindler's handwriting Brünnlitz is substituted. I take this as vital corroboration of Schindler's recollections.

From the original of this document the following details are shown: The contents are described as "Merchandise: Jews." (In the Wundheiler documentation, she makes the following comment, "Despite all my frighteningly detailed knowledge of the Holocaust, the dehumanization expressed in those words appalled me more than anything else had terrified me.") "Prisoners with guards," the document was stamped and sealed with goods of Waffen-SS. The weigh bill was dated Golleschau, January 22, 1945, but the first transport stamp was from Teschen, dated January 21, 1945, and the last stamp read Svitavy (crossed out by Schindler with Brünnlitz), January 29, 1945.

Above: The rubber stamp made by Moshe Bejski for Oskar Schindler in 1945

Right: A railway document for Jews transported from Golleschau, a branch of Auschwitz. Oskar Schindler has crossed out various stations and written in 'Zwittau', the town nearest his factory, so that he could save their lives.

Figure 66: Bill of Lading. The emendations shown are in Schindler's handwriting.
To the left: Rubber stamp forged by Moshe Bejski
Photo Credit: Author's collection

The sender's address was Golleschau Portland Cement Works; the receiver was Bartels & Co., Svitavy. The document also showed that the journey had taken ten days. The weigh bill was post-dated to January 22. The transport had already reached Teschen on the 21st, as seen from the stamp on the back of the document. Also, the document had two stamps from Svitavy, both on the 29th, when Bartels refused to take the load. The wagons were being shunted to and fro until Schindler decided to take them and unload the contents of dead and suffering Jews in the early morning of January 30, 1945. Further examination of the document shows that the transport, after leaving Golleschau, headed west, away from the Russian advance. The first calling point was at Auschwitz-Birkenau, where there was panic by the fleeing SS who were supervising the last forced marches of the prisoners. Refused refuge at Auschwitz, the transport continued on, calling at Cieszyn, Oderberg, Schonbrunn, Freudenthal, Svitavy, and finally, Brünnlitz.

Mrs. Schindler wrote:

"On the night of a terrible storm, when the temperature was 30 degrees below zero, a man came to speak with me in the middle of the night, while Oskar was still at Krakow. The man oversaw transporting 250 Jews from Golleschau, a Polish mine of terrible repute. They were crammed into four wagons to be moved to another business, which had heard of the Russians' arrival, and had stranded them. If I refused them, they would have been shot.

I phoned Oskar, and asked for authorization to accept the Jews, which I received. I went out to find Shoneborn, and we went straight to the station. It was snowing, and nearly dawn. We tried to open the locks of the wagons with large iron bars, but they were frozen shut. Schoneborn went to find a welding machine, and with patience, we opened them up.

The German Commander warned me of the sights, but I ignored him. What I saw remained in my nightmares: the men and women were indistinguishable, due to their thinness; they were almost skeletons and most weighed about 30 kilos. Their eyes shone like coals in the darkness. Twelve were dead and they had spent their last minutes, apparently in communion with God, searching for answers.

The survivors were transferred to a sort of emergency hospital immediately, where they remained for two months. They needed special attention, and had not eaten for a long time, so they had to be fed slowly mouthful by mouthful, so that they did not choke.

As they improved they were given a place at our factory, and were fed from the mill and our Black Market dealings. Our factory had become a refuge from the horrors of the concentration camps."[264]

It is almost impossible to describe what the Brünnlitz prisoners saw when they finally succeeded in opening the doors of the two cars. Jewish engineers from the camp burnt off the locks in a massive effort to release those inside. "In each car, a pyramid of frozen corpses, their limbs madly contorted, occupied the center. The 50 or more still living were seared black by the cold and were skeletal."[265] The fight to save the lives of the survivors of this transport was supervised personally by Mrs. Schindler. Moshe Bejski speaks of Mrs. Schindler's "special porridge" that was considered by many to have been the major factor in saving the lives of the survivors from Golleschau.[266]

Mrs. Schindler wrote:

"I assisted in the opening of this wagon. The sight was appalling. Dozens of shadows covered with filthy rags, half-frozen bodies were lying in frozen urine and excrement. The stench was unbelievable. We found about 12 dead and 74 just about alive. All of them were French, Dutch, Hungarian, Czech, and Polish Jews."[267]

Schindler's action, which is not shown in the film, is corroborated by Dan Granot (Adolf Grünhaut 69167) to the author: [268]

Figure 67: Dan Granot

Photo Credit: Author's Collection

**(Schindler list 69167 Dolek Gruenhaut, born February 29, 1924)
used a blow torch on the locks of the Golleschau transport to release
the Jewish prisoners. Many were frozen to death.**

Another witness was Moshe Pantirer (69040), who assisted in removing the dead and partially living Jews from the wagon:

> "I tried to move one man but the skins of their behinds were frozen, and ripped. We worked slowly and made sure the water was not too hot or we would burn them; too little, and it did not help."[269]

Another nine Jewish prisoners, who were very close to death, survived, and only, according to Moshe Bejski, with the nutrition of Mrs. Schindler's famous porridge:

1. Ladislaus Adrian, b. August 26, 1923
2. Jeno Friedmann, b. December 2, 1899
3. Arthur Golner, b. May 1, 1895
4. Josef Hasa, b. July 9, 1904
5. Moses Howes, b. April 23, 1922
6. Istvan Kosatsch, b. May 19, 1890
7. Rudolf Lowry, b. December 13, 1921
8. Alexander Schwartz, b. December 19, 1919
9. Josef Torok, b. April 6, 1893

Among other survivors of this transport were six Polish Jews:

1. Salomon Piotrkowski (77160)
2. Max Piskosz (77161)
3. Moritz Reichgott (77164)
4. Zelman Szydlo (77177)
5. Josef Hitel
6. Josef Blackermann

On the Golleschau list of January 29, ten names had been crossed out as they had died en route. These unknown Jews were all buried in the local cemetery arranged by Schindler:

1. 77101 Ladislaus Aorias
2. Jenö Friedman
3. 77102 Artur Gellner
4. Josf Hase
5. Moses Ilowicz
6. Istewar Kowatsch
7. Rudolf Löwy
8. Alexander Schwarz
9. Bela Schwarz
10. Josef Törö

In total, later confirmed in my interview with Mietek Pemper, 87 Jews arrived on the fatal transport from Golleschau, minus12 who had died.

One survivor[270] of the transport was Michael Klein, now living in Boston, Massachusetts, who was 15 years old at the time. He said, "The Schindlers saved my life, my children's lives, and future generations."

Only a few weeks after the Golleschau incident, one of the survivors, Idek Elsner (69283), was ordered by an SS guard to move a box. Elsner replied, "The box weighs 35 kilograms and I weigh only 32 kilograms. How can I carry the box?"[271] Schindler put an immediate stop to this by banning all SS from his factory workshops, an order which was never challenged by Leipold.[272]

The most distinguishing characteristic of this period was that Schindler engaged in rescue actions which were not suggested by some other individual or organization but were actually conceived and initiated by him. To mention just a few more: he made a deal with the police in the Brünnlitz area to the effect that they would send Jewish escapees to him rather than return them to the SS. Schindler also made it well-known in SS and police circles that he required carpenters and tool makers.

The dead from the Golleschau and Lanškroun trains were buried with Jewish services behind the cemetery wall in the village of Německá Bělá (today Bělá nad Svitavou) near Brünnlitz. Rabbi Levertov conducted the funeral. The grave was exhumed in 1946 and piously reconstructed in 1994.

The SS Send Stragglers to Schindler

One of the forced marches from Auschwitz contained 10,000 people, who were taken in the direction of Gross-Rosen. Out of the 10,000, only 1,200 survived. Then there was a request for carpenters and 30 men stepped forward, Moshe Hinigmann (77009) being one of them. They were all taken to Schindler's camp. After the war, Hinigmann related his story to a packed audience in Israel: "I was welcomed by a person with a friendly face. He asked me how I was doing and told me not to do any work until I had recovered. Afterwards, I knew it was Schindler." Moshe Hinigmann was on the last transport to arrive at Brünnlitz, on April 11, 1945.

Following are the other 27 who owe their lives to Schindler's rescue plan:

1. Hermann Blechmann (77001)
2. Moritz Ettinger (77002)
3. Jacob Ewensohn (77003),
4. Benjamin Feingersch (77004)
5. Leo Finkelstein (77005)
6. Selig Felsenstein (77006)
7. Meier Gartner (77007)
8. Idel Goldstein (77008)
9. Arthur Juttla (77010)
10. Leo Knobloch (77011)
11. Natan Krüger (77012)
12. Josef Kuchler (77013)
13. Berthold Hornitzer (77014)
14. Max Korzec (77015)
15. Abraham Matuschak (77016)
16. Roger Michaud (77017)
17. Josef Mozek (77018)
18. Hans Nebel (77019)
19. Ignaz Nussbaum (77020)
20. Julek Ordylans (77021)
21. Abraham Drzeboznik (77022)
22. Szaja Rosenblum (77023)
23. Chaim Salem (77024)
24. Willy Schlicting (77026
25. Albert Stillmann (77028)

26. Aron Szczapa (77029)

27. Horst Wohlgemut (77030)

The consecutive numbering indicates that the prisoners arrived in Brünnlitz together and were registered as a batch.

Another escaped Jewish prisoner, Alfred Schoenfeld (77185), had been arrested by the Gestapo in the Brünnlitz district. After interrogation he was taken by the Gestapo to Schindler's factory.[273] On another occasion, two Jewish prisoners escaped from a transport which had just left from the Gliewitz camp: Benjamin Breslauer (77182) and Roman Wilner were detained by the Gestapo in Troppau. After two weeks they were taken to Schindler's factory and safety.[274] All these were actions that required initiative and careful planning, as Dr. Wundheiler remarks:

> "Careful planning is not the mark of a person who acts from emotion and impulse alone, however compassionate that impulse might be. Rather, it is the mark of a person who has learned to rein in his impulses amid emotions so that they can serve a purpose." "To find ways to persuade one's opponents – the police, Gestapo and SS – to cooperate with a factory owner rather than foil his plans and denounce him."

Chapter Seventeen
To the Final Hour

Figure 68: The team that escorted Schindler out of Brünnlitz to safety: left to right: R. Rechin, Estera Rechen, Oskar, Emilie, Schanz, Heuberger, Dagen, Wilek, Granhaut
Photo Credit: Author's Collection

Figure 69: Richard Rechen, Estera (Pinkas) Rechen Haifa 1995
Photo Credit: Author's Collection

The greatest threat that faced Schindler now was the imminent closure of the camp. Everyone knew that the front was near collapse and that the last weeks would be the most dangerous. A group of Budzyn prisoners together with a number of other prisoners formed a resistance group in readiness for possible resistance should the Germans decide to force march the entire camp out of Brünnlitz. Worse still was the danger of entire liquidation, which was occupying Schindler's mind currently. As it happened, Schindler was to face both scenarios. The first danger was the increased activity of Wlassove units[275] stationed in the surrounding area. Schindler had implemented his own defense measures. He went directly to SS-Obersturmführer Rausch, the SS and Police Chief of Moravia, and obtained arms on the pretext of defense against the Russians. For his cooperation, Rausch received one of Schindler's last remaining items of real value, the gift of a brilliant diamond ring for his wife. Schindler returned to the camp with hand grenades, carbines, machine guns, and pistols. These weapons were concealed by one of the Bejski brothers, Uri Bejski [69384], in a storeroom at the factory.

For the second time in Schindler's war, he brought in uniforms to be used in the breakout of the camp. This time they were not uniforms of the Polish army, as they had been at Gliewitz, but uniforms of the SS and Ukrainian guard. Itzhak Stern took great care in issuing the appropriately sized uniforms to a select defense force.[276]

The climax of fear came with a solitary soldier on horseback who arrived in the camp and went directly to the Commandant's office to deliver what turned out to be orders to liquidate the camp. Mietek Pemper, who was acting as clerk to the Commandant, was the first to reveal the contents of this secret communication. All the young, the ill, and the old were to be "resettled" (killed) immediately. Only ten percent of the workers were to remain to decommission the camp. Schindler had decided that the waiting was now over, and the priority was to get rid of the SS Commandant, Leipold. With the help of Leib Salpeter (69282), the Zionist and chemist from Galicia, they got Leipold drunk, and then Schindler gave him lessons in throwing hand grenades on waste ground at the rear of the camp.[277] The explosions caused near panic to those in the vicinity.

Mrs. Schindler was horrified at what her husband was doing and begged him to calm down. Schindler's spontaneous action is another example of his well- thought out and executed ploy to defeat the Nazis at their own game. He had thrown caution to the wind and, in doing so, had proven his intuition was right. General Schoener, whose Wehrmacht headquarters were a short distance from the factory, came over to investigate the disturbance. General Schoener gave Leipold his marching orders and the following morning Leipold was seen leaving the camp, fully armed, being driven to the front at Moravska Ostrava by Schindler.[278]

A new Commandant was sent to Brünnlitz, a 68-year-old local reserve officer, by all accounts a very calm and civil individual. The threat to Schindler and his Jews had disappeared and it was now a matter of sitting out the war.

On the evening of May 8, 1945, Schindler spoke to the entire camp, including the SS guards and the Commandant. They listened together to a broadcast speech by Churchill about the surrender of Nazi Germany.[279] After Churchill's message had gotten through to those present, there was general euphoria. Schindler then gave a speech to thank everyone for their trust and help in the most difficult of circumstances. Schindler's words were taken down in shorthand by his secretary, Hilde Berger (76207).

Schindler's farewell speech:

"The non-conditional surrender of the German armed forces has just been announced. I appeal to all of you to strictly maintain order and discipline.

Once more I ask you to behave in a humane and just manner and to leave the prosecutions and revenge to those who have been assigned to these matters. If you have accusations to levy at anyone, do so with the proper authorities, because in the new Europe, there will be judges who will hear your pleas. Many of you know the persecutions, harassment and obstacles that I had to overcome in order to keep my workers during these terrible years. Although it was already difficult to protect the limited rights of a Polish worker, to help him keep his business, protect him from being deported into the Reich, protect his property and preserve his modest belongings and assets – the difficulties of protecting Jewish laborers often seemed insurmountable. Those of you who have worked with me from the beginning, through all these years, know how I made innumerable personal interventions after the closure of the ghetto, how I worked with the camp administration on your behalf in order to save you from deportation and liquidation, or how I managed to reverse orders that had already been given.

How many worries it caused me, how threatening the danger was, when you were kept away from the factory under various pretences. Very few of the workers who were sent to me had experience as skilled laborers before the war, the kind of workers that I was looking for to do this work. It is a miracle that we were able, thanks to your positive attitude, to overcome the greatest difficulties.

I have demanded some productive output from you, which must have seemed rather senseless to most of you, since you were shielded from seeing the overall situation, but it was always my will to demonstrate and defend humanity, to conduct my affairs humanely, the principle that guided all of my decisions. Continue to maintain your discipline and order.

When, after a few days spent here, the gates of freedom are opened to you, think about what many of the people who live around this factory have done for you in terms of providing additional food and clothing. I have tried and risked everything to acquire additional food for you in the past, and I pledge to continue putting everything on the line to protect you and provide you with your daily bread.

I will continue to work around the clock to do everything for you that is within my power. Do not go into the houses around here to forage and steal. Show yourselves to be worthy of the sacrifice of millions from your ranks, avoid every act of revenge and terrorism. I charge all of the capos and overseers to continue to uphold order and enforce good conduct. Tell this to all of your people, because it is in the interest of their security. Thank the Daubek Mill, whose energetic support improved your nutrition, often beyond the realm of the possible. I wish to express sincere thanks to the brave director of the mill, who personally did everything I requested in order to get food for you.

Do not thank me for your survival; thank your own people, who worked day and night to save you from annihilation. Thank the dauntless Stern, Pemper and those others who, in the course of their duty, above all in Krakow, looked death in the eye at every moment, thought of everyone and cared for everyone. This solemn hour reminds us of our obligation to remain alert and maintain order; as long as we remain here together, I ask you all, among yourselves, to decide upon courses of action that are humane and just. I thank my personal staff for their restless sacrifice for my work. To the SS guards and the marines who are assembled here, who were assigned to this duty without their consent, I thank you also. They have behaved in an extraordinarily humane and proper manner.

In conclusion, I ask all of you for three minutes of silence, to remember the innumerable victims who have fallen from your ranks in these terrible times."

It is difficult to imagine the frantic activity in the camp at this time, with the sound of gunfire in the distance. Most of the SS had been disarmed and had fled the camp. Schindler organized a home defense of the entire camp and factory. All the weapons were issued, and they prepared themselves for any situation.[280] Wehrmacht vehicles were passing on the road at the entrance to the factory. The whole camp was split into feverish activity. The Schindlers were preparing their escape to the West with the help of a select few Jews who would escort them. The Jewish prisoners who had come to Brünnlitz from Budzyn were out to settle old scores. They selected the Jewish Kapo, Willi, the most hated Kapo in the camp, who had been with them in Budzyn. Willi had been responsible for the death of several Jewish prisoners in Budzyn. Willi was seized and strung up on a factory girder, where he died.[281]

The elderly Simon Jereth (69506) of the box factory (adjacent to Emalia), took out his false teeth and from the gold fillings Hersch Licht (68987) crafted a ring out of the gold. On the inner circle of the ring, they inscribed a simple "thank you."[282] Richard Rechen volunteered to drive the lorry that was to escort the Schindlers towards the American lines. The Schindlers were to leave in their two-seater Hawk[283] taking Schindler's woman friend Marta[284] with them.

Figure 70: Oskar relaxing 1940
Photo Credit: Author's collection

Above: The lone surviving photograph of Oskar Schindler in Brünnlitz. When Schindler was about to leave Brünnlitz in May 1945, he called Viktor Dortheimer to his office and told him to take something for himself from Schindler's suitcase of valuables: Dortheimer took the photograph.

Finally, a small group of those closest workers approached Schindler and handed to him a sealed letter (in Hebrew) and reminded him, that if he ever needed to explain his conduct in the war, he was to use this letter with their blessings:

> Brünnlitz, May 8, 1945
> "We, the undersigned Jews from Krakow, inmates of the Plaszow concentration camp, have worked in Oskar Schindler's factory since 1940. Since Schindler took over management of the business, it was his exclusive goal to protect us from resettlement, which would have meant our ultimate liquidation. During the entire period in which we worked for Director Schindler he did everything possible to save the lives of the greatest possible number of Jews, in spite of the tremendous difficulties, especially during a time when receiving Jewish workers caused great difficulties with the authorities. Director Schindler took care of our sustenance, and as a result, during the whole period of our employment by him there was not a single case of unnatural death. In total he employed more than 1,000 Jews in Krakow.
>
> As the Russian frontline approached and it became necessary to transfer us to a different concentration camp, Director Schindler relocated his business to Brünnlitz near Svitavy. There were huge difficulties connected with the implementation of Director Schindler's business, and he took great pains to introduce this plan. The fact that he attained [sic] permission to create a camp,

in which not only women and men, but also families could stay together, is unique within the territory of the Reich. Special mention must be given to the fact that our resettlement to Brünnlitz was carried out by way of a list of names, put together in Krakow and approved by the Central Administration of all concentration camps in Oranienburg (a unique case). After the men had been interned in Gross-Rosen concentration camp for no more than a couple of days and the women for three weeks in Auschwitz concentration camp, we may claim with assertiveness that with our arrival in Brünnlitz we owe our lives solely to the efforts of Director Schindler and his humane treatment of his workers. Director Schindler took care of the improvement of our living standards by providing us with extra food and clothing. No money was spared and his one and only goal was the humanistic ideal of saving our lives from inevitable death.

It is only thanks to the ceaseless efforts and interventions of Director Schindler with the authorities in question that we stayed in Brünnlitz, in spite of the existing danger, as with the approaching frontline we would all have been moved away by the leaders of the camp, which would have meant our ultimate end. This we declare today, on this day of the declaration of the end of the war, as we await our official liberation and the opportunity to return to our destroyed families and homes. Here we are, a gathering of 1,100 people, 800 men and 300 women. All Jewish workers that were inmates in the Gross-Rosen and Auschwitz concentration camps respectively declare wholeheartedly their gratitude towards Director Schindler, and we herewith state that it is exclusively due to his efforts that we were permitted to witness this moment, the end of the war.

Concerning Director Schindler's treatment of the Jews, one event that took place during our internment in Brünnlitz in January of this year which deserves special mention was coincidentally a transport of Jewish inmates that had been evacuated from the Auschwitz concentration camp, the Goleszow [Golleschau] sub-camp, and ended up near us.

This transport consisted exclusively of more than 100 sick people from a hospital which had been cleared during the liquidation of the camp. These people reached us frozen and almost unable to carry on living after having wandered for weeks. No other camp was willing to accept this transport and it was Director Schindler alone who personally took care of these people, while giving them shelter on his factory premises; even though there was not the slightest chance of them ever being employed. He gave considerable sums out of his own private funds, to enable their recovery as quick as possible. He organized medical aid and established a special hospital room for those people who were bedridden. It was only because of his personal care that it was possible to save 80 of these people from their inevitable death and to restore them to life."

Signed: Nathan and Itzhak Stern and Leon Salpeter

One of the last acts Schindler was to discharge and share with his Jewish workers was to issue each one a length of cloth from the spinning mill textile store.[285] Stern and Salpeter dished out vodka and cigarettes, considered by Schindler as first-aid packages. Last farewells were offered, and the Schindler group left in a convoy. Oskar was dressed as a Jewish prisoner and was in possession of his ring, reference documents written in Hebrew, and one large diamond which he concealed in the front seat of his car. Their journey took them through the panic of the retreating Germans and the partisans who were controlling the roads. Stopped by a Russian patrol, they were stripped of their watches. At a later check point where they stayed overnight, they lost all their property, and their vehicles were damaged beyond repair. According to Emilie Schindler, in her recollections to the author, Oskar was now a mental wreck. The confrontation with the Russians had had a devastating effect on him, she says, from which he never really recovered.

Having lost their motor vehicles, they hid overnight and boarded a train the following morning heading west. According to Rechen they decided to leave the train and continue the rest of the journey on foot. It was on this last part of the journey that they became entangled with other refugees also seeking safety to the west and their meeting with Lieutenant Kurt Klein of the United States Intelligence unit with surprising results.

Brünnlitz was the turning point in the Schindler story

In the summer of 1944 Oskar Schindler had been faced with a key decision: the liquidation of the armament factory. The approaching Red Army, the uncertain future – all these factors played an important role in his actual choice. After several visits to Berlin, telephone calls with representatives of the occupation administration and armament inspectorate, Schindler rejected an offer of Swiss asylum. His vast wealth would have guaranteed a decent standard of living for years to come. But Schindler decided to invest his money in a different manner.

He knew well that the transfer of the factory to the interior was merely a temporary decision. He was aware that building and operating a new factory in the Sudetenland was an extremely difficult undertaking and he had doubts about the potential for success. But above all, there were people to consider – prisoners from the Plaszow camp, his workers. And, therefore, concepts such as humanity, compassion and protection entered into the equation. These were words that had completely disappeared from the Nazi lexicon of the "superior race." Oskar Schindler – Herr Director Schindler – created his own vocabulary and transformed the words into tangible deeds.[286]

A local doctor, Josef Lopour, from the village of Vitejevse, a few miles from Brünnlitz, kept a diary throughout the war period of the daily events in the area. From this diary, which is headed concentration camp Brünnlitz, he makes the following observations:

"This is a sad chapter. I am one of the few citizens who saw the camp before and after capitulation, and who spoke to the survivors. On May 15, 1945, as the doctor of those villages, I had the duty to transport all ill persons from the camp. Most of the prisoners were Jews from Poland. There were about a thousand men, women, and children. They had arrived at the camp in November, 1944, in a freezing winter, only dressed in trousers and shirts.

At night they slept crammed together sitting with their heads stooped over. For months they slept on straw on a concrete floor. They were covered with lice. Later on they got three tier bunks. With the sick, we tried to do our best using the chemist shop as a surgery.

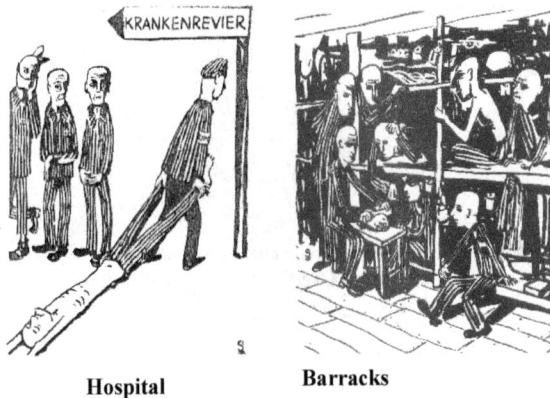

Hospital   Barracks

Figure 71: Drawings by Josef Bau
Photo Credit: Author's collection

Other prisoners slept on dirty sacks beside the beds. In a room measuring 8m x 5m x 4m with no windows and bad air there were some 170 people. When you were passing around the beds, you had the impression that you were in a warehouse of living dried flesh.

On the ground floor was a hall with howling lathes. These machines used all the power. The prisoners worked 11 hours daily without interval. Breakfast was 15 grams of bread, a spoon of jam and a liquid which was called coffee. Dinner consisted of warm watery soup and pieces of dumplings.

These poor wretches were pleased to work outside the camp where they could pick herbs and grasses to eat. The Czech people gave them bread. In the main part of the factory was a corridor which was used as the first-aid room. There, on wooden tables, the Jewish prison doctors carried out operations. Two doctors from Krakow told me that they had made many operations. Women were not allowed to become pregnant. Pregnant women were shot. The doctors admitted having carried out a number of abortions in the camp."

One of the many local inhabitants who remembers the end of the war and in particular the Jewish prisoners of the Brünnlitz camp was Vilma Odyarkova-Pachovska.

Figure 72: Vilma showing the author around Brünnlitz, 1991
Photo Credit: Author's collection

Vilma, then aged 17 years, was an assistant in the chemist shop in Brünnlitz and remembers the Jews from the camp being brought to the shop for medical treatment by Doctor Lopour at the end of the war.

Schindler's Chief, Admiral Canaris, Is Arrested

The attempt on the life of Hitler made by Colonel von Stauffenberg on July 20, 1944, brought Armageddon down upon the anti-Hitlerites and all those unfortunate people who were loosely connected to the assassination conspiracy. Himmler ordered that the Stauffenberg family was to be exterminated up to the last generation. The other main members of the plot were hanged on August 8, 1944, in Plötzensee, the Berlin prison, on hooks for meat that were borrowed from a close-by slaughterhouse, according to Hitler's order: "I want them to hang like cattle in the slaughterhouse." Altogether, there were 7,000 military men and civilians arrested, of which 5,000 were executed.

Despite the fact that neither Canaris nor his deputy, Hans Oster, participated actively in the plot, they knew about the plans but did not denounce the conspirators. Hitler realized that he was being deceived by Canaris and ordered his arrest. On February 7, 1945 Canaris was transported to the Flossenburg concentration camp where he was tortured and beaten. He maintained his ignorance of the Hitler plot and at no time did he betray his companions from the resistance movement.

Figure 73: Admiral Canaris, 1943… and death memorial plaque
Photo Credit: Author's collection

Colonel Lunding, the former head of Dutch military intelligence, was imprisoned in the adjacent cell. Canaris had previously told Colonel Lunding: "This is the end…a squandered opportunity. I have done nothing against my country. If you survive, please tell my wife…I am dying for my homeland. I am aware of what I have done. I have just fulfilled my duty trying to oppose Hitler's plans."

On April 9, 1945, just after 5.30 a.m., the SS guards put a noose made of piano wire round his neck and strangled him slowly to prolong his suffering. As he was not quite dead, they repeated the hanging and later, cut off his hands and feet. The body was burned.[287]

Chapter Eighteen
Postwar Years

**Figure 74: A key figure in Schindler's escape to safety at the end of the war
was Army Lt. Kurt Klein, himself a German-born Jew.
Photo Credit: Author's collection**

Rescued by the U.S. Army 1945[288]

In Europe, as the war came to a close, hundreds of thousands of Germans began surrendering in the occupied areas. U.S. Army Intelligence Corps officer Lt. Kurt Klein was on patrol when he was notified that a strange group of camp survivors had been found nearby all dressed in prison uniforms. They presented themselves to him as refugees from a German labor camp in Czechoslovakia. Not only had he unknowingly come across the Schindler group, he also found his future wife. In early May 1945 the group, which included a young Gerda Weissmann, had been force marched with 2,000 other camp survivors toward Czechoslovakia when the escorting SS guards abandoned them in a booby-trapped warehouse. Of the 2,000 who started out on this journey, only 150 now survived. Gerda recalled:

> "All of a sudden, I saw a strange car coming down the hill, no longer green, not bearing a swastika, but a white star. The driver of the vehicle was Lt. Kurt Klein."

Klein asked the group if anyone spoke German or English. Gerda, replying in German, told Klein that they were Jewish. Klein responded with: "So am I." Klein then asked Gerda an incredible question: "May I see the other ladies?" It was a form of address Gerda hadn't heard in six years. Gerda continued: "then he held the door for me and let me precede him and in that gesture restored me to humanity." It didn't end there…Lt. Klein and Gerda continued their relationship and were married shortly thereafter.[289]

In addition to bringing his future wife to safety, Lieutenant Klein also helped arrange safe passage into American hands for a group of suspected German prisoners who turned out to be concentration camp escapees (the Schindler group) as Emilie Schindler confirms:

> "By chance Oskar and I had been included in the group, and happily nobody bothered to contradict the words of the U.S officer. The commander, a pleasant-looking young man, said that his name was Klein and that he was also Jewish." Emilie continues, "On one of my latest trips to the United States, I met Commander Klein again. In spite of the years gone by, he still had that special shine in his eyes and that he had given us the feeling we were home at last. He welcomed me again as he had done then, and added, "I have not forgotten you, Mrs. Schindler."[290]

Only in 1987, when one of the prisoners wrote him, did Kurt Klein learn that among the group he saved was a person who became famous decades later for his own heroics. His name was Oskar Schindler. Klein received a letter from an engineer living in Haifa, Richard Rechen, who identified himself as a member of the volunteer escort party who had undertaken to deliver their beloved Herr Direktor Schindler first to the American lines and ultimately to Switzerland. The group had been organized by Dr. Chaim Hilfstein, one of the most respected figures among the Schindler Jews. In his letter, Rechen said that for 41 years he had been trying to locate the American soldier who ensured Schindler's safe passage. Rechen's letter described the journey from Schindler's factory to his meeting with Klein in the second week of May 1945. These facts were later corroborated to the author by the late Dan Granot (formerly Dolek Gruenhaut, who had help save the Jews on the Golleschau transport and who later escorted Schindler out of Brünnlitz to safety) in a London Hotel in 1995.

The Wiesenthal Connection

Figure 75: Simon Wiesenthal: photograph given to the author 1990
Photo Credit: Author's collection

Simon Wiesenthal (1908-2005) devoted his postwar life to searching for Nazi war criminals and bringing these individuals to justice. Wiesenthal came from a family of Galician Jews. He studied architecture in Prague and worked in this profession until Galicia was taken over by the Soviet Union. He was persecuted by the NKVD (secret police) and later by the Nazis. He survived the war and was freed from the Mauthausen concentration camp in Austria. After the war he became chairman of the Jewish Central Committee in Austria and the founder of the Jewish Documentation Centre in Linz and Vienna. Wiesenthal had Schindler on *his* list and by his investigations into his background was able to clear him of Nazi war crimes and SS association.

Simon Wiesenthal's letter to the Central Bavarian Committee in Munich from October 1, 1945:

> "As director of the enamelware factory in Krakow and later in Brünnlitz Schindler saved a great number of Jews. The best that we can do now is to show our gratitude for the protection of 1,200 Jews. In the name of the Jewish Committee of Upper Austria I ask you kindly to do everything you can to help Director Schindler."

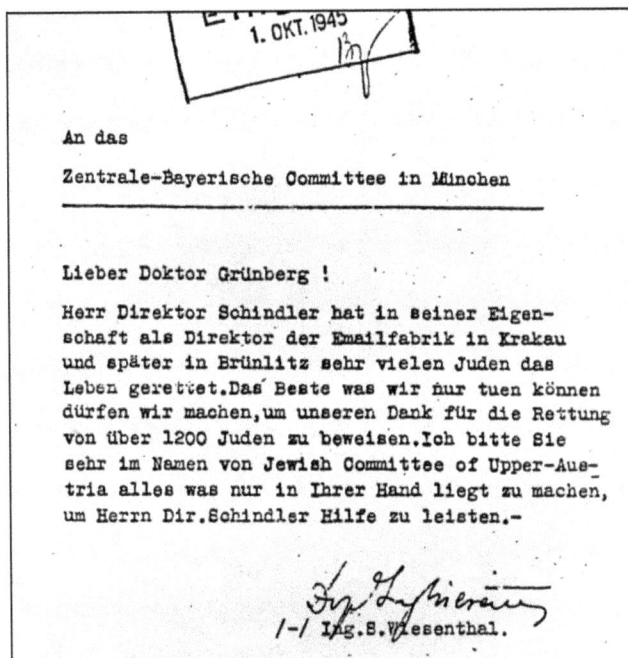

Figure 76: Wiesenthal letter to the Jewish Committee, October 1, 1945
Photo Credit: Author's collection

In November 1990, the author, who was investigating Nazi war crimes in Poland, was making his own investigation into Schindler's wartime activities. The author visited Simon Wiesenthal at his offices in Vienna where Wiesenthal reiterated his opinion (that he had set out in the October 1 letter to the Barvarian Committee above) regarding the ethics of Schindler which he had displayed in the rescue of his Jewish workers during the war years. This view by Wiesenthal was later confirmed by a letter to the author:

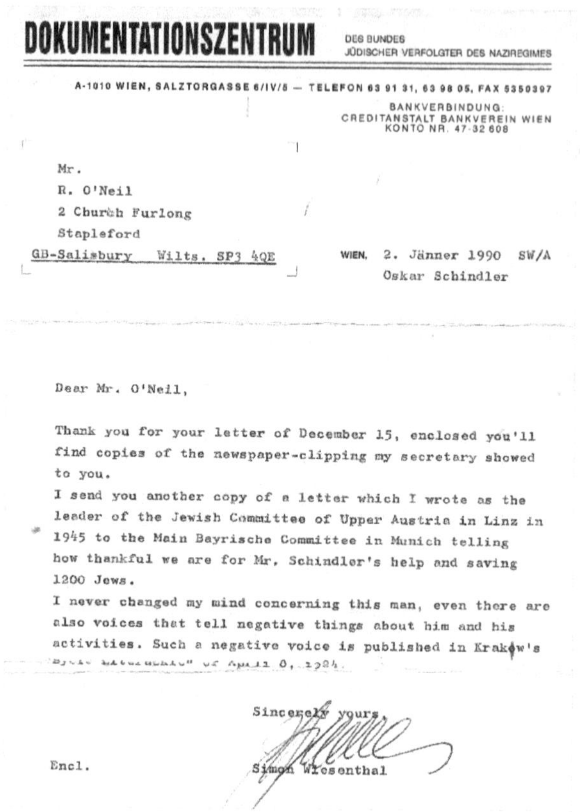

DOKUMENTATIONSZENTRUM DES BUNDES
JÜDISCHER VERFOLGTER DES NAZIREGIMES

A-1010 WIEN, SALZTORGASSE 6/IV/8 — TELEFON 63 91 31, 63 98 05, FAX 5350397

BANKVERBINDUNG:
CREDITANSTALT BANKVEREIN WIEN
KONTO NR. 47-32 608

Mr.
R. O'Neil
2 Church Furlong
Stapleford
GB-Salisbury Wilts. SP3 4QE   WIEN, 2. Jänner 1990 SW/A
                                         Oskar Schindler

Dear Mr. O'Neil,

Thank you for your letter of December 15, enclosed you'll
find copies of the newspaper-clipping my secretary showed
to you.
I send you another copy of a letter which I wrote as the
leader of the Jewish Committee of Upper Austria in Linz in
1945 to the Main Bayrische Committee in Munich telling
how thankful we are for Mr. Schindler's help and saving
1200 Jews.
I never changed my mind concerning this man, even there are
also voices that tell negative things about him and his
activities. Such a negative voice is published in Krakow's

Sincerely yours,

Simon Wiesenthal

Encl.

Figure 77: Wiesenthal letter to the author, December 2, 1990
Photo Credit: Author's collection

There is more: In 1949 Schindler received the following reference letter
from the American Joint Committee:

The American Joint Distribution Committee in New York
hereby confirms that it possesses verified testimony on the
active measures Mr. Oskar Schindler took to save Krakow
Jews from extermination during the period of Nazi
occupation. The Committee sincerely requests all
organizations and individuals do all that is in their power to
help Oskar Schindler on account of his important role in
saving Jews in occupied Poland. Oskar Schindler saved
women and men from death in concentration camps such as
Auschwitz and others (Belzec in particular). Schindler's
camp in Brünnlitz was a remarkable phenomenon – it was the
only camp in Nazi-occupied Europe where Jews were not
terrorized and no Jew was killed. On the contrary, Schindler
always treated his Jews with great decency. Now, as Oskar
Schindler is forced to begin a new life, please help him as he
helped our sisters and brothers. With this written
confirmation by the Joint Committee from 1949 the entire
case of Oskar Schindler is hereby concluded.

After his departure from Brünnlitz and following his release from American detention, Schindler and his wife soon found themselves in a hopeless situation without any money. In liberated Czechoslovakia in the autumn of 1945, a security search was launched to arrest Schindler for his work with the Abwehr. A year later, Schindler was charged in his absence for capital offences committed against the State. In the meantime, the Schindlers had found a flat in Regensburg, Bavaria…and celebrations:

Figure 78: Josef and Rebecca Bau 1945
Photo Credit: Author's collection

One last act of revenge was to be enacted in Regensburg: Hersch Licht (68987) and Ryszard Lax (69254) had spotted commandant Leipold in Regensburg. Schindler was informed and did not hesitate for a moment and went to the police station where Leipold had been placed on an identification parade. Schindler went directly to Leipold and said, "You are Leipold and do not continue to deny it. If you continue to do so, there are 300 Jews outside who will massacre you." Leipold, faced with this direct action, admitted his guilt.[291]

The Schindlers Go to Argentina

Why the Schindlers chose Argentina to become their new home remains a mystery. However, Argentina in the 19th and 20th centuries was a country where many Jewish immigrants from Russia and Eastern Europe moved; today the country has a Jewish population of over 230,000. The country also has over 400,000 German-speaking residents. The Schindlers decided to leave for Argentina in 1949 with the financial assistance of rescued Jews. Schindler set up a nutria farm in the town of San Vincente, but the venture was unsuccessful and led to bankruptcy. The marriage deteriorated and Oskar fled the country in turmoil leaving Emilie to fend for herself.

The unsuccessful stay in Argentina, the failure of his activities, debts and loans, all led Schindler to a desperate situation. The efforts of Jews themselves, their financial support and aid from the Jewish Joint Distribution Committee failed to produce the intended effect and Schindler, instead, lost the money in risky enterprises. Schindler again turned to alcohol to solve his problems. Still, his rescued Jews continued to financially support him and his wife. Schindler's attempt to seek compensation for wartime damages from the German government, assisted by Mieczyslaw Pemper, Moshe Bejski, and others, also failed. Schindler's marriage was in ruins and Oskar finally left his wife for good. On a trip to Germany in 1957 financed by Jewish organizations, Schindler met with several of the Jews he had saved and, in 1958, he moved to Frankfurt am Main.

Living in a small flat in a dirty street near the train station, he tried again to start a business. But all his efforts ended in fiasco and his health rapidly deteriorated. In 1964 he suffered a heart attack and had to seek treatment in a sanatorium. He sold his story of his life to a publishing company, but the money quickly disappeared in wild business ventures. Schindler received assistance again from Pemper and Bejski, but all to no avail.

Mietek Pemper on reflection to the author on Schindler:

> I believe it is necessary to view Schindler in various phases of his life; this leaves us, then, with several different Schindlers – Schindler before the war, during the war, and after the war, when he had problems and when nothing worked out for him. For us, he was naturally a fearless knight, a benefactor, and an angel, and God knows what else. We didn't see his shortcomings, nor did we look for any. And even if he had loads of shortcomings, we still would have forgiven him. Schindler was an energetic brawler with a vibrant sense of humor. He wasn't a master who controlled our life and death, but he was our patron or sponsor. He played a very risky game, but maybe he wasn't even aware of it because he was caught up in some kind of sporting excitement. He made it clear to us that he was more cunning than were his explosive colleagues and he looked forward to manipulating them. He represented the most humane aspects of the German character. He had been given a large amount of good in his genes. This complicated and difficult-to-understand man possessed a lot of courage and humanity.
>
> Signed: Mietek Pemper

1961-1963: First International Recognition: Schindler's Olive Tree

The rescued Jews never forgot about Schindler and, therefore, on the occasion of his birthday, a celebratory reception was organized for April 28, 1962 in Tel Aviv. Three hundred of the Jews he had saved waited at the airport in Tel Aviv for Schindler's arrival. The reception became an extremely emotional affair, particularly when his wartime accomplishments were read aloud. Over 400 of Schindler's Jews and their families attended the reception. Each of the former prisoners was to stand and say a few words in honor of Schindler. Moshe Bejski wrote down all the speeches on napkins and small scraps of paper which he showed to the author on one of his many visits to his house.

Figure 79: Waiting for Schindler at Lod (Ben Gurion) Airport
Photo Credit: Author's collection

Oskar Schindler was to plant an olive tree in the Garden of the Righteous at Yad Vashem in Jerusalem on May 2, 1962, Yom Hashoah – Holocaust Remembrance Day – but Schindler fell ill and could not attend. By May 8, he had recovered enough for the ceremony to take place with a circle of close friends.

Figure 80: Oskar planting his tree
Photo Credit: Author's collection

Schindler received international honors in the mid-60s. Nevertheless, he battled deep depression and became increasingly dependent upon support from Jews in Israel and the U.S.A. The same was true for Emilie, who was still in Argentina. Schindler testified at the trials of former Nazis. President Heinrich Lubke of West Germany awarded Schindler the Cross of Merit, First Class, on November 5, 1965, and gave him, as well, an honorable pension. In 1967, he received the Martin Buber Peace Prize.

Pope Paul V1 named Schindler a Knight of the Order of St. Sylvester in October 1968.

Figure 81: Reception in Israel May 1962[292]
Photo Credit: Author's collection

October 9, 1974 – Death and Burial

Schindler was a guest in Israel on 13 occasions. His financial difficulties continued to plague him. Serious health problems added to his troubles; he suffered another heart attack and, at the same time, was diagnosed with diabetes.

At the Beth Am Synagogue in Los Angeles in 1969, Schindler accepted an award for the protection of Jews and, with the support of Holocaust victims, a foundation bearing his name was established. Schindler was also involved in the creation of an exchange program between West Germany and Israeli students. In 1974, he suffered further heart problems brought about by smoking and heavy drinking. On October 9, 1974, he died in Hildesheim. His funeral was held in Frankfurt on October 16. At Schindler's request, he was laid to rest in the Catholic cemetery on Mt. Zion in Jerusalem on October 28.

Richard Rechen, who was the driver of the car in which Schindler escaped to the West after his flight from Brünnlitz, was the person chosen to go to West Germany and claim Schindler's body. Rechen, interviewed by the author in Tel Aviv, summed up his feelings:

"When I heard from my friends that Oskar had died, I was terribly sad. He was 66 years old. I felt awful – it was as if my brother had died. Oskar Schindler not only saved our bodies, he saved our souls. Thanks to him we didn't lose our faith in man. He proved that there were, and are, Christians who, like the Good Samaritan, poured healing oil and wine into our wounds. Oskar, you are our Samaritan! It was your wish to find your final resting place in the holy city of Jerusalem. We promise to do everything in our power to fulfill your wish.

Figure 82: Viktor at Schindler's final resting place 1995
Photo Credit: Author's collection

Figure 83: Viktor Dortheimer and author 1995
Photo Credit: Author's collection

"When Oskar Schindler arrived in Krakow love had been outlawed by the Germans and was met, instead, by derision. But this stopped and love, humanity and decency reappeared. What Oskar and Emilie began and continued to do until the end of the war is impossible to describe in words.

Chapter Nineteen
Consequences and Just Punishment

Figure 84: The Nuremberg Trials
Photo Credit: Svitavy Museum Collection

The horrifying number of victims of the Holocaust and the Final Solution produced by investigative commissions is merely an estimate.

Before the start of the war the greatest number of Jews – approximately three million – lived in the Soviet Union. Nearly one million of these Soviet Jews perished in the Holocaust. Of the three million or so Jews living in pre-war Poland, the main killing grounds of Jews during the war, only 300,000 survived. Approximately 3.5 million European Jews died at six death camps in Poland. But Polish anti-Semitism didn't subside even after the war and numerous pogroms broke out against Jews who returned to Polish cities.

In 1939 a total of 252,000 Jews lived in the Baltic States; 223,000 perished during the war. Of the 140,000 Dutch Jews deported, 106,000 never returned. In Hungary 560,000 of approximately 800,000 pre-war Jews did not survive. Prior to the start of the war around 720,000 Jews lived in France and its colonies; nearly 90,000 never returned home. Before the war Belgium had a Jewish population of 75,000; 29,000 did not survive deportation. Germany recorded over 170,000 Holocaust victims, Austria approximately 65,000. Romania with Bukovina and Bessarabia had 365,000 victims. Nearly 130, 000 deported Jews came from Greece and Yugoslavia. In 1939 the Protectorate of Bohemia and Moravia had a Jewish population of over 118, 000 Jews; 73,000 perished in the Final Solution. Over 80,000 Jews were deported and only 10,000 returned from the concentration camps.

Having miraculously survived Allied bombing, the Nuremberg Palace of Justice became the venue for the International Military Tribunal, established on the basis of the London Charter for the prosecution of war criminals. Defendants were the main representatives of the Third Reich and the trial lasted from November 20, 1945 until verdicts were returned on October 1, 1946. In addition to individuals, the Nazi organizations NSDAP, SS, the Gestapo, and SD were declared criminal organizations. A total of 200 defendants were tried directly at Nuremburg on charges of crimes against humanity and peace and as war criminals. An additional 600 defendants were tried before traditional military tribunals.

A total of 177 Nazis were convicted of crimes; 12 were sentenced to death, 25 received life sentences, and the remaining convicted defendants received long unconditional sentences. Between 1945 and 1951 a total of 5,028 Nazis were convicted, 806 of whom were sentenced to death. A United Nations commission compiled a list of 36,529 war criminals, the majority of whom contributed to the genocide of Jews, Roma, and other ethnic minorities. A total of 3,470 individuals were tried in supplemental post-war trials, while 150,000 people were charged in other countries involved in the war. Over 100,000 defendants were convicted of crimes committed against Jews. Following the renewal of the judicial system in Germany, over 6,000 people were tried up to 1970, 12 of whom were sentenced to death and 98 to life imprisonment.

The Nuremberg Trials had a great influence on the development of post-war international law, including, for example, the Genocide Convention.

The Commandant of the Plaszow Camp on Trial

Figure 85: Amon Goeth on his way to Court, Krakow 1946
Photo
Credit: Svitavy Museum Collection

Even the former commander of the Plaszow camp, Amon Leopold Goeth, was brought before the Highest National Tribunal. Goeth was captured by the Allies in the SS sanatorium at Bad Tölz and brought to Dachau for interrogation, after which he was transferred back to Krakow. Goeth was the first defendant to stand trial in Poland on charges of direct involvement in mass murder. Plaszow Jews liberated from the Brünnlitz camp served as witnesses against the accused. The key witnesses against Goeth were his former office worker Mieczyslaw (Mietek) Pemper, as well as Artur Biberstein and Helena Hirsch. Goeth was declared guilty on all counts on

September 5, 1946 and sentenced to death. He was executed on September 13.

Other war criminals accused of mass murder in the Holocaust were hunted down and put on trial; on November 9, 1948 Josef Leipold, the commandant of Brünnlitz, was executed for crimes committed in concentration camps. Leipold had been apprehended in Regensburg, Germany with forged identification papers. Oskar Schindler was among those who provided testimony against Leipold.

Belzec: Final Resting Place of Many of the Krakow Jews

Many of Schindler's Jews succumbed to the racial treachery of the Nazi State by being transported to the Aktion Reinhardt death camps of Belzec (600,000 murders), Sobibor (250,000 murders) and Treblinka (900,000 murders). In June and October 1942, Schindler witnessed the deportation of many thousands of Jews to the extermination camp at Belzec.

Belzec was where mass murder was committed with military precision on an industrial scale, a human abattoir that operated on a conveyor-belt system.

Immediately after the end of war, Belzec was still just a rumor. A hint of its existence and the colossal numbers of people who were murdered there only started to emerge during post-war investigations. Judge Moshe Bejski's parents, sister, aunts and uncles were shipped to Belzec from the home-town of Dzialoszyce; Viktor Dortheimer's mother, who had sought the safety of Skarwina on the outskirts of Krakow, Bau's family, and many of the relatives mentioned before, suffered the same fate.

Oskar Schindler knew about Belzec and its function but was never able to penetrate the tight security that surrounded the camp. According to Mrs. Schindler, Oskar was turned away at Tomaszow-Lubelski, five kilometers from the camp.

Oskar Schindler's activities within the framework of the Holocaust are minimal when considering what was going on elsewhere. My book, *Belzec: Stepping Stone to Genocide* (JewishGen Inc., 2008; http://www.pickmanmuseumshop.com/jewishgen.html), sets out the background to Jewish genocide in Galicia. To assist and guide the reader when traversing this unique period in history, I will set out the background to our present understanding of these events, centering on the activities of Aktion Reinhardt and the Belzec death camp.

State of Current Research

The research that constitutes the basis of this study was undertaken on a number of different but related fronts. It includes critically important data derived from an archaeological survey of the mass graves at Belzec by forensic archaeologists from Torun University in Poland. By comparing this information with other data of the transports to Belzec from the Jewish communities of the Lublin district, Galicia, and elsewhere, we are able to envisage the scale of murder committed in the name of the "Final Solution" in a way that is independent of eyewitness testimony. Consequently, this evidence constitutes substantial proofs of Nazi war crimes against the Jewish people and an incontrovertible body of evidence to confront Holocaust denial.

In the context of a number of important and hotly debated studies of recent years which deal with the background, indoctrination and ideological commitment of those who carried out Nazi war crimes, the evidence of this study provides an important perspective. The detailed investigation of the German and Austrian personnel who ran the camp offers a number of insights into the way in which Aktion Reinhardt and its precursor, the euthanasia program, were staffed.

Belzec was commissioned by the highest authority of the Nazi state and acted outside the law of both civil and military conventions of the time. Under the code Aktion Reinhardt, the death camps were organized, staffed, and administered by a leadership of middle-ranking police officers and a specially selected civilian cadre who, in the first instance, had been initiated into the euthanasia program. Their expertise was then transferred to operational duties in the death camps. The hands-on extermination of European Jewry in the death camps of Reinhardt, the author suggests, was police-led, from start to finish.

While this was a top-secret operation, many of those involved were not committed Nazis or even members of the SS, but ordinary Germans engaged not so much in gratifying congenital murderous, anti-Semitic impulses, but either under personal threat from the leadership or as opportunists hoping to avoid combat duties and amass personal wealth looted from their victims. Aktion Reinhardt staff was protected by the highest authority from military and civilian discipline or regulation. They were, in effect – for the duration of the war – a band of brothers.

The principle of police leadership in the Reinhardt camps was unprecedented and was never extended or repeated in any other penal establishment in the areas of German occupation. The combination of police and civilians appears to have been a direct policy of the Nazi State. The majority of Reinhardt personnel operating in these camps became a maverick unit and were given the spurious cover of SS insignia to facilitate their objective. These men, operating under a Geheime Reichssache (Secret Reich Affair) became "the untouchables." All outside influences concerning rank, status and human decency meant absolutely nothing to this group. Within the Reinhardt establishment there was a complete negation of any recognized principles of law and order, discipline, or basic humanitarian considerations.

The men engaged in Reinhardt were practiced in institutional murder since 1940 and were psychologically conditioned to continue similar duties elsewhere. After all, if they could engage in the murder of their "own" through euthanasia, they could hardly be expected to have any inner moral conflict with murdering Jews. Even so, in practice, clinical institutionalized murder was a far cry from what these men were later faced with in Belzec –which called for an extra dimension of personal commitment. Among the Reinhardt personnel, the motivation for carrying out the base murder of men, women and children varied according to the individual. Fear predominated among the lower echelons of the leadership, but others were attracted by generous pay and conditions of service with extra leave, allowances and opportunities for further advancement. Others were motivated by the spoils of extermination: corruption, greed, and in some cases crude prejudices and sadistic self-gratification. Exemption from frontline duty was an added inducement. In due course all these men, even those who self-righteously proclaimed abhorrence of Belzec's purpose, became corrupted when given the power of life and death over people whom they were encouraged to treat as sub-human.

In the lower ranks, Nazi ideology and anti-Semitism were not the prime driving forces behind the majority of the mass murderers. It is in the leadership that political indoctrination and rabid anti-Semitism were to be found. One man in particular, the Stuttgart police officer Christian Wirth, exemplifies this. He was the central cog in the destruction process, even more so than his immediate superior, the designated overlord of Reinhardt, SS-Brigadeführer Odilo Globocnik. Unlike Himmler and his immediately following, who were driven by a pseudo-religious ideology, or a "holy" mission, Wirth remained an enigma, a crude man with uncouth habits spurred on by an old-fashioned sense of "duty" and a hatred for Jews.

Recent Scholarship and Study

The destruction of European Jewry has been treated in a number of ways by specialists who are at the cutting edge of Holocaust research: Gerald Reitlinger's *The Final Solution* (originally published in 1953) is thought-provoking but focused primarily on Jewish extermination and gives little indication of the inner power struggles within the General Government.[293] Reitlinger's work has been superseded by Raul Hilberg's magisterial three-volume *Destruction of the European Jews* (1985), which in my view remains the definitive work. It is breathtaking in scope and systematically deals with every aspect of the mechanics of destruction, including German material on this tragedy. Hilberg also includes an excellent account of the administrative conflict in the General Government. Martin Gilbert's *Holocaust* (1987) considers Reinhardt from a broader perspective, while Daniel Goldhagen's widely discussed, well-documented, and controversial *Hitler's Willing Executioners* (1997) only refers to Belzec on three occasions within its references to Reinhardt. Only Yitzhak Arad's *Belzec, Sobibór, Treblinka - The Operation Reinhard Death Camps* (1987), and the latest published research by Michael Tregenza in Lublin, *Belzec – Das Vergessene Lager des Holocaust* (2000) focus on Belzec in some depth within the context of Reinhardt. Christopher C. Browning's prolific scholarship – *Fateful Months* (1985); *Path to Genocide* (1992); *Essays on the Final Solution* (1995); *The Final Solution and the German Foreign Office* (1978); *Ordinary Men*; *The Reigner Telegramme Reconstructed*; *Nazi Policy, Jewish Questions, and Policies*; *Nazi Policy, Jewish Workers,*

German Killers – are major contributions. The SS training camp at Trawniki near Lublin was the most important element in providing manpower for Reinhardt. The interesting and most welcome research paper by David Rich et al enhances our understanding of this subject.

Among the Polish sources, of particular interest are the works of E. Szrojt, and T. Chrosciewicz. For the deportation operations from the Galician District see T. Berenstein. Other useful sources are *An Outline History of the Lwów Railways 1942-3*, which contains interesting facts regarding the deportation transports from Lvov to Belzec. See also Dr. Janusz Peter (Kordian), *W Belzcu podczas okupacji (In Belzec during the Occupation)*. When discussing the Generalplan Ost see Czeslaw Madajczyk's *Forschungsstelle für Ostunterkunft* (Research Center for Eastern Resettlement) and the European-wide Jewish extermination program. On the fate of the Christian Poles who were left to face the German and Russian onslaughts, there are thought-provoking personal recollections of this period in Tomasz Piesakowski's *The Fate of Poles in the USSR, 1939-1989* and the *Zygmunt Klukowski Diary 1939-44*. See also Zoë Zajderowa's *The Dark Side of the Moon*. For the fate of German Jews in Dresden, see the Victor Klemperer diaries.

From the German side see the diary of Alex Hohenstein, *Oberbügermeister (Senior District Mayor) of Poniatowec in the Warthegau 1941/2*; *Das Diensttagebuch des deutschen Generalgouverneurs in Polen* (Hans Frank Diaries); *Die Tagebücher von Joseph Goebbels* (Goebbels Diaries); *[Diensttagebuch Himmler] Der Dienstkalender Heinrich Himmler 1941/2*. These are rich sources indeed.

Dr Hans Frank's Diary, *Tagebuch des Herrn Generalgouverneurs für dies Besetzten Polnischen Gebiete, 25 Oktober 1939 bis 3. April 1945* is crucial for understanding the power struggle within the General Government between Himmler, Frank and Krüger. The original Frank Diaries can be found in the archives of the former Archiwum Glownej Komisji Badania Zbrodni Hitlerowskich w Polsce (Main Commission for Investigation of Nazi Crimes in Poland), today the Izba Pamiêci Narodowej (Institute of National Memory) in Warsaw, Poland. The Tagebuch is a detailed although not personal record of the civil administration divided into 38 volumes. The diary is compartmentalized according to subject matter – agriculture, labor, security, etc. There is an abridged English translation of this work (Hans Frank's Diary, *Pañstwowe Wydawnictwo Naukowe*, Warsaw 1961). See also *International Military Tribunal, Trial of the Major German War Criminals* (42 volumes). Vol. XX1X, Document Number 2233-PS, 356-725 contains material from the Tagebuch.

For the purposes of this study, I have been selective when quoting the Tagebuch, usually citing secondary sources as indicated, where appropriate. The main source of material used in this study is Larry V. Thompson, *Nazi Administrative Conflict: The Struggle for Executive Power in the General Government of Poland, 1939-1945* (unpublished thesis), University of Wisconsin, USA, 1967. Importance is attributed to this work because the central theme focuses on the personal and institutional conflict, or SS & Police v Gouverneur, General Government, Poland 1941-1943. See also Robert L. Koehl, *German Resettlement and Population Policy, 1939 – 1945*, Cambridge (HUP) 1957.

More recent material concerning the Frank Diaries can be seen at the Deutsches Historisches Institute (German Historical Institute) in London, under references SH 5/9030 and SH 2/149. Other recent publications deal with the subject or parts thereof from different viewpoints. When placed in context, Browning's *Ordinary Men* (1991), together with Goldhagen's *Willing Executioners*, deal controversially with events outside Reinhardt that have no direct bearing on events within the death camps. Browning's thesis suggests a mundane perspective of the Nazi decimation of the Jews, explaining how ordinary men, once engaged in unbridled mass killing, went about their task with diligence and efficiency. The Reinhardt personnel were no less ordinary and they, too, took on the role of executioners in T4; and then, in a far more deadly environment, became the principals in a brutal industrialized genocide. What we have, therefore, are "ordinary men" outside Reinhardt, committing mass murders with the protection of the Reich Security Main Office Executive, with the choice of being engaged or not in mass killings. Conversely, within Reinhardt, these "ordinary men" had no protection, right of appeal, or choice of withdrawing from the slaughter. They were ruthlessly driven in their terrible mission by an untouchable, heartless police leadership, which acted on orders from the highest authority, whose purpose was the complete extermination of Jewry. One particular aspect is the scholarly consensus that perpetrators had the choice of refusing to obey an order to kill. This contention is largely supported and underpinned by judicial pronouncements by SS courts and in subsequent post-war criminal trials. I have argued that these conclusions do not hold with regard to Reinhardt.

Another important contribution to be assessed here is the only published account of the Belzec death camp by a Jewish survivor, Rudolf Reder's *Belzec*. Reder's account, recently translated, has been liberally used by historians simply because it is the only comprehensive record by one of two sole victims who escaped and survived the camp.

Oddly, no major German scholarship, although represented elsewhere, has emerged about Belzec per se.

Although the euthanasia program in general has been well documented, especially from the medical aspect (Klee, Burleigh, Friedlander, Platten-Hallermund, Mitscherlich and Mielke, et al.), it is worth bringing into perspective its relevance to Reinhardt. The mechanics and principles of euthanasia were to emerge finally as the answer to fulfilling the Nazi genocidal policies. Mass shootings had been ruled out due to the enormous numbers of victims involved, its impracticality, and the adverse psychological effects on the executioners. There was the additional factor that secrecy could not be guaranteed. The methods and technical advances of the euthanasia program as the precursor to genocide are noted.

The central issue discussed in this reappraisal is the focus on the middle and lower echelons of recruits to the euthanasia program and their subsequent transfer to Reinhardt. Henry Friedlander in *Origins of Nazi Genocide* pursues a similar line of inquiry, but he restricts his research to the opening phase of T4, whereas this inquiry is a more robust and comprehensive analysis. More extensive treatment of the psychiatric institutions has been explored in Michael Burleigh's *Death and Deliverance: 'Euthanasia' in Germany 1900-1945*, Ernst Klee's *Euthanasie im NS-Staat: Die Vernichtung lebensunwerten Lebens*, and more recently in Patricia Heberer's *Targeting the Unfit and 'Exitus Heute' in Hadamar*. See also *Conference paper, Lublin, 8 November 2002: A Continuity in Killing Operations: T4 Perpetrators and Aktion Reinhard.*

A new generation of German scholars has emerged and continues to emerge – Götz Aly, Peter Chroust, Christian Pross, et al, who are penetrating and opening up past Nazi medical crimes and forcing a certain amount of soul-searching by the present-day medical establishment in Germany. For a useful background to the psychiatric institutions during the Nazi period, see Bronwyn McFarland-Icke's *Nurses in Nazi Germany*. Gitta Sereny's *Into the Darkness: the Mind of a Mass Murderer* (personal interviews with Franz Stangl), is an extraordinary exposure of the Nazi system and genocidal policies in Reinhardt. Regarding archival material, the voluminous files relating to perpetrators prosecuted for the crimes committed during the euthanasia and Reinhardt operations are of the utmost importance.

Exploring the literature relating to events during and after the euthanasia (T4) period is vital for an understanding of Reinhardt. Attention has again focused on the new generation of German scholars – Dieter Pohl, Götz Aly, Thomas Sandküler, Peter Longerich, Karen Orth, Ulrich Herbert, Peter Witte, and Bogdan Musial, to name but a few – who have directed their research in a wide-ranging re-assessment of the circumstances surrounding the Final Solution. The Nazi crimes committed in Galicia in particular have attracted a lively and wide divergence of opinion. Contributions by Christian Gerlach were of immense value when discussing the fate of European Jews, especially those from the Greater Reich.

Other scholars, whose significant contributions in the wider context, particularly in dating the decision-making process of the Final Solution, have also been helpful. When discussing the German Security Services I have very much depended on George Browder's *Hitler's Enforcers*.

One of the difficulties encountered during the course of this research was coming to terms with the actuality of events that occurred in Belzec. It is only now, after a joint initiative by the Polish government, the United States Holocaust Memorial Museum in Washington, D.C., and the American Jewish Committee to carry out an archaeological survey at the site of the Belzec death camp, that we have the first scholarly topographical report of the camp. I was both fortunate and privileged to have been present during the course of these investigations. This work resulted in the publication of a unique archaeological document by Andrzej Kola (Professor of the University of Toruń), *Belzec: the Nazi Camp for Jews in the Light of Archaeological Sources. Excavations 1997 - 1999* (English version), which, for the first time, exposes – without fear of contradiction – the purpose and enormity of this perhaps greatest and most brutal of crimes. In addition, several short histories of the Lublin ghetto and Lublin district are of interest.

A bibliography referring to Schindler's deeds can be found in the Appendices.

"Shreibt un farschreibt!"
(Yiddish: Write and record!)[294]

Chapter Twenty
In Search of the Star of David

Figure 86: Museum Administrators: Mgr. Blanka Čuhelová
(director of the town museum) and Mgr. Radoslav Fikejz (historian)
Photo Credit: Author's collection

Svitavy Honors its Famous Son

The Town Museum and gallery administer the large Oskar Schindler collection, which contains over 300 items including valuable manuscripts, photographs, and documentary films, many of which I donated.

The project of the permanent exhibition displayed in the Town Museum, called "In Search of David's Star – Oskar Schindler – The Righteous Among Nations," as well as the establishment of the plaque commemorating Oskar Schindler, were promoted by the Town Mayor Mgr. Jiří Brýdl and Václav Koukal, a senator of the Czech parliament.

Many of these items are on display in this exhibit. Thanks to cooperation with foreign institutions, the museum was able to obtain certain works that have not yet been published in the Czech Republic. The Schindler story enjoys great public interest, especially in Poland, Israel, the USA, Germany, United Kingdom, and Russia. Since 1994, in response to Spielberg's film and the related Shoah project, which attempts to map the fate of as many Jews from the Holocaust as possible, an inexhaustible number of journalistic articles have been published on the Schindler topic.

These works have tried to describe the Schindler story in various contexts, sometimes creating a halo around Oskar Schindler's head. Also available are a great number of memoirs, the diaries of the rescued, and Schindler's letters found in 1999 in the "Schindler suitcase." Materials and many valuable documents are stored today at the Yad Vashem Memorial in Jerusalem.

In 2000 a small lecture hall with a capacity of 30 visitors was set up in the temporary spaces of the museum. A total of 14 display panels present the life of Oskar Schindler, the Svitavy native who saved the lives of 1,200 Jews during the Holocaust. Exhibits include 90 photographs, maps, and documents, the majority of which come from the museum collection. Presented in Czech and German, the display captions describe Schindler's life in Svitavy, Krakow, and at the work camp in Brünnlitz. Also on display is a copy the famous Schindler's List and the postwar honors Schindler received. Czech, German, and English documentary films the museum was able to acquire for its archives are also available for viewing.

The Town Celebrates

The Town of Svitavy commemorated the deeds of Oskar Schindler with a memorial of two granite columns connected by a bronze plaque bearing the inscription, "To the unforgettable savior of the lives of 1,200 persecuted Jews." The plaque was unveiled in Jan Palach Park opposite Oskar Schindler's childhood home on March 9, 1994, the day of the advance premier of *Schindler's List* in Svitavy.

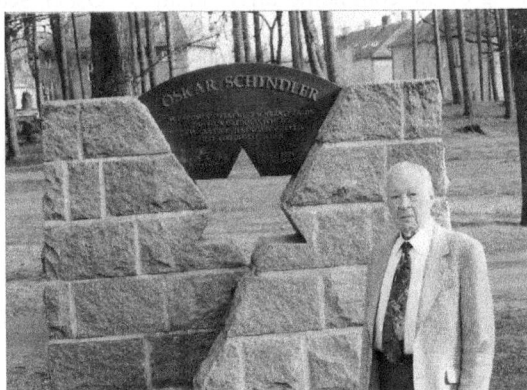

Figure 87: Viktor at the Schindler memorial Svitavy 1998
Photo Credit: Author's collection

The ceremonial unveiling was attended by Chief Rabbi Karol Sidon, German Ambassador Rolf Hofstetter, Israeli Ambassador Moshe Yegar, and representatives from the American Embassy, and the author. The Czech Republic was represented by deputies from the Czech Parliament and ministry workers. Representatives from the Jewish communities and civic groups from the Czech Republic and Germany were also in attendance.

Memorial Event in 1998

The Town of Svitavy prepared a memorial event for April 26, 1998 to celebrate the 90th anniversary of Oskar Schindler's birth. The memorial event held in the Ottendorfer House was attended by the distinguished guests Chief Rabbi Karol Sidon, Israeli Ambassador Raphael Gvir, German Charge d´Affaires Werner Wrendt, representatives of Ackermann Gemeinde and the author. Over 150 Schindler Jews from around the world were invited. Numerous letters of apology have been kept in the museum archives, as advanced age and health problems prevented the trip to Svitavy. Nonetheless, they recalled that it was Oskar and Emilie who had liberated them from the hell of the Holocaust. In addition to political and cultural personalities, Viktor Dortheimer, one of the Schindler Jews, and I were invited to sign the Svitavy guest book.

The Svitavy memorial and commemorative plaque recalling the deeds of Oskar Schindler are meant to symbolize humanity and tolerance. It's as if a Czech and German being was connected by a Star of David and wanted to show that Svitavy was not the only place where people of different nationalities and faiths lived side by side in harmony. This moral appeal for reconciliation, relevant in 1994 in connection with the crisis in the Balkans and in connection with resolving ongoing Czech-German disagreements, was promoted by Spielberg's film and the lifelong tale of Oskar Schindler and his Jews. The Svitavy memorial was designed by Roman Svojanoský.

The unveiling of the commemorative plaque to Oskar Schindler, like the entire gala advance premiere of the film, received a great deal of media attention. All nationwide Czech television stations broadcast live coverage and dozens of reporters and photographers were present. The lives of Oskar and Emilie Schindler became a popular point of discussion in publications.

Figure 88: Chief Rabbi Karol Sidon (right) and Svitavy Mayor Jiří Brýdl (left).
Photo Credit: Author's collection

**Figure 89: The author with Viktor Dortheimer
at the Jewish Cemetery Svitavy 1998
Photo Credit: Author's collection**

**Figure 90: Refurbished Jewish Cemetery Svitavy 2003
Photo Credit: Author's collection**

A Jewish cemetery with charnel house was founded in Olomoucká St. on the very edge of the town in 1892. The cemetery was surrounded by a brick wall, though only the foundation of this wall with the ground plan of the charnel house remains today. The cemetery was deserted after being vandalized for the first time in 1938. This neglected historical landmark with broken and relocated tombstones finally underwent reverent repairs in 2002-2003.

Emilie Re-surfaces After the Film *Schindler's List*

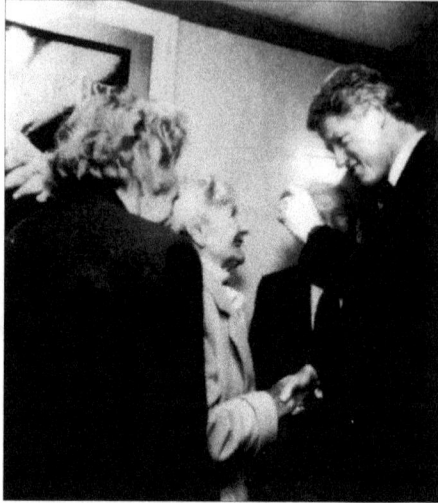

**Figure 91: Emilie Schindler speaking with President Bill Clinton
at the gala premiere of Schindler's List in New York in 1994
Photo Credit: Author's collection**

**Figure 92: Her audience with Pope John Paul II at the Vatican
was an unforgettable experience for Emilie
Photo Credit: Author's collection**

Emilie Schindler came to Svitavy in 1999 with a German film company. The documentary film made here followed the footsteps of Emilie from Starý Maletín to Svitavy and Brünnlitz. The 92-year-old widow remembered a place she knew well as a young lady, the Church of the Visitation of the Virgin Mary, where she married in 1928. Emilie spent nearly seven months at Brünnlitz helping her husband save the lives of Jews.

Following emigration to Argentina in 1949 it appeared that her marriage to Oskar was improving, but the idyllic moments soon ended. Oskar Schindler returned to his old way of life and Emilie felt deceived. In 1957 Emilie remained in Argentina, alone and without any means. She received assistance from Jewish organizations and associations. In her memoirs she recalls with bitterness that she lived in the shadow of Oskar Schindler, who was honored in the 1960s.

The Jews themselves realized this and at the celebratory banquet in Tel Aviv in 1962 the name of Emilie Schindler, Angel of Brünnlitz, was invoked a number of times. She finally gained satisfaction in 1993. Emilie received high honors from the Argentine government, and was paid royalties from Keneally's book, including Oskar's share. She died on October 5, 2001, in Strassberg near Berlin.

Figure 93: Emilie, left, and Erika Rosenberg in church in Svitavy
Photo Credit: Author's collection

Figure 94: Emilie Schindler with the author at the King David Hotel, Jerusalem 1995. Emilie is holding the author's unpublished mauscript *The Man from Svitavy* Photo Credit: Author's collection

Chapter Twenty-One
Conclusions

So, who was this Righteous Gentile? Has Keneally told the whole story, and if he has, did he get it right?

Schindler was a naive optimist, a chronic alcoholic, a lover of women outside his marriage to Emily Pelzl. The Jews he saved used to say, "Thank God he was more faithful to us than to his wife." Will the enigma ever be solved? Schindler is not here to tell us, and the survivors are uncertain and differ in their opinions. The establishment and Schindler's business associates in Krakow had opposing views of his ethics and would have preferred to sit on the fence and hope the Schindler story would retreat into the archives.

Schindler's friends and enemies accept that he was a very unusual man. A few of the Jews that he saved maintain, after all these years, that they still consider him a Nazi and exploiter of Jewish slave labor. Others swear their love for the man. That he used Jewish slave labor to enrich himself is not questioned, nor are his endeavors to eventually save his Jewish laborers.

Schindler must have been aware of the penalties confronting him when dealing in the merchandise of corruption, and if that be so, then his courage is true, too. He may have considered his Nazi friends were too corrupt and greedy or simply too preoccupied with their own approaching doom to act against him. Even so, the calculated risk must have remained high. There is no doubt Schindler received protection from the Wehrmacht, the Abwehr, and the Armaments Inspectorate. He convinced the Wehrmacht and the Armaments Inspectorate that his works were indispensable to the German war effort. He was useful because of his infiltration into the closed and guarded culture of the SS. We must not forget that he was a high-ranking officer of the Abwehr, and, I believe, very loyal to Canaris and all that he represented.

By 1942, when the intended genocide of the Jews was apparent to him, he went on playing the game of bluff and counterbluff with the likes of Goeth and Leipold. On a number of occasions, Goeth could have blown the whistle on Schindler, but he kept his own counsel. I believe that there was a true friendship between these two men and the gifts given by Schindler to Goeth were considered, by Goeth, to be the spoils of war.

The only possible conclusion seems that Oskar Schindler's exceptional deeds stemmed from just that elementary sense of decency and humanity that our sophisticated age seldom believes in. A repentant opportunist saw the light and rebelled against the sadism and vile criminality all around him. The inference may be disappointingly simple, especially for all amateur psychoanalysts who would prefer the deeper and more mysterious motive that may, it is true, still lie unprobed and unappreciated.[295]

It is a strange coincidence that my very first interview with a Schindler survivor remains probably the most enlightening and lasting image of the man himself:

Figure 95: Mrs. Rosalia Kornhauser
Photo Credit: Author's collection

"Schindler was a man of convincing honesty and outstanding charm. He usually had a cheerful smile on his strong face. His frank grey-blue eyes smiled too, except when they tightened in distress as he talked of the past.

Rosalia Kornhauser

Was Oskar Schindler a righteous person? The criteria I adopted in formulating my conclusions were in the form of three questions: (1) Did he save life? (2) Did he have any pecuniary interest? (3) Did he put his own life in danger?

In answer to (1) is that there is abundant evidence that he did save life. The answer to (2) is more difficult. The evidence suggests that in the early days of the war, Schindler did take advantage of the situation and benefited personally, but this was just a blip when considering the extraordinary events that followed. There is evidence to suggest that he amassed great wealth and there is also evidence that this wealth was used to facilitate his program of saving lives. On count (2), I think a jury verdict would exonerate him on a 10-2 majority. The answer to (3) is that there is overwhelming evidence that Schindler's life was on the line on a number of occasions.

In conclusion, what of Tom Keneally's book? I have consciously avoided traveling the same road as Keneally, as my task was to independently research his conclusions. Although it was a road with many crossroads, much of the way forward had already been cleared by him, making my task that much easier. His research was exemplary. Whatever extras Keneally may have added or painted for the sake of the novel, the essential facts are true. It was never my intention to supplant *Schindler's List,* only to supplement it and perhaps add by my research as a basis for further study.

Robin O'Neil, Salisbury UK 2009 & 2021

Mrs. Schindler's final statement after completing her book, *Where light and Shadow Meet:*

> "A toast to all of you my fellow human beings. I hope that as you close this book, you will want to make a toast for my husband...And for me, too."

Who could disagree with her?

Acknowledgements

To personally thank the many individuals who have helped and contributed to my research over many years was an impossible task. To close friends, survivors of the Holocaust, archivists, and academia in general, I pay due acknowledgment. My thanks are extended to my long-tested mentors: the late Sir Martin Gilbert, the late Professor John Klier, Professor Michael Berkowitz, et al, and to my editors: Joyce Field (CJ), Lance Ackerfeld, Pamela Russ and Beth Galleto.

Special mention must go to Mrs. Emilie Schindler who, during the furor of the Spielberg gathering at the King David Hotel, Jerusalem, in 1995, kindly made time to receive an unknown and uninvited Englishman who had penetrated the security cordon. Mrs. Schindler answered my questions regarding her husband, Oskar, and related her own recollections of the war years. A lady in every sense of the word.

To the late Herbert Steinhouse who in 1996, sent his personal recollections of his meetings with Schindler and Itzhak Stern and has my early research period until his untimely death shortly after.

Photographs and documents come from the author's own collection, the Jewish Historical Institute in Warsaw, United States Holocaust Memorial Museum, the Yad Vashem Institute of National Remembrance, the Krakow Ghetto Pharmacy Museum, the Svitavy Museum, Auschwitz Museum, and the Klein Foundation (USA). Many photographs and documents come from individuals I have met and interviewed over the years: Simon Wiesenthal, Dr. Moshe Bejski, Viktor Dortheimer, Dan Granot, Rosalia Kornhauser, Josef and Rebecca Bau, Richard and Estera Rechen, Professor Aleksander B. Skotnicki, Mietek Pemper, Sophie Stern, Dr Chani Smith, to name but a few.

To Dr. David Silberklang, Editor of Yad Vashem Studies, for permission to quote from Moshe Bejski's assessment of Schindler: Yad Vashem Studies 24 (1994), 317-348.

The completion of this book could not have been concluded without the help of the Svitavy Museum, which kindly offered manuscripts of historical interest concerning Oskar Schindler: Mgr. Blanka Čuhelová and Mgr. Radoslav Fikejz.

Lastly, but not least, to my family and close friends who had to endure my obsession with Oskar over many, many years.

Appendix A: Sources

The late Dr. Moshe Bejski, former Chairman of the Commission for Recognition of the Righteous Gentiles and a former Justice of the Supreme Court in Israel, is central to the Schindler story. It was my privilege to have met Dr. Bejski in the early 1990s in Israel when he kindly edited my first attempt to reconstruct the Schindler story. Dr. Bejski remained a good friend and mentor until his untimely death in 2007.

Moshe Bejski was born in 1920 in the Polish town of Dzialoszyce, near Krakow. After the Nazis invaded Poland, Bejski's family was deported to the Belzec death camp. He and his brother Uri were saved by Schindler when the industrialist drafted them to work in his factory. Officially, the Bejski brothers were listed as a machine fitter and a draftsman, but Uri was known for his expertise in weapons and Moshe was a master document-forger. Throughout the war, Moshe Bejski created rubber stamps with the Nazi regime's symbol on them, and forged papers and passports that Schindler used to smuggle Jews out of harm's way.

In the 1960s, Bejski testified at Adolf Eichmann's war crimes trial. Bejski remained close with Schindler for many years, giving him money and defending him against critics who accused the industrialist of alcoholism and womanizing. In 1974, he delivered the oration at Schindler's funeral in Jerusalem.

From 1970 to 1975, Bejski chaired Yad Vashem's Commission of the Righteous, where he was tasked with identifying gentiles who saved the lives of Jews during the Holocaust to be honored as Righteous Among the Nations. The commission made several controversial decisions during the time he was chairman, sifting through those who hid Jews while simultaneously aligning themselves with the Nazis and others who saved Jews in exchange for payment. As part of his work with the commission, Bejski created the principle of "the inherent consistency of the rescuer's gesture," ruling that a person could only be Righteous Among the Nations if his actions were spurred by a genuinely humanitarian spirit.

Bejski was appointed to the Israeli Supreme Court in 1979 and served there until he retired in 1991.

In 1994, Yad Vashem Studies published Moshe Bejski's personal thoughts about Oskar Schindler. This appraisal is now offered as an introduction to set the scene for what is to follow:

Oskar Schindler and *Schindler's List*

Moshe Bejski

It appears that Steven Spielberg's film *Schindler's List* has by now reached the peak of public interest in the Holocaust. The film brought the horrors of the Holocaust – to the extent that they could be cinematically reconstructed – to the consciousness of hundreds of millions of people who until now had little or no knowledge of what had happened to the Jewish people in Nazi-occupied Europe.

From the moment Spielberg's film was screened in cinemas all over the world, many asked whether the events depicted in *Schindler's List* are factually grounded and whether the figure of Schindler, as portrayed by the American director, corresponded to the actual person and his conduct.

The answer is not simple, and a preliminary clarification is in order: Spielberg's movie is largely an adaptation of a book by Australian writer Thomas Keneally, *Schindler's List,* published in 1982. Although before writing his book Keneally interviewed many survivors who had been saved by Schindler and availed himself of archival material related to the story, he did not intend to – nor did he – write a documentary-historical book. Even though the characters, both Jews and non-Jews, bear the names of actual persons, and the events described in the book did take place, their fictional representation belongs to the realm of poetic license; that is, deviation from actual facts in order to enhance the artistic effect.

Descriptions of certain events are only loosely related to historical-documentary realities, just as dialogues between characters were conceived in the writer's imagination. Moreover, there are several factual errors in the book that stem from faulty memories of the survivors. Nevertheless, all these qualifications do not detract from the general accuracy of the depicted events, with one important exception: even a writer as gifted as Keneally cannot reconstruct in full the horrors of existence in a concentration camp, simply because these horrors defy human imagination.

Spielberg did not aspire to make a historical-documentary feature, and *Schindler's List* certainly does not belong in this category. I do not regard myself as qualified to pass professional judgment on the artistic merits of the film; but, as a person who went through the actual experience, I do feel entitled to say that, even though in numerous instances the film is at variance with facts, it remains firmly grounded. This notwithstanding certain modifications dictated by the need to make the film appealing to a wide audience.

Despite its considerable length (three and a quarter hours), the film describes only a part (probably a small part) of Schindler's undertakings during the five and a half years of the war. The film passes over the Brünnlitz period in almost complete silence and does not depict the greatest rescue act of the Schindler couple; namely, bringing in the freezing prisoners from the Golleschau camp. They had been travelling back and forth for two weeks in sealed boxcars without food or water.

The occasion does not permit me to do justice to Oskar Schindler's personality, to relate the full story of his efforts on behalf of the Jews who worked for him, his individual approach to each one of them, his efforts to protect and rescue them. The truth is that the details of his story were not widely known before 1962.

When Schindler came to Israel for the first time, the survivors who lived in the country (240, many of them with families by then) gathered for a festive reception with their wartime benefactor in a Tel Aviv hotel. That evening, May 2, 1962, was the first time they spoke out about what Schindler had done for each of them individually and for the whole camp to protect and rescue the prisoners. The venue did not provide an opportunity for all those gathered to bear testimony; only 14 survivors spoke. But their stories were recorded as direct, reliable, and independent testimony regarding the "Schindler affair" and were subsequently deposited in the Yad Vashem archives. There is no doubt that they constitute the most direct and reliable record, particularly those testimonies of survivors who were close to Schindler. But they were not made into a book or a film, and even they do not tell the entire story.

Included here are selected excerpts from testimonies given by survivors on that night as well as several other documents. This selection of documents bears out the conclusion that, essentially, both Keneally's book and Spielberg's film are based on actual events. The material also offers some information about Schindler the man, his relationship to the Jews, his unique and numerous efforts that led to the rescue of 1,200 men and women, including the list of names of the 300 women whom he saved from the inferno of Auschwitz.

There are three aspects of Spielberg's film that I find of great importance:

(1) The film has reached an audience of tens, perhaps hundreds, of millions, offering them an opportunity to learn something about the Holocaust that struck the Jewish people.

(2) In recent years there have been hundreds of publications that seek to deny that the Holocaust ever took place. Spielberg's film, based on testimonies of persons who are still alive, provides an effective means to blunt the impact of these nefarious undertakings.

(3) Oskar Schindler, together with some 12,000 persons that have been honored by Yad Vashem as Righteous Among the Nations, including those who acted in concentration and death camps, is yet another example and proof that it was possible to help and rescue persecuted Jews everywhere and under every circumstance. There were simply not enough people with the will and courage to render assistance. Perhaps the film will awaken the world to the fact that during the war humanity failed the persecuted Jews.

Moshe Bejski

The firestorm of Jewish genocide

The Final Solution, Nazi Germany's plan for the extermination of European Jewry, turned the eastern occupied territories into a mass grave for six million Jews – men, women, and children. Rising from the ashes and learning the tragic lessons of the Holocaust, the State of Israel chose to never forget. Through a special Knesset (Israeli Parliament) law, Yad Vashem was established in 1953, to enshrine and preserve the memory of the six million Jews annihilated and the thousands of flourishing communities destroyed.

On August 15, 1953, the Knesset unanimously passed the Martyrs and Heroes Remembrance (Yad Vashem) Law, which outlined the objectives of Yad Vashem and its organizational framework. Section 1(9) deals specifically with commemorating the high-minded Gentiles who risked their lives to save Jews.

This recognition carries with it the privilege of planting a tree on the Avenue of Righteous Gentiles, and the award of a medallion inscribed in Hebrew and French, with words from the Talmud: Whosoever saves a single soul, it is as if he has saved the whole world.

In 1963, Oskar Schindler was nominated a 'Righteous Person,' only the third individual to receive the privilege of planting a tree. His contemporaries, Julius Madritsch, Raymond Titsch, and Oswald Bousco were also recognized.

The Speaker of Israel's Parliament said: "It is our duty to discover these knights of morality, to establish contact with them, to pay them our debt of gratitude, and to express to them our admiration for their courage … These few saved not only the Jews but the honor of man."

The Jews named the Holocaust *Shoah* (I will give them an everlasting name, Isaiah 56:5).

The Shoah was a turning point in history – a logical progression of the persecution of the Jews, dating back over a thousand years, culminating in the Berlin suburb of Wannsee. It was there, on January 20, 1942, that the bureaucratic destructive process of the Jews was determined. The final seal of approval came in a two-paragraph letter from Herman Goering (Hitler's deputy) to Reinhard Heydrich (the principal architect of the holocaust) in July 1941, with orders to proceed with the Final Solution.

The wheels of destruction slowly started to turn. Nothing was committed to writing and there was no specific plan. All was left to inferences and inventions conjured up in the minds of the architects and technicians of human destruction.

The Jews had lived for centuries with discriminatory edicts: firstly, 'you may not live amongst us as Jews'; then, 'you may not live amongst us'; and finally, from the Nazis, 'you may not live'.[296]

In 1942, when Jews in the whole of Poland were being rounded up and sent to extermination camps, Oskar Schindler distanced himself from the Nazi racial policy. He operated his own rescue mission to save as many Jews as possible, by taking them with him when he moved his factory from Poland to Czechoslovakia. To some, his actions were that of a saint. To others, he remained a Nazi who made money from Jewish slave labor. He remains a controversial figure, an enigma of his times.

A letter from Oskar Schindler to Director Dr. Ball-Kaduri at Yad Vashem shows the essence of the man's character and thinking: the conflict between obedience and conscience which he experienced in 1939, and the decision he took to follow the latter regardless of the consequences that might result from his dangerous and adventurous existence.[297]

Schindler wrote:

"In judging my actions, I want people to keep in mind, that in all my decisions, I acted as a free human being who had everything life could offer. In critical and hopeless situations, I was often able to inspire weaker characters and pull them along with me.

Let me give you a few details about myself and my change of opinions. I will try and explain some of my actions as well as it is possible in the circumstances in which I now find myself.

Ultimately, I am a German. When the Prussians marched in and occupied the Sudetenland, my homeland; when they made a colony of it, pillaged it like enemy territory and used the inhabitants as second-rate people, only finding use for them as cannon fodder; when the last of my Jewish school friends and acquaintances immigrated as quickly as possible, I started thinking. The memory of a happy childhood, spent with those friends, became for me a moral obligation that drove me on.

Then, when I experienced the German occupation in the Protectorate and in Poland for a few months, I knew clearly that I and a million other non-Reich Germans were being taken for a ride by the convincing propaganda about a 'New' Europe with nationalistic and economic advantages. I was not going to become subordinate to a bunch of sadistic murderers and deceitful impostors who surreptitiously got the government of a very straight and ordinary nation on their side.

This realization may have been in many German minds, but because of the fear of being ruined professionally, or disadvantaged economically, they kept quiet in spite of their doubts and carried on as if nothing had happened because it was easier and safer to do so.

Thank God, I had the courage to see the consequences of this disastrous time and jumped off the bandwagon to save what was still possible to save. Many like-minded people, mainly former Austrians, allied with me. It was important to remember that this change did not take place after July 20, 1944, (the attempt on Hitler's life) when all frontiers had broken down and many had given up. It started four years prior to this date, when the German Blitzkrieg made the world hold its breath. The political uncertainty of the war years put me under enormous mental pressure. My upbringing to respect orders, to be obedient and follow the law, made me battle with myself, until I finally buried all those instilled doctrines.

I was not going to be uncritical anymore. I was going to follow my instinct and judgment; to do something for humanity and to make room for compassion.

Like-minded friends, and the sight of the daily suffering, helped me overcome all my conflicts. I am not a religious man, far from it. As an immoderate man, I have far more faults than the average person who goes modestly through life.

'Respect for humanity', as Albert Schweitzer says. 'I could hold and defend it.'

Who could understand the inner conflict I felt, after sending a dozen women to the SS 'super humans,' to whom alcohol and presents had already lost their attraction? Some of the women knew what was asked of them, although they were only aware of fragments of my difficulties. The pain I experienced was certainly not jealousy, but disgust with myself. To throw pearls before the swine and say that the end justifies the means was poor comfort to me.

When the German war success neared its end and friends repeatedly called to persuade me to leave with them for Switzerland, take all my possessions with me and leave everything else to chance (for example, the destruction and extermination, which was relentless), I found that, morally, I could not do this. Instead, I drove to Krakow, taking my reserves of dollars, and bought large quantities of food and medicines. These I dispatched as express goods to my camp at Brünnlitz in new ammunition boxes, which I registered as ammunition parts.

In the last months of the war, I paid hundreds of thousands of Marks to the SS as wages for totally senseless work, but it kept the gangsters satisfied and left me in peace.

What would have been said if I had gone to Switzerland? The survivors of my factory would have said, 'He was quite decent, but a pity he had to run away.' I know some quite decent people who today live far better than I, but who failed when it was important.

And, what of my wife, Emilie? I wonder if the wives of any of those so-called 'decent men' would have traveled 300 kilometers in the bitter cold weather, with a case full of schnapps, a case far too heavy for her, to exchange the contents for medicine in order to help those starving and suffering Jews from the Golleschau transport who had lost their last spark for life through German barbarism. For my wife, this task was self-evident. Whenever there was a need to help people in peril, she would care, regardless of the dangers. She had the courage to treat SS leaders as butlers and valets.

'I felt the Jews were being destroyed – I had to help. There was no choice.

Oskar Schindler, September 9, 1956

The 1982 publication of Thomas Keneally's book, *Schindler's Ark* (re-published later as the novel *Schindler's List*), and the 1993 release of Steven Spielberg's film *Schindler's List* brought world-wide prominence to the Holocaust in general, and to Oskar Schindler in particular, as the embodiment of all those who risked their lives to save Jews and other victims of the Final Solution. The Holocaust and Oskar Schindler both remain inexplicable in their entirety, but I hope my efforts will shed light on one aspect of those terrible times.

In Dr. Luitgard N. Wundheiler's analysis[298] of Schindler in 1986, she poses the question: "Why, then, is Oskar Schindler not better known? Why is he never mentioned together with Raoul Wallenberg, Elizabeth Abegg or André Trocme?" Twenty years later, we scratch our heads over Abegg and Trocme but are more conversant with Wallenberg and Schindler.

Among the Righteous now commemorated at Yad Vashem, one asks oneself, how does he fit in with all these other heroes, how was he different, what makes us sit up and take notice? Dr. Moshe Bejski, himself a Schindler survivor, put it quite plainly: "Schindler was different for two reasons: first, his exploits were on a very large scale; and second, he carried them on for a very long time."[299]

The story of Oskar Schindler is not the history of a man born to be a hero, like Raoul Wallenberg; rather it is the story of a common – even a base man. Before the war, Schindler had been something of a ne'er-do-well. After the war, he was a financial failure. Yet, under the right circumstances, he became a savior. It is only the presence of monstrous evil that makes Oskar Schindler a good man – finally, an exceptional one.

While many of us would like to think we would have acted in a similar fashion towards oppressed people of any race, the difference was that Schindler found himself in a position of some authority and power, and this, together with his charisma, enabled him to influence the events that unfolded before him.

During the entire course of the war, in so far as the many hundreds of Jews who were touched by Schindler are concerned, not one single Jewish life was lost by unnatural causes. As Dr. Wundheiler remarks: "...and if a human being with so many shortcomings could do that, is there anyone among us who can say, 'I am not good enough or powerful enough to help?' It is uncomfortable to know about Schindler because he stirs our conscience precisely because of his weaknesses."

My purpose is to re-examine and analyze the novel *Schindler's List* by Thomas Keneally. As the novel lacks notation of primary and secondary sources, we are at the mercy of the writer regarding the credibility of the facts surrounding Schindler's activities during the Holocaust. I also consider it important to accurately document Schindler's story because of the many publications and films now being produced which rely entirely on the Keneally book as source material.

I am writing this account biographically and proceeding in chronological order from the years 1908 to 1945. Each section is subdivided into chapters, analyzing Schindler's behavior within the historical context of the times. New evidence is introduced which challenges existing facts, and I present my own assessments and opinions.

Documentation, Sources and Direction of Travel

In researching documentation on the life of Oskar Schindler, I interviewed and corresponded with many of the Schindler Jews who have become celebrated survivors of the Holocaust.

When Spielberg was asked why he used the American publication title *Schindler's List*, in preference to the more widely known and original title, *Schindler's Ark* (in America, this title was considered too religious), he replied, "I want to make a lot about lists."[300] He was right. The Schindler story is all about lists; there are right lists and wrong lists, long lists and short lists, personal lists, official lists, and the lists to which I attach most evidential value – the Madritsch list and the Davar list.

The list of Oskar Schindler is not as straightforward as one might think. Although it remains the framework from which everything radiates, it takes on different and perplexing guises as the Schindler story unfolds. What one must appreciate is that the list one identifies with Schindler – i.e., the list of names he selected for the exodus of his Schindler Jews on the transport from KL (concentration camp) Plaszow[301] to Brünnlitz in October 1944 – should not be directly identified with the list in the archives at Yad Vashem. The Yad Vashem list is a German document drawn up from a list of names presented to them on behalf of Schindler and subsequently processed (with alterations and replacement names made for personal gain) by the Jew Marcel Goldberg (69510).[302] This presentation first took place in the labor office of Plaszow, then later in the administration department of the Gross-Rosen concentration camp.

However, it is not that simple. There are more complications to examine before one arrives at any sensible understanding of how the list or lists came into being. One can safely disregard the notion that Oskar Schindler personally dictated a list of his Jewish personnel for transfer to the safer camp at Brünnlitz. All the evidence suggests that he was away from Krakow currently, securing the factory in Brünnlitz.

Schindler's original list was based on the 300 Jews retained for decommissioning purposes in the Emalia[303] factory when it was being closed down in August 1944. It was these Jews who were the first batch to be transferred to Brünnlitz. The remainder of his workers, some 800, had been sent to Plaszow. Apart from a small number of personally sanctioned Jews chosen by Schindler,[304] the remaining names that were to make up the Brünnlitz transport were left in the hands of Marcel Goldberg (69510) and SS-Unterscharführer (Corporal) Smith of the Jewish labor office in Plaszow.[305] This is when the wheeling and dealing and corruption took place, and when the diamonds talked. Some of the most distinguished community leaders were removed from the list and replaced by those who could pay.[306] In the post-war analysis of Schindler's list, there are added complications with claims and counterclaims by survivors who profess to have had some part in the formulation of the list.

The pro-forma list perceived to be Schindler's is in fact the standard form for the transport of prisoners filled in by the German authorities, in this case for Gross-Rosen. When the Schindler men arrived at Gross-Rosen from Plaszow, they were selected in groups and processed accordingly. Each man received a number, obliterating him as a person, before being transferred to the Schindler factory camp at Brünnlitz.

The Schindler's lists held by Yad Vashem and widely circulated as "The List" is nothing more than a regulated form of accounting. To support and to corroborate my argument I refer to Emilie Schindler's recollection on arriving at the Brünnlitz camp:

> "Miss Kronovsky had come with us from Zwittau (Svitavy) to work at the plant (Schindler's factory in Brünnlitz). She was remarkably meticulous and punctual, and as the secretary she also had to keep up to date the lists of all those who worked at the plant. These lists had to be submitted every eight days when the food rations were delivered, supposedly calculated according to the required number of calories per person."[307]

The scene in Spielberg's film where Itzhak Stern (69518) is shown typing the list at Schindler's dictation is the colorful imagination of a Hollywood film director. Stern, according to my research, was never an employee in Schindler's Emalia factory. One of the greatest misconceptions in the Schindler story – in books, film, and in other literature – is that Itzhak Stern worked as Schindler's accountant in the Emalia factory. Stern only occasionally worked for Schindler. Schindler's accountant and factory manager was the Jew Abraham Bankier (69268). Bankier was the previous owner of Emalia under its former commercial business name – Rekord. Ousted from his factory through bankruptcy, Bankier became the manager for Schindler, and many of the Schindler Jews that the author has interviewed said he was the kingpin behind most of Schindler's activities. In Spielberg's *Schindler's List*, the characterization of Stern should mainly have been that of Bankier. The scene in the film where Stern is shown being swept into a departing train for the death camps, only to be saved at the last minute by Schindler, who is seen running along the platform shouting his name, was in reality Bankier. Nevertheless, this does not lessen Stern's contribution.[308]

Schindler's women traveled from Plaszow, but instead of going directly to Brünnlitz, found themselves in Auschwitz-Birkenau. The bureaucrats of Auschwitz-Birkenau processed the women exactly as the men had been processed at Gross-Rosen, with one exception: the men were listed by consecutive numbering only and not by name alphabetically, whereas the women were listed both by consecutive numbers as well as by alphabetical name. Gross-Rosen, Plaszow, and Brünnlitz were all satellite camps within a spreading arc of penal establishments working to a standard set of rules and regulations. To simplify matters, the men's list was restructured into alphabetical order for easy reference to the individuals concerned.

The list throws up many anomalies; name changes, dates of birth, and occupations are not what they seem. Generally, they are correct, but for several reasons, some of the prisoners chose to give inaccurate information, while other inaccuracies were simply the result of typing errors made by the German authorities.

The interviewing technique I adopted, was, from the outset, based on the realization that memory is not history. It stands to reason that much of the events described and dialogue recalled form a memoir – a compilation of recollections of incidents and conversations as elderly witnesses remembered them happening 50 years earlier. It has been a challenge for the researcher to disentangle the mass of testimonies, which have – for many reasons – been exaggerated or mistaken, to arrive at the probable true course of events. I was more comfortable in relying on written evidence made at the time or immediately after the described events occurred.

Much of the dialogue came through the filter of translation, whether in the form of personal interviews with witnesses or in dealing with documentation. Eyewitnesses heard or spoke the original in one language and repeated it to me in another, often through an interpreter. Most of the time, the oral translations were just about adequate but mostly grammatically incorrect, as the interpreter switched from direct to indirect quotations. Fortunately, the majority of witnesses forming the core of my research spoke English.

I was not so fortunate when dealing with documentation extracted from archival sources in Israel, Poland, Germany, and the Czech Republic. Apart from English press reports and the odd book in English which referred to the subject, I was at the absolute mercy of friendly translators. Many of the translators were Schindler Jews who were spread far and wide and were able to feed me further information when requested. I had to take advantage of every opportunity that presented itself, sometimes in very odd situations. A brief example of one such incident is illustrative: I had just secured some material from the archives in Svitavy, Czech Republic. Waiting at a bus stop, I entered into conversation with a complete stranger[309] who was eager to converse in English, so I immediately asked him to translate some documentation, which he did directly into a tape recorder, one eye on the lookout for the bus and one eye on the document.

Tape recorders were an essential part of my equipment when dealing with foreign-language documents. I was heavily reliant on this practice, and initially sent each document to a translator who would translate the document onto tape. Upon its return, the translation was transferred from the tape directly into print. All tapes have been kept in my archives. On some occasions, I obtained independent clarification of a particular translation and found this practice was able to verify the accuracy of the original translation.

The Schindler investigation I began some 20 years ago was protracted and sometimes difficult. However, on occasions luck came my way: staying at the City Hotel in Tel Aviv I left each day for Yad Vashem to interview survivors or other witnesses.

Figure A1: Yaël Reicher, City Hotel, Tel Aviv 1995

Photo Credit: Author's Collection

At the hotel I met Yaël Reicher, who was interested in my research. Each day I left her sheets of Hebrew documents and the following morning I would find this material translated and left at the hotel desk for my attention. My grateful thanks, Yaël.

Appendix B: Principal Research Documents

1. Dr. Ball-Kaduri Documentation
2. Steinhouse Documentation
3. Madritsch List and Documentation
4. Czech Security Documentation
5. Emilie Schindler Documents and Memoir (1996)
6. Keneally's *Schindler's List'*
7. The *Davar* List

1. The Ball-Kaduri Documentation[310]

Much of the information about this period comes from a detailed and lengthy report and from documentation and observations (in German) by Dr. R. Ball-Kaduri. The documentation deals with both Schindler and Stern and the protagonists surrounding them at that time.

In 1945, Ball-Kaduri represented a Jewish Agency dealing with the evidence of Holocaust survivors and restricted his investigations solely to German- speaking witnesses. Any matter that arose in other languages was passed over to another department. In 1956, he was working under the auspices of Yad Vashem; all the references are in the archives at Yad Vashem, Jerusalem.

The information collated by Ball-Kaduri was obtained with the help of Stern, and, later, through direct communication with Schindler. There are a large number of very interesting documents – some originals, some photocopies. The letters Schindler sent to Ball-Kaduri in which he writes about himself are of great value.

The accounts may be divided into sections covering the period 1939-1945:
1. Itzhak Stern
2. Oskar Schindler
3. Stern in Krakow
    a. Work at J.L. Bucheister and Co.
    b. Work for TOZ and the Joint
    c. Work for armed forces in Unkelbach; the Progress factory
4. Schindler in Krakow
    a. Schindler's factory and Schindler's camp in Krakow
    b. Schindler and the Nazi system
5. Stern in Plaszow
    a. End of outside work at Progress factory
    b. Commandant Goeth, liaison between Stern and factory management
    c. General observations
6. Collaboration, Schindler/Stern, Krakow/Plaszow
7. Transition from work camp Plaszow to concentration camp Plaszow
8. Move of Schindler's factory to Brünnlitz

9. Work camp Brünnlitz
    a. Schindler's welfare of the Jew
    b. Salvage [Saving? Rescue? Liberation?] of the Golleschau transport of 100 Jews in January 1945
10. Liberation of Brünnlitz

When Ball-Kaduri was compiling his report, he had to use a special method. As he received Stern's statements, he found it impossible to write them down in chronological sequence. At the time he presented his evidence, Stern resided in Tel Aviv and was the manager of a factory. It is said that he was a first-rate organizer and was an expert on factory statistics. These characteristics, however, did not appear to help him as he related the details of the war years with Oskar Schindler to Ball-Kaduri.

According to Dr. Ball-Kaduri, Stern would bubble over when thinking of the past. He spoke very quickly and recounted isolated incidents very vividly, just as they entered his mind. There was no chronological order in his narrative, and he seemed to lack an understanding of the interviewer's difficulties.

Dr. Ball-Kaduri decided to take detailed notes in shorthand while Stern was speaking, and then transfer the notes that same evening or the next day to a typewritten account. It was only after about five meetings with Stern that Dr. Ball-Kaduri started to see the whole of the extraordinary story Stern and Schindler had experienced. Through specific questioning, the account became clearer.

These interviews lasted six months, during which time Stern would repeat an incident many times, until he was halted. Nothing of importance changed throughout the repetition of incidents. The report was completed in December 1956 and signed by both Yitzhak Stern and Dr. Ball-Kaduri as a true statement of the events that took place during that critical time.

We have, in Stern's deposition, a unique insight into his dealings with Schindler. He provides an account which would otherwise be impossible for us to realize.

2. The Steinhouse Documentation[311]

Figure A2: Herbert Steinhouse in Paris, 1949
Photo Credit: Author's Collection

Unknown to Keneally, Spielberg, Ball-Kaduri, and other interested parties, another writer had stumbled onto the Schindler story over 40 years earlier. In 1949, Herbert Steinhouse worked for the Canadian Broadcasting Corporation in Paris, and was the first journalist to interview Schindler and Stern about their wartime exploits. Being the professional he is, Steinhouse arranged several interviews with both Stern and Schindler, conducted under strict conditions. Translators of German and Yiddish were present, and a shorthand typist recorded the interviews, verbatim. Also present was Al Taylor, a professional photographer who captured pictures of the most telling truth, revealing the symbiotic relationship between Schindler and Stern since their first meeting on November 19, 1939. Evidence of the love and understanding that existed between these two men has not been shown since, in writing or in film. Al Taylor does it with one photograph of great symbolic tenderness.

Figure A3: Itzhak Stern and Oskar Schindler, Paris 1949 (Al Taylor)
Photo Credit: Author's Collection

It is interesting how closely the article written by Steinhouse 50 years earlier supports *Schindler's Ark* by Keneally, who never met Schindler.

The Steinhouse documentation makes Schindler even more extraordinary than either the book or the film, both of which depict him as someone who started out wanting cheap labor to make money and who became a humanitarian in the process. The Steinhouse papers wrestle with the answer to the question that we all want to know: What made Schindler tick? Why did he do what he did? Herbert Steinhouse's interviews would appear to have more validity than the speculative writing of both the book and the film.

The Steinhouse documentation is important for several reasons: for the corroboration it gives to the established record; for the additional details and anecdotes not contained in either Keneally's novel or Spielberg's film; and, most importantly, for the direct access it gives us to Schindler himself. **See Appendix G for the collaboration between the author and Herbert Steinhouse when the author submitted to him his early draft of the Schindler story, "The Man from Svitavy".**

3. The Madritsch Documentation[312]

One cannot discuss Oskar Schindler without incorporating into the dialogue his contemporaries in Plaszow – Julius Madritsch, Raymond Titsch[313] and Oswald Bousco.[314] These four, recognized by the State of Israel as Righteous Persons, occupy a unique place in the hearts and minds of the Jews formerly incarcerated in the ghettos and labor camps of Krakow and Tarnow. The four conspired to lessen the hurt and deprivation of the Jews interned in the most appalling circumstances. Much of my information comes from a personal record kept by Madritsch – original German documents of the time recording his dealings with the SS bureaucrats in Berlin. The Titsch documents, by way of affidavit, were made after the war to counter allegations against his employer, Madritsch. The recollections of both men are also important for the memory of Oswald Bousco, who was executed by the Nazis in Krakow.

Figure A4: Julius Madritsch. Figure A5: Raymond Titsch[315]
Photo Credit: Author's Collection

4. Czech Security Services Documentation 1938 and 1946[316]

The documentation dated 1938 deals with Schindler's arrest and interrogation in Svitavy on August 18/19, 1938. The documentation of 1946 deals with the aftermath of the war when the Czechoslovakian government was tracking down known Nazis, Schindler included, and when the arrest and interrogation of Joseph Aue took place.

Finding these police reports was quite significant. In Keneally's account of Schindler, he appears to have skipped a chapter – the period when Schindler was engaging with the Abwehr in 1938 and was imprisoned on a capital charge of espionage against the Czechoslovakian state. Sentenced to death by hanging, he languished for some months in jail until Hitler took over the whole of Czechoslovakia, at which time all political prisoners were released.

Mrs. Schindler has noted, "Oskar was condemned to death for his offence. The German invasion of Czechoslovakia in 1939 saved his life."[317]

This material exposes Schindler's direct connection with the German security services and his appointment as second-in-command of the security services in Moravska Ostrava,[318] a town on the Czech/Polish border. It also delineates his role in the recruitment of Joseph Aue as an agent and the transfer of Aue to the premises of J.L. Bucheister and Co., Stradom Street, Krakow. Keneally's reference to the Bucheister premises centers on the first meeting between Schindler and Stern on November 19, 1939; Stern was the Jewish accountant working directly under Aue, the German-installed Treuhänder. Keneally nearly got it right, but for the missing piece in the jigsaw, found in this Czech security documentation. In short, Schindler was a high-ranking officer of the Foreign Section of the Abwehr in Moravska Ostrava and Krakow. Aue was a committed agent operating and residing at the premises of Bucheister, used by the Abwehr for its undercover work in Krakow. Stern appears to have been ignorant of this.[319]

5. Emilie Schindler's Documentation

This was of exceptional help not only because of her close personal relationship with Oskar,[320] but also because of her direct involvement in his activities as an agent of the Abwehr in Ostrava and his early activities in Krakow. Emilie was also directly involved in the Brünnlitz camp and the incident concerning the Golleschau tragedy. My material began with the help of Jon Blair, the film director, who gave me access to a full schedule of interviews he had had with Emilie Schindler in Argentina in 1981. This was followed up by my own personal interviews with Mrs. Schindler in Israel and subsequent correspondence. Finally, I used information in Emilie Schindler's memoirs later published in Argentina.

6. Keneally's *Schindler's Ark* (later *List*)

My problem with this book was that sources were not attributed, nor was there an index from which to work. Generally, it is accurate, with parts painted in, or out, for the sake of the novel. The research, however, is impeccable. I deliberately put the Keneally book aside and worked from my own notes, but I used his book as a guide to the Schindler story and was impressed with Keneally's attention to detail and his progress as the story unfolded.

7. The *Davar* List: The original Schindler's List?

The *Davar* publication is of considerable importance considering the list's controversial legacy. The list of Schindler's Jews given by Schindler to the Committee for Aid to Jews was published in Palestine's daily newspaper *Davar* between August 31 and September 5, 1944. The list with 901 names and birthdates was created in March 1944.

The quoted documentation (section 1-7) remains the author's main source of information covering a broad spectrum of Schindler's activities between 1938 and 1945. There are many other documents and witness accounts covering the periods prior to, and after, the war years and these are incorporated into the text.

Appendix C: Historical Synopsis

Schindler's Home-Town Svitavy – A Town in the Bohemian-Moravian Borderlands

The history of Svitavy, a feudal town of the Olomouc bishops, dates to the year 1256. Up until 1945 the main language heard in town streets and on the Renaissance Square was German. The arrival of the railroad in Svitavy in the 19th century led to the heavy industrialization of the entire area. While many factories determined the industrial character of the town, the historical town square became an important tourist attraction.

The town of Svitavy underwent dramatic changes in the 19th century. The textile industry, the main livelihood of town citizens, entered a phase of tumultuous expansion. The complexes of factories that were founded gave Svitavy an unmistakable industrial character. The vast majority of the 9,029 residents recorded in the 1900 census were Catholics. A mere 75 individuals declared themselves to be Czech-speaking citizens. Over 100 societies and associations, including organized labor, had an important impact on town life. Despite all their difficulties, the citizens of Svitavy coexisted in relative peace. But the "Manchester of Moravia," as the town had been called, found itself at a historical crossroads during the period of the First World War. A deep economic crisis, the loss of markets for produced goods and social tension were a portent of unrest in 1918.

The declaration of a free Czechoslovakia and the demise of the Hapsburg monarchy were not accepted with enthusiasm in Svitavy. The town was situated in the German-speaking enclave of Hřebečsko and the leaders of Svitavy tried to align the town with German Austria. While the occupation of Svitavy by the Czechoslovak army in December 1918 calmed the situation, it did nothing to resolve the prevailing attitudes of town citizens. Life in Svitavy over the next 20 years developed peacefully, but with the rise of Adolph Hitler the exemplary German-Czech cooperation came to an end in the small town in the Bohemian-Moravian borderlands.

Jews in the Bohemian-Moravian Borderlands

Life moved at a slow pace on the border between Bohemia and Moravia. The region had been settled by Czechs and Germans; towns were founded by monarchs, the nobility, and Church authorities. Jews began taking up residence in this region in the 14th century. The first Jews appeared in the town of Jevíčko, others in Svitavy, followed by Litomyšl. It wasn't until the 18th century that reports about the Jewish community began to increase. Jews settled in larger towns, wherever it was permitted. It took a long time before they were allowed to practice trades and own farm the land. Jews leased distilleries, made a living in banking, and in the 19th century, having already been granted equal rights, they established factories. Nevertheless, despite their hard-earned accomplishments, the tragedy of the Holocaust destroyed this pillar of national and denominational life in the Bohemian-Moravian borderlands.

The Jewish Community in Svitavy

While Svitavy had obtained the right to supervise and control Jewish moneylenders as early as the 14th century, the first Jew in written town records was Jakob Donat in 1715. Jews were not allowed to reside in the town until 1848. After this date Jews moved to Svitavy from the Jevíčko and Boskovice areas and their numbers continued to grow. This growth was the impetus for the formation of a prayer congregation. In 1888 this congregation was transformed into a Jewish community under the administration of the Boskovice rabbinate. The community became independent in 1890 and the first rabbi appointed was Daniel Fink of Boskovice, who focused his efforts on building a synagogue for the 189 Jews registered in Svitavy in 1900.

The independent synagogue of the Svitavy Jewish community, from plans by Ernst Gotthilf, was consecrated on September 27, 1902, by Dr. Felix Kanter, a man who also played a role in the story of Oskar Schindler. Kanter lived near the Schindler family home in Jihlavská Street (today Poličská St). According to witnesses the young Oskar Schindler often played with the rabbi's children, a fact that may help explain Schindler's special relationship with Jews which, in the fury of the wartime period, blossomed into friendship.

Figure A6: Daniel Fink. Figure A7: Dr Felix Kanter
Photo Credit: Author's Collection

Figure A8: Independent Synagogue, Svitavy
Photo Credit: Author's Collection

The Nuremberg Laws

Upon taking power in 1933, Adolph Hitler used the anti-Jewish sentiment prevalent in Europe over the centuries for massive and targeted propaganda purposes. Jews were declared the "root of all evil" and this myth, along with the myth of the "superiority of the Aryan race," was elevated to the level of German state policy in two constitutional laws. These laws were announced by the Reichstag on September 15, 1935, in Nuremberg during a Nazi Party rally.

The first of these laws – The Reich Citizenship Law – established that only people of German blood or people with "related blood" could be Reich citizens. This meant German Jews were stripped of all civil rights. The second law – The Law for the Protection of German Blood and German Honor – prohibited marriages between Germans and Jews.

German Annexation of the Sudetenland October 1938

Figure A9: <u>Wehrmacht enter the Sudetenland</u> **October 1**
Photo Credit: Author's Collection

As part of the 5th occupation zone Svitavy was taken by German military units on October 10, 1938. The Germans crossed the border on October 1 but didn't enter Svitavy until the 10th. The occupation of the town received a thunderous welcome by throngs of citizens.
Celebrations climaxed the following day with a review of the assembled forces on the square.

As agreed, to in the Munich Agreement, the Wehrmacht began moving into the Sudetenland on October 1, where they were received with jubilation. The press in London published accounts of the jubilation of the Sudeten Germans along with photographs showing the cascade of flowers greeting the German soldiers. This is, of course, not what these peoples are cheering about; the emotional display is largely an outburst of nationalism and patriotism. The people in the images saw themselves being liberated and finally united with the German Reich. One of the Sudeten Germans impressed with the Nazis was a young Oskar Schindler.[321]

Occupation of Poland

On September 1, 1939, the German army invaded Poland and provoked the largest military conflict in the history of the world. Krakow was occupied by the 14th Wehrmacht Army on September 6 and the first anti-Jewish decrees were issued shortly thereafter. All Jewish shops, businesses, restaurants, and cafes were to be marked with the Star of David. The first 25 Jews were killed in the prison of St. Michael on September 13. Jewish doctors were permitted to treat only Jews and Jewish butcher shops were closed. Beginning October 26 all prayer rooms and synagogues were closed, and Jews were ordered to perform mandatory work on Saturdays. Krakow became the capital of the General Government – a part of divided Poland with a population of 12 million people. Thirty prisons and camps of various types were established in the city during the occupation and tens of thousands of people passed through these facilities. Between 1940 and 1945 a total of 210 trains with over 17,000 prisoners, including 2,400 women, departed from Krakow. No other city in Poland had so many Germans' living in it during the war – 10,000 police and SS forces alone were in Krakow at the beginning of 1940. The rest is history…

The Holocaust – 1935-1945

When the extermination camp at Auschwitz, Poland, was liberated by the Red Army on January 27, 1945, many people were still unaware that one of the most terrible and spine-chilling stories in the history of human civilization had occurred there and behind the barbed wire fences of other camps. The genocide of Jews, Roma, Slavs, and other groups deemed "inferior" by the Nazis involved over 11 million people, half of whom were murdered in concentration camps and ghettos. This period in history was designated as the Holocaust, or in Hebrew "Shoah," meaning disaster. Today, January 27th is commemorated around the world as International Holocaust Remembrance Day. In the Czech Republic this day is named Memorial Day for the Victims of the Holocaust and the Prevention of Crimes against Humanity.

The Final Solution

At the Wannsee Conference held on January 20, 1942, in suburban Berlin, a meeting convened by Reinhard Heydrich discussed the coordination and implementation of the genocide of European Jews. The genocide, **Endlösung,** or the final solution to the Jewish question, involved 11 million European Jews who were to be "displaced" to the East, where they were to receive "special treatment." Translated into real terms, this meant the continuation of the mass murder of Jews in extermination camps. At the beginning of 1942 the concentration camps in occupied Poland were renamed extermination camps. Names such as Auschwitz, Treblinka, Chelmno, Sobibor, Belzec and Maly Trostenets became synonymous with death and suffering.

The Nazi's pretense for legalizing the anti-Jewish measures in Germany was the assassination of Ernst vom Rath, a legation secretary at the German embassy in Paris, on November 7, 1938. The assassination provoked an outcry of emotion among Germans, resulting in an anti-Jewish pogrom, later named Kristallnacht. During the night of November 9-10, 1938, synagogues and prayer rooms were plundered, shops were ransacked, and tens of thousands of mainly wealthy Jews were shipped to concentration camps at Dachau, Buchenwald, and Sachsenhausen. Over 100 people were killed during the pogrom.

Kristallnacht, named after the shards of broken glass from windows and display cases reflecting the moonlight, continued in other locations of the Reich. In many towns of the occupied Sudetenland the pogrom continued the following days. Not even the Svitavy synagogue escaped the fury. On the morning of November 10, the building was surrounded by firemen who prevented the flames from spreading to adjacent buildings. Max Pirschl carried several Hebrew books from the burning synagogue and used the flyleaves of these volumes to keep a journal of the course of the Svitavy pogrom. The books are part of the museum collection today. The wreckage of the synagogue was soon removed, and a square was established in its place. The square was named Lübecker-Platz after the Wehrmacht regiment that occupied Svitavy in October 1939.

Appendix D: Schindler Timeline

Figure A10: Schindler Museum Office Montage
Photo Credit: Author's Collection

April 28, 1908 - Oskar Schindler is born in Svitavy (Zwittäu), an industrial city in Moravia, a province of the Austro-Hungarian Empire. Moravia is nestled between Bohemia in the north and Slovakia in the south. The region is also known as the Sudetenland.

August 1, 1914 - World War I begins. Austria-Hungary joins with Germany to fight France, Britain, Italy, and (in 1917) the United States.

November 11, 1918 - World War I ends with collapse of three empires: Russia, Germany, and Austria-Hungary. Moravia, which included Schindler's hometown of Svitavy, is detached from Austria and annexed by the new republic of Czechoslovakia. As a result of the war, several million Sudeten Germans find themselves a minority people in the new Czechoslovak state. Schindler is ten years old. Schindler attends German-language school –gymnasium – in Svitavy. Among his classmates and playmates are two Jewish boys, sons of the local rabbi.

1920s - Schindler works as salesman for his father's farm-machinery factory.

May, 1928 - Schindler races motorcycle, a Moto-Guzzi, in high class competition.

1928 - Schindler marries Emilie. His father disapproves of marriage, and apparently Schindler leaves his job working as a salesman as a result of a tiff. He becomes a salesman for Morovia Eklectric and travels to Poland on business.

January 30, 1933 - Hitler is appointed Reichs Chancellor in Germany.

1935 - Schindler family factory goes bankrupt. Oskar's parents separate. Schindler joins the pro-Nazi Henlein party in Czechoslovakia.

September 29, 1938 - Hitler meets British Prime Minister Chamberlain and French Premier Daladier in Munich, Germany. The western leaders step back before Hitler's threats of war and force the Czechoslovak government, an ally, to cede the Sudetenland to Nazi Germany. The Jews and Czechs of the Sudetenland were summarily expelled and their property confiscated. They fled to Prague and to the regions of the rump Czech state not yet occupied by the Nazis. That would come six months later.

Autumn 1938 - Schindler joins German military intelligence, Abwehr, under Admiral Canaris. As a salesman, Schindler travels to southern Poland and reports to Abwehr regarding points of military importance in Poland. His affiliation with Abwehr excuses Schindler from military service.

November 9, 1938 - Kristallnacht, The Night of Broken Glass: Throughout the Greater German Reich (Germany, Austria, and the Sudetenland), Nazi storm troopers smash and burn Jewish shops and synagogues. The glass littering the street in the aftermath gave the event its name, The Night of Broken Glass. Tens of thousands of Jewish men are arrested and sent to the concentration camp, Buchenwald.

March 15, 1939 - German troops occupy the rump state of Czechoslovakia and enter Prague to the gloom of the populace. Slovakia becomes a cooperative satellite of the Nazis. The Czech lands of Bohemia and Moravia are absorbed into the Reich and named the Reichs Protectorate of Bohemia and Moravia.

September 1, 1939 -German troops attack Poland. Three and a half million Jews live in Poland. The southern Polish city of Krakow, the ancient seat of Polish kings, is occupied on September 6, 1939. Oskar Schindler arrives shortly thereafter.

October 12, 1939 - The Nazis establish Krakow as the seat of their General Government of occupied Poland. Hans Frank, Hitler's lawyer, is designated Reichsfüehrer of Nazi-occupied Poland. He orders the "voluntary" departure of all but "work-essential" Jews from Krakow. After several months, the Germans take matters into their own hands and expel 32,000 Jews to Warsaw, Lodz, other Polish cities, and the nearby countryside. Schindler makes initial contact with Stern.

December 3, 1939 - Schindler informs Stern of an impending SS raid in the Jewish ghetto of Kazimierz, a suburb of Krakow. "Tomorrow, it's going to start," he said. "Jozefa and Izaaka Streets are going to know all about it!"

December 4, 1939 - SS Einsatzgruppen descend on Jewish ghetto at Kazimierz, a suburb of Krakow. They terrorize Jews on Jozefa and Izaaka Streets, searching for diamonds and gold, and then set fire to the synagogue of Stara Boznica, the oldest in Poland.

January 1940 - Schindler opens Deutsche Emailwaren Fabrik factory at 4 Lipowa Street in Krakow neighborhood of Zablocie.

April - June 1940 - Hitler attacks and conquers Western Europe.

August 1, 1940 - Hans Frank issues deadline for all but "work-essential" Jews to depart Krakow voluntarily. There is a mad scramble as Jews search for "essential" jobs. Through the urging of Stern, Schindler accepts 150 Jews as employees at his factory.

October 1940 - Hans Frank, in a speech, says, "My dear comrades, I would not eliminate all lice and Jews in one year (public amused, he notes in his diary), but in the course of time, and if you help me, this end will be attained."

November 1, 1940 - By this date, 23,000 Jews have been expelled from Krakow.

November 10, 1940 - Nazis issue decree: "All Jews and Jewesses over the age of nine through the General-Government must wear a four-inch arm band in white, marked with 'the star of Zion' on the right sleeve of their inner and outer clothing."

February 1941 - Two Krakow rabbis, Kornitzer and Rappaport, are sent to Auschwitz and killed for having protested the expulsions from Krakow.

March 20, 1941 - Jewish ghetto established in Krakow in neighborhood of Podgorze. As historian Lucy Dawidowicz has written, "The Krakow ghetto was enclosed within walls in the form of Jewish tombstones, symbols of a terrifyingly literal character." The Jewish police in the ghetto, the OD (or Ordnungsdienst), is formed.

June 22, 1941 - Hitler attacks the Soviet Union.

End of 1941 - Schindler is arrested by Gestapo for black market activities. He manages to be released by way of his high-ranking friends and bribery.

December 1941 - In a speech Hans Frank says, "As far as the Jews are concerned, I want to tell you quite frankly that they must be done away with in one way or another . . . .Gentleman, I must ask you to rid yourself of all feelings of pity. We must annihilate the Jews. Difficult to shoot or poison the three and half million Jews in the General-Government, but we shall be able to take measures which will lead, somehow, to their annihilation."

April 28, 1942 - Schindler's thirty-fourth birthday. He kisses a Jewish girl at his birthday party.

April 29, 1942 - Schindler arrested a second time, having been denounced as "a Jew kisser." He again wins his release.

June 1, 1942 - Beginning of first Krakow deportation to Belzec.

June 3, 1942 - Schindler goes to Krakow train station to rescue his office manager, Abraham Bankier, and other workers from deportation to Belzec. (In the film, Itzhak Stern is given the role of the rescued.)

June 4, 1942 – 7,000 Jews are deported from Krakow ghetto. In the afternoon, Schindler rents two horses and he and his mistress watch the SS's liquidation of ghetto from a nearby hill. Schindler becomes fixated on a little Jewish girl dressed in red who stands out from the crowd of Jews being herded to the train.

October 28, 1942 – 2,000 Jewish children and 6,000 Jewish adults are deported to Belzec death camp.

End of October 1942 - Six Jews killed in forests near Krakow, having been betrayed by local peasants.

Autumn 1942 - Schindler travels to Budapest, Hungary, to inform Jewish leaders there of the extermination campaign going on in Poland. In general, Hungarian leaders do not believe him. It is, says one, "an insult to German dignity."

Forced labor camps established at Plaszow, a suburb of Krakow. Amon Goeth is commandant.

December 22, 1942 - The Jewish Fighting Organization blows up several cafes in the heart of Krakow frequented by German officers. They are led by Jewish commander Adolf Liebeskind. "We are fighting for three lines in a history book," he said.

By **February 1943** - All members of the Jewish Fighting Organization in Krakow are arrested or killed.

March 13, 1943 - Final liquidation of Krakow ghetto begins.

March 14, 1943 - Several hundred small children shot in entrance of house, and several hundred old people and sick are killed in street. 2,000 Jews sent to Auschwitz-Birkenau. Children and old people are slaughtered at Jewish hospital. Dr. Zygmunt Fischer is ordered to abandon his patients, but he refuses and is shot with his wife and child. The patients are killed in the wards. Schindler establishes a Jewish sub-camp (a Julag) at his Emalia factory.

Spring 1944 - At Chujowa Gorka forest, Nazis unearth and burn bodies of Jews executed earlier. Jews await deportation to death camp, but Schindler goes to train station and arranges through Goeth for a fire brigade to spray the cattle cars with water.

July 20, 1944 - German officers attempt to assassinate Hitler. The effort fails.

Emalia factory ordered dismantled; the prisoners sent to Plaszow. Schindler plays a game of cards with Goeth for Helen Hirsch.

Autumn 1944 - Schindler prepares a "list" of Jews whom he argues are "essential" workers and are needed at his new factory in Czechoslovakia.

Schindler establishes factory at Brünnlitz, Czechoslovakia.

September 13, 1944 -Amon Goeth is arrested by the SS and charged with black market activities. 300 Schindlerjuden are sent to Auschwitz-

Birkenau instead of to Brünnlitz.

November 1944 - Schindler women are transferred from Auschwitz-Birkenau to Brünnlitz. Schindler greets them, "You're safe now; you're with me."

April 28, 1945 - Schindler's thirty-seventh birthday. He gives a speech.

May 8, 1945 - Schindlerjuden give Schindler gold ring. The gold is extracted from the bridge in a prisoner's mouth and engraved with the inscription: "He who saves a single life saves the entire world." Schindler and his wife, Emilie, both dressed in prison uniforms, flee the Russians in a Mercedes. They are accompanied by eight Schindlerjuden who are there to protect them. A letter written by the Jews testifies to Schindler and Emilie's actions.

May 11, 1945 - Brünnlitz camp is liberated by lone Russian officer on a horse.

September 13, 1946 - After a trial, Amon Goeth is hanged in Krakow.

1949 - Schindler departs Germany for Argentina to try his hand at a nutria factory.

1957 – Schindler's nutria farm goes bankrupt. B'nai B'rith purchases the Schindlers a house in San Vicente, a southern suburb of Buenos Aires.

1958 - Schindler returns to West Germany, leaving his wife and mistress behind. With funding from Joint Distribution Committee and "loans" from a number of Schindler Jews, Schindler establishes a cement company.

1961 – Schindler's cement factory goes bankrupt. Schindlerjuden invite Schindler to Israel. Eichmann trial is underway.

April 28, 1962 - Schindler is awarded honor Righteous Gentile.

October 9, 1974 - Schindler dies in Frankfurt, West Germany. He is buried at the Latin cemetery on Mount Zion in Jerusalem.

Appendix E: Schindler's Deeds and Legacy

1.   At the beginning of December 1939 Schindler warned Itzhak Stern of the SS plan to pillage the Kazimierz quarter and appropriate valuables and money.

2.   In mid-December 1939 Schindler protected Leon Bosak from arrest by the Gestapo due to the fact that his business had been taken over by administrator Karol Gomola, an acquaintance of Schindler's from Moravská Ostrava.

3.   Schindler saved many young Poles from being shipped to Germany to perform forced labor by employing many more people at Emalia than he actually needed.

4.   Schindler provided his workers food, clothing, and enamelware they could sell for money. Workers could buy food in a well-stocked factory canteen.

5.   Schindler managed to secure the release of Kessler from Auschwitz. The former director of the Commercial Bank in Krakow had Jewish ancestors.

6.   When Jozef Adam Skąpski fell ill, his mother asked Schindler, who rented a flat from her, to take the sick boy to the clinic in Koperníkova St. Schindler obliged, saving his life.

7.   Schindler secured release from Auschwitz of Mianowski, the director of the Krakow electric plant who had provided Schindler with a wagon of coke for firing enamel when the factory was launching operations. Schindler protected him until the end of the war.

8.   On October 27, 1942 Schindler warned his workers on the night shift of the planned SS raid on the ghetto. Schindler allowed the workers to spend the night on factory grounds, saving them from deportation to Belzec.

9.   Schindler gave his workers the same warning in March 1943 before the liquidation of the ghetto.

10.   Schindler saved several Polish workers from arrest by the Gestapo.

11.   He warned the Jews ahead of time of visits by Amon Goeth and informed Jews of planned inspections by SS officers at the camp. Schindler used alcohol and small gifts as bribes to prevent more thorough inspections by Nazi officials, thus eliminating the danger threatening his camp and prisoners.

12.   The Jewish assistance organizations JSS and JUS (1942-1943) functioned well at the camp. With Schindler's approval these groups provided condensed milk for the sick, health supplies, surgical tools, children's food, and disinfection agents.

13.   Schindler allowed the Zegota Jewish organization to deliver food and shoes to the sub-camp in Lipová St. (and later to Brünnlitz).

14.   Poles employed at Emalia helped Jews maintain contact with the city and exchange trade.

15.   Schindler gained approval to set up a sub-camp at Emalia. The sub-camp housed Jews from Schindler's factory and several surrounding businesses. Schindler spent 300,000 zloty of his own money to build an infirmary and camp facilities.

16.   Jewish workers at Emalia sent food to other sub-camps in Plaszow.

17.   Prisoners were not watched by guards during their work at Emalia. Schindler frequently intervened to help prisoners terrorized by the camp commander or guards.

18.   Not a single execution was recorded at the Emalia camp.

19.   Prisoners at Schindler's camp were not bullied as prisoners at the main camp were; Jews were able to maintain community life. Schindler permitted cultural performances on Sundays.

20.   Schindler had Jewish prisoner Feliks Kamiński, who had lost an eye at a previous camp, taken to the hospital, where a German doctor gave him a glass eye. This saved the prisoner's life during selections and Feliks Kamiński survived to gain his freedom upon the liberation of Brünnlitz.

21.　　At the request of his workers Schindler brought infirm prisoners – relatives of his workers – from the Plaszow camp to his sub-camp in Lipová St. At the request of Stern he employed Rabbi Jakob Lewertow. Schindler arranged meetings between Jews at Emalia and the caretakers of their children.

22.　　Schindler saved his prisoners who had been sent to their death – Romek Wohlfeiler, the Danziger brothers, Lamus, Jan Dresne, and the five members of the Wohlfeiler family.

23.　　Schindler saved 14 of his employees from transport wagons at the Prokocim station, including Abraham Bankier, Jerzy Reich, and Jakob Leser.

24.　　According to Chairman Michal Weichert, Oskar Schindler was one of the German informers who provided news of planned Nazi measures against Jews.

25.　　Personally or through the use of couriers Schindler sent the Jewish Defense Committee in Budapest information about the tragic fate of Jews in the General Government. Schindler distributed secret Hebrew letters concerning the situation and conditions in the Plaszow camp, deportations, and Nazi terror.

26.　　Schindler funneled financial support that arrived in 1942-1944 from Budapest.

27.　　He informed the Jewish Center in Istanbul about the situation of Jews.

28.　　Schindler cooperated with so-called "decent Germans" – Major von Kohrab (representative of the head of the Abwehr in occupied Poland and a secret collaborator with the Budapest central office), Julius Madritsch, Raymond Titsch, and Rudolf Sedlaczek from Vienna.

29.　　Schindler was taken into custody by the Gestapo three times, including on charges of "fraternization" with Jews and for accounting inconsistencies at his factory in 1942-1944.

30.　　He ordered train wagons holdings prisoners from his factory to be hosed down as they stood sealed at the Plaszow station on a steamy summer day.

31.　　At Brünnlitz Schindler housed prisoners directly in the factory building above the production hall, thus preventing them from being subjected to bullying by SS guards.

32.　　Schindler gained the release of 300 women on the list and ensured their safe passage to Brünnlitz.

33.　　Schindler obtained food for the Brünnlitz camp in cooperation with the neighboring Daubek Mill, whose director Schindler had known before the start of the war. Schindler brought weapons, clothes, and boots to the camp and organized the defense of the camp against potential SS aggression.

34.　　Schindler accepted refugees from other camps at Brünnlitz. He gave them food and clothing, saving them from death.

35.   Prior to the liberation of Krakow in 1945 he gave away money to his workers and clerks from Emalia, which was still in operation, to purchase food.

36.   On January 29, 1945 the stationmaster at the Svitavy train station informed Schindler that a sealed wagon with prisoners from Golleschau was standing at the station. Schindler arranged for the train to be taken to Brünnlitz. After being unsealed, 86 freezing Jews were carried out, 12 of whom had already perished. The remaining prisoners were treated at a provisional infirmary at Brünnlitz. Part of the small rations for the other prisoners was taken and Emilie Schindler gave the seriously ill Jews porridge and milk. Leipold, the commander of Brünnlitz, ordered the prisoners to begin work immediately, but Schindler argued that he paid large sums to the SS treasury – even for the sick. And despite the fact that there were no medications, clothes, beds, and food in the camp for another 74 people, Schindler took them in, took care of them, and saved their lives.

37.   Camp commander Leipold tried to liquidate the Brünnlitz camp, but Schindler managed to stop his plans and instead gave prisoners weapons for their defense.

38.   In April 1945 Schindler managed to have Leipold sent to fight at the front.

39.   Prior to fleeing the camp on May 8, 1945, Schindler gave each prisoner several meters of wool cloth and vodka. The prisoners were able to survive their first days of freedom by selling these goods.

40.   Schindler fled the camp on the night of May 8-9 accompanied by a group of his former prisoners. Before leaving he was given a letter testifying to the fact that he had saved the lives of many Jews at Brünnlitz.

Appendix F: Recollections

During World War II, millions of Jews died in the Nazi death camps, but Oscar Schindler's Jews miraculously survived Hitler's genocide. The boy **Moshe Rosenberg** was one of them.

In his book *The Boys - Triumph Over Adversity*, Sir Martin Gilbert tells how Moshe Rosenberg, then 16 years old, was being whipped one day at the KZ camp Plaszow by Nazi guards for daring to take a rest while road-building. After 25 lashes the whipping unexpectedly stopped. The boy looked up – and he saw Oscar Schindler. "I'll take care of this one," Schindler told the guards, and proceeded to drag the boy to a nearby stable.

Moshe Rosenberg later recalled: "Loud enough for the Germans to hear, he shouted, 'What's this shit?' Then he threw some food wrapped in paper and walked out. It was his way of smuggling food to the Jews. Without him stepping in, the guards would have beaten me until I was dead."

A few months later, while he was working in Schindler's factory DEF, Moshe Rosenberg sat down for a moment. At that very moment Schindler came in to the factory, followed by the SS Commandant Amon Goeth. Rosenberg later recalled how Schindler "raced ahead of Goeth, grabbed my jacket and slapped my face, shouting, 'Get back to work!' It was an act. Schindler never hit anyone or raised his voice. If Goeth had found me sitting down he would have shot me on the spot."

On another occasion a young Schindler-worker **Isak Pila** had made the mistake of falling asleep under a table at the factory the same day that Amon Goeth came by for an inspection. When Goeth saw the sleeping young man, he told Oscar Schindler to kill him instantly. Schindler desperately tried to find a way out and hit the boy on one side of the face, then the other. Finally he said to Goeth, "He's had enough. I need him. We've got a war to win. This can always be settled later."

Schindler's usual technique, but Amon Goeth complied – and Isak Pila survived.

In his book *Schindler's Ark* Keneally tells the story of the **Danziger brothers**, who cracked a metal press one Friday. Oscar Schindler was away on a business trip and someone denounced the brothers to Amon Goeth. They were immediately arrested and their hanging advertised in the next morning's roll call in Plaszow.

Oscar returned at three o'clock on Saturday afternoon, three hours before the execution. News of the sentence was waiting on his desk. He drove to the SS headquarters at once, taking cognac with him and some fine kielbasa sausage. He found Goeth in his office and no one knows the extent of the deal that was struck that afternoon. It is hard to believe that the SS Commandant was satisfied simply with cognac and sausage. In any case, he was soothed by Schindler, and at six o'clock, the hour of their execution, the Danziger brothers returned to Schindler's factory in the back seat of Oscar's plush limousine.

Poldek Pfefferberg was instrumental in publicizing the story of Oscar Schindler. He and his wife Ludmilla were saved by Schindler. The rest of his family was not as lucky; almost 100 perished, including his parents, sister, and brother-in-law.

One day, in November 1939, a man knocked on the door, and Pfefferberg thought it was the Gestapo. It wasn't. It was Oscar Schindler, a German businessman who had purchased an enamelware factory that had been confiscated from Jews. Schindler had come to ask Pfefferberg's mother, an interior designer, to redecorate his new apartment.

"I was hiding in the next room," Pfefferberg later said, "but listening to Schindler, I knew he wasn't Gestapo. Even then I could tell he was a good man. I began to talk to him and we became friends."

He began to work a little for Schindler, procuring rare commodities for him on the black market. In 1940, he met Ludmila Lewinson, and the two were married in the Krakow ghetto, where Jews were confined. They subsequently worked for Oscar Schindler in his factory.

Schindler promised the Jews who worked for him that they would never starve, that he would protect them as best he could. And he did, building his own workers barracks on the factory grounds to help alleviate the sufferings of life in the nearby Plaszow labor camp. He gave safe haven to as many Jewish workers as possible, insisting to the occupying Nazi officials that they were "essential" workers, a status that kept many from certain death.

"Oscar Schindler was a modern Noah," Pfefferberg said, "He saved individuals, husbands and wives and their children, families. It was like the saying: 'To save one life is to save the whole world.' Schindler called us his children. In 1944, he was a very wealthy man, a multimillionaire. He could have taken the money and gone to Switzerland .... He could have bought Beverly Hills. But instead, he gambled his life and all of his money to save us."

After the Liberation in May 1945, Poldek and Ludmila went first to Budapest and eventually to Munich where Poldek – a physical education instructor before the war – organized a school for displaced children. Oscar Schindler, too, had settled in Munich where his best friends, the people he regarded as "his children," were the Jews he had helped survive.

It was there, in the midst of a card game, that Poldek Pfefferberg made his promise, vowing he would tell the world what had happened, how even on the days when the air was black with the ashes from bodies on fire, there was hope in Krakow because Oscar Schindler was there. "You protect us, you save us, you feed us – we survived the Holocaust, the tragedy, the hardship, the sickness, the beatings, the killings! We must tell your story." Poldek Pfefferberg spent 40 years trying to drum up interest in the Schindler story – and the story was told so the whole world knew it by heart.

Mejzesz Puntierer – today Murray Pantirer – was the only one of his family to survive. He lost both his parents, two sisters, and four brothers during the war, all murdered by the Nazis.

He himself was saved because Oscar Schindler gave him work at his factory, provided him with food, and protected him from the Nazi reign of terror. Murray Pantirer later recalled the time a prisoner stole some potatoes. "An SS man put a potato in his mouth. He had to stand outside like that in the cold weather, and it was written on him, 'I'm a potato thief.' When Schindler saw it, he took the potato out of his mouth, and said to the guy, "Go back to your work." And he told the SS man, "In my camp you don't do those things."

During World War II **Abraham Zuckerman** spent his teenage years in Nazi concentration camps, never hearing about Oscar Schindler until he was sent as a worker to his factory, known as Emalia, at Plaszow in 1943.

"The moment that I arrived, I knew that my life had changed," Abraham Zuckerman later recalls. "There was food and mountains of potatoes. One never went hungry. The movie showed one thing, but there were other things that he did in camp, little things," says Zuckerman. "He was a chain smoker, so he used to take a puff and throw it away. For the survivors, the people who were smoking, it meant a lot to them to pick it up and have a puff. He would do it on purpose, knowing that people would pick it up."

He couldn't just give them cigarettes or extra food because there were Nazi guards in the factory who might squeal if they witnessed behavior deemed too humane; indeed, says Zuckerman, Schindler was arrested a couple of times because somebody reported him.

Despite the conditions, Oscar Schindler was always a perfect gentleman to the inmates, he says. "He bowed to you, and he said good morning to you," Zuckerman says, which may not sound like much of a favor, but to those beaten-down Jews, that small acknowledgement of their dignity gave them enormous hope.

Abraham Zuckerman has devoted himself to memorializing Oscar Schindler. Zuckerman published his memoirs in 1991. His *A Voice in the Chorus* is a moving and powerful addition to the library of works on the Holocaust.

Bronia Gunz spent World War II largely under Schindler's protection: first at Plaszow and later at the factory in Brünnlitz, Czechoslovakia.

She later recalled how Schindler told the prisoners to dig graves to deceive the Nazis. But he assured them he could save them and then he disappeared for days. "We were digging the graves and thinking, 'This is the end,'" Gunz said. Then Schindler returned. "One day this beautiful, gorgeous man shows up with a piece of paper, and he says, 'Saved, no digging anymore.'"

By 1944, when the workers on Schindler's list were transferred to Brünnlitz, their feelings of security were unshakeable. "Doubts? No, never!" insisted Bronia Gunz. "He was for us like God."

Rena Ferber, today Rena Finder, was only ten years old when the Nazis invaded Poland. Her father was killed at Auschwitz and she and her mother were sent to KZ Plaszow.

They began working at Emalia, Schindler's enamel and ammunition factory. The conditions in Schindler's factory were more humane than Rena and her mother would have encountered in any other circumstance during the war. She later recalled that Schindler "treated us with kindness and respect ... Schindler bribed Goeth and others to get food and better treatment for the Jews during a time when all Germans were killing the Jews."

She later told how a Nazi guard was about to shoot her for mistakenly breaking a factory machine, and Oscar Schindler intervened. "He said, 'You idiots, this little girl could not break that machine.'"

"He was wonderful," Rena said of Schindler: "He was tall and he was handsome and he had a twinkle in his eye. He was our hero and our God. How can you say thank you for someone who saved your life? I wish he were here today so I could hug him and kiss him."

She added, "I would not be alive today if it wasn't for Oscar Schindler, my mother survived and so did my grandfather. It's a tragedy that Oscar Schindler died young before the world could acknowledge his heroism. His countrymen considered him a traitor; to us he was our God, our Father, our protector.

In his book, *Witness The Making Of Schindler's List*, Franciszek Palowski tells about **Janina Olszewska**, who had worked for Oscar Schindler at his office and had known him well during World War II. She later told that Schindler not only saved Jews but also helped many Polish people.

When her husband was arrested and sentenced to death for his work with the Polish underground, Schindler miraculously got him out of the prison and thus saved his life.

Janina recalled once when a friend came to her in tears: the Nazis were taking her son to slave labor in Germany. She asked Schindler for help and he arranged the boy's release, employing him in his factory until the end of the war.

On another occasion an escaped Polish prisoner from Auschwitz showed up at Janina's. When Schindler was asked for help, he hired the man as his chauffeur.

Helen Beck, then Hela Brzeska, No. 18 on Schindler's List, was torn from her family as a teenager and was 15 when she was thrown into KZ Plaszow as a kitchen helper. She later recalled the SS Commandant Amon Goeth as being "incredible[*sic*] bloodthirsty – he would walk the line with his dogs and order them to rip people apart. And after a few minutes of torture, Goeth would shoot them in front of everyone."

At an evening line-up in Plaszow the Nazi guard smacked Helen so hard that the girl collapsed and the guard ordered her death. But she was spared, saved by Oscar Schindler as she suddenly was enlisted in his work forces.

Today, she still doesn't know how Schindler did it. But the next morning in Schindler's factory, the tall man with soft blue eyes and a Nazi lapel pin walked by her and said, "Just keep working, keep working."

Helen later recalled when she worked in the kitchen at one of Schindler's parties. At the end of the party, in front of some of the top Nazis, Schindler asked the Jewish servants to come out and take a round of applause for their hard work and good service. Scared, they came out and to their surprise, the drunken Nazis applauded them.

Only after the war, as Helen searched for her family, did she learn that she had lost six of her nine siblings, along with her parents. Helen Beck later said, "We gave up many times, but he always lifted our spirits ... Schindler tried to help people however he could. That is what we remember."

Anna Duklauer Perl had her name on Oscar Schindler's List – No. 76235, Anna Duklauer, Metallarbeiterin or metalworker, it says in German next to her name.

Long before Steven Spielberg ever heard of him and decided to make his movie, Oscar Schindler's name was kept nearly as close to Anna Duklauer Perl's heart as the names of her own children and grandchildren. For almost five decades, she never said much about the Holocaust or the salvation of becoming one of Schindler's Jews. She later said, "I just told them that without a man named Oscar Schindler, I wouldn't be here." But she didn't tell them the whole story until Spielberg's movie was made.

In 1942 Anna, barely 20 years old, was sent to the forced labor camp of Plaszow. Here the conditions of life were made dreadful by the SS Commandant Amon Goeth. She didn't think she would survive very long; she was beaten regularly and her life was almost unbearable.

Then one day in the laundry, in the spring of 1943, she was approached by a small Jewish man who told her he needed women to work in Oscar Schindler's factory. "I don't know why I was chosen that day," she later said. "It's a question I've asked myself hundreds and hundreds of times. Why me? Why was I chosen to live?" At first, Anna did not want to go and leave her sister Erna. "But she begged me. 'Go. With Schindler, there is life. You must go,'" Anna later said.

At Schindler's enamelware factory DEF Anna worked 12 hours a day, alternating her time between making pots and pans and working in the kitchen preparing meals. But she was away from harassment and the killings. At Schindler's factory, nobody was hit, nobody murdered, nobody sent to death camps. Anna Duklauer worked at Schindler's factory until the Liberation. "Schindler was a good man. You could tell that… Schindler and us grew together. And in the end, he gave away all his money," Anna later commented.

Over the years Anna heard bits of news about Oscar Schindler from others on "The List." Unloved and unrecognized at home, he reached for the bottle. He had become an alcoholic during the war and struggled to wean himself off the habit. "He was like in the movie," Anne said, "very handsome. A lady's man. And he had this huge ring. We used to say you could see him coming from the light of his ring."

She didn't remember the exact day, but it was sometime in 1974 when she heard that Oscar Schindler had died. "I think a little bit of us all died, too," she said. "If it weren't for Oscar Schindler, we wouldn't be here."

Another time at Schindler's factory, during an inspection by Amon Goeth and his SS officers, the attention of the visitors was caught by the sight of the old Jew, **Lamus**, who was pushing a barrow too slowly across the factory courtyard, apparently utterly depressed. Goeth asked why the man was so sad, and it was explained to him that Lamus had lost his wife and only child a few weeks earlier during the liquidation of the ghetto. Goeth ordered his adjutant Grün to execute the Jew "so that he might be reunited with his family in Heaven." Then he guffawed and the SS officers moved on.

Someone from the metal hall rushed up to Oscar Schindler's office and alerted him. Oscar came roaring down the stairs and reached the yard just as the SS man ordered Lamus, "Slip your pants down to your ankles and start walking." Dazed, the old man did as he was told.

Schindler called out desperately, "You can't do that. You are interfering with all my discipline." The SS officer just sneered. Schindler continued, blurting out the words, "The morale of my workers will suffer. Production for der Vaterland will be affected." The SS adjutant took out his pistol, ready to shoot.

"A bottle of schnapps if you don't shoot him," Schindler almost screamed, no longer thinking rationally. "Stimmt!" To Schindler' astonishment, the SS man complied. Grinning, the officer put the gun away and strolled arm in arm with the shaken Schindler to the office to collect his bottle of schnapps. And old Lamus, trailing his pants along the ground, continued shuffling across the yard, waiting sickeningly for the bullet in his back that never came.

On another occasion, three SS men walked onto the factory floor without warning, arguing among themselves. "I tell you, the Jew is even lower than an animal," one was saying. Then, taking out his pistol, he ordered the nearest Jewish worker to leave his machine and pick up some sweepings from the floor. "Eat it," he barked, waving his gun. The shivering man choked down the mess. "You see what I mean," the SS man explained to his friends as they walked away. "They eat anything at all. Even an animal would never do that."

Abraham Zuckerman spent five of his teenage years in Nazi KZ camps. He recalls Oscar Schindler this way. "There were SS guards but he would say 'Good morning' to you. He was a chain smoker and he'd throw the cigarette on the floor after only two puffs, because he knew the workers would pick it up after him. To me he was an angel. Because of him I was treated like a human being. And because of him I survived."

Sol Urbach was 15 years old when he was taken to the Plaszow concentration camp. He was one of the fortunate saved by being on Oscar

Schindler's list. For Sol Urbach, the Holocaust meant the death of almost his entire family. After the war he emigrated to the United States.

William Schanz, then **Zew Schanz,** was saved by Oscar Schindler. At the war's close Schanz was selected to accompany Schindler and his wife on a journey west, protecting them from Russian troops. Later Schanz moved first to France, then in 1949 to the United States, where he successfully entered the travel business, becoming chairman of Regency Cruises.

Three hundred women, all Schindler Jews, were deported in cattle cars to certain death in Auschwitz; among them Marianne, now **Manci Rosner.** Oscar Schindler got them released: the only shipment out of Auschwitz. When the women returned, Schindler met them in the courtyard. Surrounded by SS guards he gave them an unforgettable guarantee: " Now you are finally with me, you are safe now. Don't be afraid of anything." Manci Rosner said, "I am so thankful to Oscar Schindler. We never would have survived it."

Murray Pantirer lost both his parents, two sisters, and four brothers during the Holocaust. After the war he built up a great fortune as a magnate in the United States. He honored Schindler in his own special way. Every time a new town was planned and built, at least one street was named after Schindler. In New Jersey alone there are 21 Schindler Streets, and even a Schindler Plaza.

Edith Wertheim, then **Etka Liebgold,** recalls how 300 Schindler women were interned at Auschwitz. "One night they took us to the gas chamber. We were waiting the whole night. In the morning we found out: Schindler is here!" He had come to rescue them, bribing the Nazis to retrieve the women on his list and bring them back. Years later Oscar Schindler attended her wedding.

Ignacy Liebermann and his family were deported to the Krakow ghetto; upon the liquidation of the ghetto he was transferred to the Plaszow camp. He worked as a tailor in the uniform factory of the Righteous Gentile, Julius Madritsch, and was chosen by Oscar Schindler to be his personal tailor. He passed away in 1969.

Wiktor Lezerkiewicz, now Victor Lewis, was put on Schindler's List on page 2, No. 108. He considers it a miracle. He was electrician in Oscar Schindler's factory, though he knew absolutely nothing about the trade. He emigrated to the United States in 1949.

Leib Lejzon, today Leon Leyson , says he was "just a skinny kid" during World War II. But Oscar Schindler developed a fondness for him, nicknaming him "Little Leyson" and showing him many kindnesses, such as extra soup and bread. And when his vision began to blur from the factory work, he was excused from the night shift. The most important act was putting him on the final list. His two eldest brothers did not survive the war, but he, his parents, and brother and sister were saved by Oscar Schindler.

Amon Goeth's maid **Helena Hirsch** was saved by Oscar Schindler from a life of terror and humiliation and certain death in the Auschwitz death camp. He outwitted the commandant of Plaszow, Goeth, and "won" her in a card game. Today she lives in Israel.

Hela Brzeska, today Helen Beck, was 15 when she was thrown into Goeth's camp a kitchen help. She describes Goeth as being "incredible bloodthirsty - he would walk the line with his dogs and order them to rip people apart. And after a few minutes of torture, Goeth would shoot them in front of everyone ..."

Kuba and Helen Beck, No. 18 and No. 611 on Schindler's List – both were torn from their families as teenagers and sent to the Plaszow concentration camp. In 1944, Helen was among 300 women routed to Auschwitz. She miraculously was rescued by Schindler. Only after the war, as she searched for her family, did she learn that she had lost six of her nine siblings, along with her parents.

Appendix G: Lists

1. The Davar List

The first authentic Schindler's List was compiled by Director Oskar Schindler on September 5, 1944, in Krakow: the Davar List. This list contains 202 names selected by Schindler for transfer to the Newe Kuhler Fabrik – NKF, a factory where refrigerators and aircraft parts were manufactured.

The original list, written in Hebrew, was taken by Schindler on a clandestine visit to Hungary where he met influential Zionist sympathizers. Schindler acquainted the world with what was going on in Poland at that time. This is a unique document.

Serial No.	Surname	First Name	Year Born
1	ABRAHAMER	Yacov	1918
2	ANFANG	Perec	1923
3	ASPITZ	Josef	1908
4	BADER	Chaim	1921
5	BADER	Siga	1902
6	BAND	Eduard	1919
7	BAUMANN	Jacov	1897
8	BERGER	Alter	1924
9	BERGLEISEN	Mendel	1922
10	BLAWAT	Eliezer	1895
11	BLINDERMANN	Wolf	1912
12	BRANDSTATER	Asher	1925
13	BIRNBAUM	Aron	1914
14	BIRNBAUM	Izak	1921
15	BUKIET	Alter Simon	1918
16	CELNIK	Markus	1913
17	CUCKIER	Mordechai	1919
18	CUCKIER	Naftali	1903
19	DEBINSKI	Marek	1925
20	DORNSTEIN	Leo	1919
21	DREIER	Serel	1925
22	DRESNER	Meir	1918

Serial No.	Surname	First Name	Year Born
23	EINTIN	Josef	1916
24	EISENBERG	Abraham	1905
25	ENGLARD	Chanoch	1915
26	EPSTEIN	Abraham	1921
27	EPSTEIN	Shebs	1905
28	FALK	Norbert	1906
29	FAURER	Chaim	1921
30	FAUST	Josef	1896
31	FEIGENBAUM	Milech	1923
32	FEIGENBLATT	Izak	1903
33	FEIGENBLATT	Kalman	1905
34	FELDSTEIN	Josef	1894
35	FELER	Lipa	1912
36	FERBER	Mieczyslaw	1925
37	FEULDICZ	Alter	1900
38	FORSTER	David	1914
39	FRANCUZ	Fishel	1923
40	FRAUMAN	Josef	1912
41	FRENKEL	Mozes	1911
42	FRENKEL	Osiasz	1905
43	FRAUNDLICH	Izak	1923
44	FRIEDNER	Yoachim	1924
45	GARTNER	Jonas	1927
46	GEMEINER	Efraim	1898
47	GESUNDHEIT	Leib	1919
48	GLASS	Josef	1890
49	GLEITMANN	Asher	1905
50	GOLDBERG	Joszua	1903
51	GOTTLEIB	Naftali	1927
52	GRUNER	Hirsch David	1905
53	GRUNER	Yacov	1928

Serial No.	Surname	First Name	Year Born
54	GUTENBERG	Mendel	1925
55	GUTMAN	Abraham	1896
56	GUTMAN	Mozes	1922
57	GUTMAN	Natan	1925
58	HAFTER	Yeshayahu	1926
59	HAUBESTOCK	Nechemia	1898
60	HAUSTOCK	Beniamin	1922
61	HELLER	Salomon	1899
62	HERNDORF	Eliza	1911
63	HERZOG	Gershon Chaim	1912
64	HILFSTEIN	Yoel	1907
65	HIRSCHPRUNG	Adolf	1928
66	HIRSCHPRUNG	Izak	1909
67	HIRSCHPRUNG	Moritz	1924
68	JASKIEL	Abrahan	1908
69	JUDA	Abraham	1905
70	JUNGWIRTH	Israel	1910
71	JUNGWIRTH	Natan	1906
72	KAHN	Sasha	1914
73	KATZ	Abraham	1906
74	KIRSCHNER	Arthur	1915
75	KLAGSBRUN	?	1918
76	KLEIN	Hillel	1923
77	KLEINER	Chaim	1907
78	KLEINER	Natan	1924
79	KLESSNER	Josef	1928
80	KOHN	Joachim	1907
81	KOHN	Moniek	1906
82	KORBER	Leizer Lew	1907
83	KRAUSS	Jakov	1904
84	KRONFELD	Nuta	1912

Serial No.	Surname	First Name	Year Born
85	KUHN	Moritz	1904
86	LAUFER	Sol	1920
87	LEHRFELD	Shimon	1922
88	LEHRFELD	Wilhelm	1925
89	LERNER	Mieczyslaw	1905
90	LEWIT	Mordachai	1920
91	LEWIT	Mozes	1914
92	LICHTENSOHN	Henryk	1921
93	LICHTENSOHN	Gershon	1905
94	LITMANOWICZ	Salomon	1915
95	LOFFELHOLZ	Chezkel	1912
96	LUSTGARTEN	Karol	1897
97	LUSTGARTEN	Rishard	1924
98	MANDELBAUM	Meir	1920
99	MANDELBAUM	Mendel	1924
100	MARKOWICZ	Israel	1909
101	MEER	Jacov	1916
102	MEITLIS	Israel	1897
103	MILLER	Lipman	1918
104	MOLLER	Shaul	1926
105	MONDSCHEIN	Binem	1918
106	MOTLECZ	Izak	1922
107	NADEL	Leon	1889
108	NESSEL	Salomon	1924
109	NEUMAN	Yeshayahu	1894
110	NIEBELSKI	Rubin	1917
111	PARNASS	Israel	1916
112	PECHNER	Susman	1897
113	PECHNER	Wolf	1928
114	PERELKA	Szulin	1898
115	PERLMANN	Naftali	1891

Serial No.	Surname	First Name	Year Born
116	PERLMUTER	Leon	1910
117	PERLROTH	Abraham	1927
118	PILLER	Melech	1925
119	PILLER	Salomon	1914
120	PILLER	Samuel	1920
121	PINELES	Maksymilian	1921
122	PINKASOWICKI	Jacov	1912
123	PIRLOCZ	Aron	1926
124	PRZECHADZKI	Israel	1914
125	RABER	Pinkas	1913
126	RATZ	Chaim	1923
127	RATZ	Fiewel	1920
128	REISMAN	Jacov	1915
129	RIGER	Mendel	1927
130	RILS	Natan	1925
131	RITTER	Izydor	1911
132	RITTER	Simcha	1907
133	ROSENBAUM	Dawid	1926
134	ROSENBAUM	Hersch	1925
135	ROSENBERG	Motek	1921
136	ROSENFELD	Moris	1924
137	ROSENHAHN	Samuel	1925
138	ROZENWIEG	Naftali	1923
139	ROTTBERG	Moris	1908
140	SARNA	Yonka	1921
141	SCHEINER	Shmul	1897
142	SCHELLER	Abraham	1920
143	SCHENIRER	Tolo	1927
144	SCHIMEL	Aleksander	1927
145	SCHIPPER	Salomon	1912
146	SCHLOSSEL	Abraham	1914

Serial No.	Surname	First Name	Year Born
147	SCHMALZ	Aron Josef	1897
148	SCHNUPFTABAK	Leon	1902
149	SCHNUR	Moris	1907
150	SCHONWETTER	Dawid	1912
151	SCHUMACHER	Kalman	1912
152	SCHWARZBAUM	Dawid	1910
153	SCHWARZMEER	Leib	1921
154	SILBERSTEIN	Abraham	1909
155	SILBIGER	Gerad	1923
156	SINGER	Henryk	1903
157	SKAMSKI	Jacov	1921
158	SPIEGEL	Melech	1912
159	SPIEGEL	Yechiel	1913
160	SPINNER	Chaim	1890
161	STEPLER	Jacov	1912
162	STILL	Eliasz	1912
163	STOPNICKI	Salomon	1923
164	SWASCHKENTIL	Dawid	1909
165	SZAWSZOWSKI	Israel	1921
166	TEITELBAUM	Abraham	1916
167	TEITELBAUM	Dawid	1913
168	TEITELBAUM	Dawid	1917
169	TEITELBAUM	Josef	1920
170	TEITELBAUM	Menachem	1918
171	TUSS	Hirsch	1911
172	UNGER	Meir	1898
173	UNGER	Mozes	1928
174	UNTERMANN	Abraham	1933
175	WASSERMAN	Baruch	1925
176	WASSERMAN	Jacov	1905

Serial No.	Surname	First Name	Year Born
177	WEIGEL	Maksymilian	1914
178	WEINER	Yechiel	1919
179	WEINREB	Ada	1926
180	WEINSTEIN	Hersch	1919
181	WEINSTEIN	Yechiel	1895
182	WEISS	Aron	1918
183	WEISS	Chaim	1915
184	WEISS	Jozua	1908
185	WENZELBERG	Moris	1919
186	WERDIGER	Dawid	1920
187	WERTHAL	Bernard	1922
188	WERTHAL	Josef	1927
189	WERTHEIMER	Henryk	1906
190	WIENER	Natan	1903
191	WOLFMAN	Adolf	1921
192	WOLFMAN	Jacov	1913
193	WOLFMAN	Salomon	1935
194	WORTMANN	Leon	1894
195	WORTMANN	Moris	1926
196	WURZEL	Anselm	1924
197	WURZEL	Moris	1926
198	WURZEL	Stefan	1927
199	ZAHN	Asher	1917
200	ZOLLMAN	Max	1923
201	ZOLLMAN	Mozes	1911
202	ZUCKER	Israel	1906

2. Julius Madritsch List

The exact lettering details may vary due to smudging by the typewriter keys on the original document. Prisoner number was allocated within the Madritsch factory complex. There were approximately 10,000 prisoners.

Men

Serial No.	Surname	First Name	Prisoner No.
1	BERENHAUT	Josef	6950
2	FEIGENBAUM	Jakub	7414
3	FEIGENBAUM	Ludwik	7415
4	HUDES	Leib	7105
5	KARP	Izaak-Szyja	7114
6	LEWI	Dawid	7168
7	OBERFELD	Adolf	7122
8	STERN	Natan	240
9	WOHLFEILER	Ignacy	7365
10	HUDAS	Naftali	7106
11	HUDE	Isak	4119
12	KINSTLINGER	Moses	3600
13	GRUSS	Abraham	7416
14	GOLDSTEIN	Bernard	7068
15	SALPETER	Leib	3940
16	TAUBE	Maksymilian	7341
17	TAUBE	Emanuel	7340
18	SEGAL	Chaim	7295
19	KINSTLINGER	Joachim	7149
20	LIEBERMANN	Ignacy	7174
21	LIEBERMANN	Maurycv	7175

Serial No.	Surname	First Name	Prisoner No.
22	LAMENSDORF	Leib	7151
23	WINSTOCK	Josef	11290
24	WEINSTOCK	Manek	11292
25	WEINSTEIN	Barel	7379
26	TILLES	Jakub	7350
27	WACHTEL	Chaim	4216
28	KISEN	Kiwa	7013
29	STERNBERG	Jakub	7325
30	STERNBERG	Jerzy	7326
31	GOLDSTEIN	Adolf	7067
32	KLINGENHOLE	Aron	7128
33	GRUN	Abraham	7073
34	GOLDSMIED	Aron	7066
35	HERZ	Ludwik	7095
36	ZIMET	Dawid	3520
37	SPERBAR	Chaim	7315
38	SCHLESINGER	Moses	7280
39	SCHLESINGER	Chaskel	77274
40	KRIEGER	Chaskel	7143

Women

Serial No.	Surname	First Name	Prisoner No.
1	FEIGENBAUM	Necha	8044
2	FEIGENBAUM	Janina	8045
3	HUDES	Estera	2256
4	KARP	Fajga-Raca	8088
5	KARP	Celina	8087
6	LEWI	Adela	8105
7	LIEBERMANN	Salomea	1022
8	STERN	Leontyn	2589
9	WOHLFEILER	Rosa	8022
10	WOHLFEILER	Halina	8020
11	WOHLFEILER	Rena	8021
12	REICHAR	Bluma	8126
13	KINSTLINGER	Chana	2289
14	LAWINSKA	Natalia	8107
15	ZWETSCHKENSTIL	Jenta	8076
16	WEINSTOCK	Balka	11211
17	GAMS	Genia	2453
18	TILLES	Tanba	367
19	STERNBERG	Klara	685
20	SCHLESINGER	Maria	8450

3. Brünnlitz List

Men

Alphabetized by Surname: * indicates the person is referred to in the text

Gross-Rosen KL Brünnlitz/Liste D. Mannl. Haftlinge-18.4.45

Ldf Nr.	H.Art. U.Nat.	H.No	Vorname	Name	Geburts Datum
226	Ju.Po.	69061	Abramoczyk	Szyja	15.09.17
271	Ju.Po.	69109	Abusch	Jos	28.10.12
264	Ju.Po.	69102	Abzug	Emanuel	10.06.04
269	Ju.Po.	69107	Adler	Alexander	25.08.23
241	Ju.Po.	69077	Allerhand	Salo	15.06.28
244	Ju.Po.	69081	Altmann	Dawid	09.05.17
182	Ju.Po.	69016	Ameizen	Josef	16.08.06
209	Ju.Po.	69044	Anglister	Mojzecz	25.01.21
219	Ju.Po.	69054	Ankier	Chaskiel	03.02.16
232	Ju.Po.	69068	Apfel	Moses	17.08.08
216	Ju.Po.	69051	Appel	Fryderyk	15.01.17
596	Ju.Po.	69453	Armer	Jakob	18.09.25
230	Ju.Po.	69066	Auerbach	Abraham	11.10.14
255	Ju.Po.	69093	Ausubel	Dawid	31.03.09
272	Ju.Po.	69110	Baldinger	Izak	11.11.22
222	Ju.Po.	69057	Balicki	Abraham	15.06.03
251	Ju.Po.	69089	Balsam	Salomon	04.04.03
227	Ju.Po.	69062	Bankier	Abraham	03.04.10
421	Ju.Po.	69268	Bankier	Abraham	09.05.95
41	Ju.Po.	68865	Baral	Samuel	26.10.04
228	Ju.Po.	69063	Barth	Eliasz	04.10.06
236	Ju.Po.	69072	Barth	Nysen	17.11.04
718	Ju.Dt	77102	Barush	Siegfried	03.05.01
247	Ju.Po.	69084	Bau	Josef	18.06.20
523	Ju.Po.	69379	Bauer	Josef	12.12.09
253	Ju.Po.	69091	Baum	Juliusz	17.10.07
268	Ju.Po.	69106	Baum	Naftali	11.09.13
256	Ju.Dt	69094	Beck	Friedrich	25.06.86

Ldf Nr.	H.Art. U.Nat.	H.No	Vorname	Name	Geburts Datum
611	Ju.Po.	69468	Beck	Kuba	31.08.22
242	Ju.Po.	69078	Beckmann	Samuel	12.07.21
258	Ju.Po.	69096	Beder	Fischel	15.06.14
246	Ju.Po.	69083	Beer	Alter	11.11.11
238	Ju.Po.	69074	Beer	Chaim	15.06.13
235	Ju.Po.	69071	Beer	Hirsch	28.02.21
617	Ju.Po.	69474	Begleiter	Stefan	06.04.25
301	Ju.Po.	69142	Behrenhaut	Josef	06.06.99
529	Ju.Po.	69385	Bejski	Izrael Berek	02.03.18
531	Ju.Po.	69387	Bejski	Moszek	01.01.21
528	Ju.Po.	69384	Bejski	Urysz	14.06.24
719	Ju.Ung	77103	Berger	Adolf	29.03.09
262	Ju.Po.	69100	Berger	Chaim	01.03.10
565	Ju.Po.	69422	Berger	Josek	15.07.25
183	Ju.Po.	69017	Berger	Majer	19.07.07
458	Ju.Po.	69307	Berger	Wladyslaw	17.05.26
266	Ju.Po.	69104	Berlinerblau	Lewi	25.12.99
270	Ju.Po.	69108	Bialywlos	Alexander	04.06.23
83	Ju.Po.	68913	Bieberstein	Alexander	01.08.95
3	Ju.Po.	68823	Biedermann	Hirsch	07.09.25
606	Ju.Po.	69463	Biedermann	Max	18.01.13
229	Ju.Po.	69065	Bierer	Jakob	17.02.08
252	Ju.Po.	69090	Binder	Alter	21.03.06
208	Ju.Po.	69043	Birnbaum	Juda	22.11.09
192	Ju.Po.	69026	Birnfeld	Markus	24.01.04
20	Ju.Po.	68841	Birnhack	Ignazy	17.02.17
233	Ju.Po.	69069	Birnzweig	Simche	10.06.15
190	Ju.Po.	69024	Bittersfeld	Leon	12.03.28
6	Ju.Po.	68826	Blammer	Jakob	04.05.15
223	Ju.Po.	69058	Blasenstein	Henryk	29.10.25
220	Ju.Po.	69055	Blatt	Aczer	09.09.20

Ldf Nr.	H.Art. U.Nat.	H.No	Vorname	Name	Geburts Datum
276	Ju.Po.	69114	Blatt	Henryk	31.50.22
275	Ju.Po.	69113	Blaufeder	Jakob	12.08.09
261	Ju.Po.	69099	Blecheisen	Mendel	01.06.06
688	Ju.Po.	77001	Blechmann	Hermann	12.12.26
44	Ju.Po.	68868	Bleiweib	Efroim	23.12.06
201	Ju.Po.	69035	Blum	Icek	12.02.04
199	Ju.Po.	69033	Blum	Markus	20.10.20
188	Ju.Po.	69022	Blum	Mozes	14.08.96
534	Ju.Po.	69390	Blumenfrucht	Hersz	17.04.17
196	Ju.Po.	69030	Blumenkranz	Adolf	12.12.97
720	Ju.Ung	77105	Bolaczy	Tibor	25.07.18
721	Ju.Po.	77106	Borenstein	Josef Hilel	01.09.98
360	Ju.Po.	69207	Borger	Adolf	02.08.96
722	Ju.Dt	77107	Borger	Michael	25.12.97
605	Ju.Po.	69462	Borger	Viktor	04.01.01
200	Ju.Po.	69034	Bossak	Mark	21.05.12
248	Ju.Po.	69085	Bottner	Mojzesz	02.05.18
331	Ju.Po.	69176	Brambrot	Szmul	12.05.25
265	Ju.Po.	69103	Bramm	Rafael	09.06.25
159	Ju.Po.	68992	Brandeis	Josef	19.07.01
254	Ju.Po.	69092	Bratkiewicz	Natan	08.07.11
723	Ju.Ung	77108	Brauer	Natan	06.06.01
218	Ju.Ung	69053	Braun	Moritz	24.06.03
259	Ju.Po.	69097	Brauner	Jerzy	23.07.26
661	Ju.Po.	69520	Brautmann	Henryk	20.10.00
795	Ju.Fr	77190	Brayntich	Josef	24.03.04
496	Ju.Po.	69350	Brechner	Rudolf	06.11.01
239	Ju.Po.	69075	Brenner	Adolf	6.05.25
195	Ju.Po.	69029	Bres	Moszek	15.08.13
789	Ju.Po.	77182	Breslauer	Benjamin	07.02.20
724	Ju.Tsc	77109	Brock	Robert	04.09.16
224	Ju.Po.	69059	Brodor	Markus	08.02.21

Ldf Nr.	H.Art. U.Nat.	H.No	Vorname	Name	Geburts Datum
240	Ju.Po.	69076	Bronner	Leopold	16.02.00
225	Ju.Po.	69060	Brotmann	Chaim	27.01.11
499	Ju.Po.	69353	Buchen	Moses	25.11.06
725	Ju.Dt	77100	Buchhalter	Fritz	09.00.28
257	Ju.Po.	69095	Buchsbaum	Jakob	03.04.21
380	Ju.Po.	69227	Butfuhrer	Norbert	12.06.22
70	Ju.Po.	68896	Cajg	Szmul	13.08.20
194	Ju.Po.	69028	Chajkin	Chaskiel	15.11.10
798	Ju.Po.	77193	Chewel	Hirsch	26.08.14
170	Ju.Po.	69003	Chiel	Pinkas	12.05.22
800	Ju.Po.	77195	Chlebowiski	Josef	05.12.22
614	Ju.Po.	69471	Chojna	Moniek	01.01.22
622	Ju.Po.	69479	Danzig	Hirsch	29.12.09
245	Ju.Po.	69082	Danziger	Eduard	16.02.09
658	Ju.Dt.	69517	Davidowitsch	Erwin	15.07.97
726	Ju.Hol	77101	Davidson	Jakob	01.09.17
577	Ju.Po.	69434	Degen	Leopold	19.02.25
352	Ju.Po.	69199	Dembitzer	Teodor	04.10.97
727	Ju.Ung	77102	Desci	Peter	13.02.23
340	Ju.Po.	69185	Deutelbaum	Samuel	25.04.2
629	Ju.Po.	69486	Dienstag	Markus	23.02.15
635	Ju.Po.	69493	Diktorczyk	David	25.02.09
393	Ju.Po.	69240	Domb	Izrael`	23.01.08
285	Ju.Po.	69124	Dortheimer	Wigdor	16.09.18
263	Ju.Po.	69101	Dreiblatt	Majer	21.05.09
297	Ju.Po.	69136	Dresner	Jonas	04.09.23
300	Ju.Po.	69141	Dresner	Juda	26.03.93
211	Ju.Po.	69046	Dressler	Joachim	14.07.95
597	Ju.Po.	69454	Dressler	Keinz	22.10.19
277	Ju.Po.	69115	Dringer	Dawid	18.10.21
592	Ju.Rus	69449	Drisin	Chaim	22.70.22
709	Ju.Po.	77022	Drzeboznik	Abraham	01.04.20

Ldf Nr.	H.Art. U.Nat.	H.No	Vorname	Name	Geburts Datum
207	Ju.Rus	69042	Dubnikow	Eli	28.07.23
76	Ju.Po.	68903	Eckstein	Chaskel	14.12.08
728	Ju.Ung	77103	Eckstein	Jgnaz	12.03.00
543	Ju.Po.	69400	Ehrlich	Hirsch	07.03.17
191	Ju.Po.	69025	Ehrlich	Samuel	01.09.04
206	Ju.Po.	69041	Eichenholz	Szyja	20.01.25
588	Ju.Po.	69445	Eichental	Meier	12.05.21
398	Ju.Po.	69245	Eidner	Pinkus	20.12.14
552	Ju.Po.	69409	Eilberg	Bernard	27.07.11
92	Ju.Po.	68923	Eintrecht	Alexander	02.03.06
486	Ju.Po.	69340	Eisen	Kiwa	02.05.93
234	Ju.Po.	69070	Eisenberg	Georg	06.06.06
729	Ju.Ung	77104	Eisenstein	Aron	20.04.14
630	Ju.Po.	69487	Eisland	Jakob	10.09.09
212	Ju.Po.	69047	Ejbuczyc	Fiszel	08.11.20
197	Ju.Po.	69031	Elefant	Wolf	18.08.08
434	Ju.Po.	69283	Elsner	Adolf	30.01.02
450	Ju.Po.	69299	Elsner	Ludwig	30.05.21
730	Ju.Hol	77105	Emden	Louis van	06.07.15
731	Ju.Ung	77106	Emmerien	Karol	23.07.11
217	Ju.Po.	69052	Essig	Michal	23.11.13
214	Ju.Po.	69049	Essig	Mojzesz	02.08.17
181	Ju.Po.	69015	Ettinger	Henryk	02.12.22
180	Ju.Po.	69014	Ettinger	Michal	10.07.13
689	Ju.Po.	77002	Ettinger	Moritz	29.11.12
653	Ju.Po.	69512	Eule	Isidor	14.01.12
690	Ju.Po.	77003	Ewenschn	Jakob	07.04.19
193	Ju.Po.	69027	Faber	Hirsch	05.06.07
594	Ju.Po.	69451	Falk	Israel	03.04.04
559	Ju.Po.	69416	Federgrun	Moses	10.04.12
550	Ju.Po.	69407	Feeitag	Leizon	25.11.04
305	Ju.Po.	69146	Feigenbaum	Jakob	08.12.00

Ldf Nr.	H.Art. U.Nat.	H.No	Vorname	Name	Geburts Datum
298	Ju.Po.	69137	Feigenbaum	Ludwig	28.11.24
639	Ju.Po.	69497	Feil	Oskar	29.10.01
618	Ju.Po.	69475	Feiler	Abraham	23.01.21
620	Ju.Po.	69477	Feiler	Salomon	09.03.23
358	Ju.Po.	69205	Feilgut	Aron	28.06.06
575	Ju.Po.	69432	Feinberg	Chaim	05.01.25
400	Ju.Po.	69247	Feiner	Josef	16.05.15
401	Ju.Po.	69248	Feiner	Wilhelm	21.10.17
691	Ju.Dt.	77004	Feingersch	Benjamin	17.12.25
626	Ju.Po.	69483	Feit	Lazar	25.04.13
146	Ju.Po.	68979	Feldmann	Herman	02.11.16
80	Ju.Po.	68908	Feldstein	Wolf	08.12.23
693	Ju.Po.	77006	Felsenstein	Selig	14.04.06
316	Ju.Po.	69160	Ferber	Arje	15.07.81
641	Ju.Po.	69499	Ferber	Israel	13.07.99
598	Ju.Po.	69455	Fertig	Chaim	17.02.24
733	Ju.Ung	77108	Feuermann	Bernard	10.11.93
734	Ju.Ung	77109	Feuermann	Sandor	01.06.27
556	Ju.Po.	69413	Figowicz	Pejsach	21.06.13
670	Ju.Po.	69655	Filzmacher	Mendel	29.10.14
601	Ju.Po.	69458	Finder	Maurycy	23.06.07
692	Ju.Po.	77005	Finkelstein	Leo	11.03.22
625	Ju.Po.	69482	Fischer	Ismar	12.11.05
580	Ju.Po.	69437	Fischgrund	Leopold	26.12.01
647	Ju.Po.	69505	Fleischmann	Chaim	15.11.06
636	Ju.Po.	69494	Flint	David	22.01.06
637	Ju.Po.	69495	Flint	Hersz	30.12.04
507	Ju.Po.	69362	Florenz	Benzion	13.04.14
509	Ju.Po.	69364	Fluss	Izak	14.01.01
732	Ju.Ung	77107	Foldesz	Sander	14.09.98
735	Ju.Ung	77120	Forkos	Hermann	28.11.99
736	Ju.Ung	77121	Frankel	Adolf	22.12.13

Ldf Nr.	H.Art. U.Nat.	H.No	Vorname	Name	Geburts Datum
623	Ju.Po.	69480	Frankel	Salomon	03.04.22
789	Ju.Hol	77183	Franken	Fritz	10.08.06
631	Ju.Po.	69488	Frei	Moses	18.01.25
581	Ju.Po.	69438	Freihof	Fischel	04.12.02
584	Ju.Po.	69441	Freimann	Anschel	06.10.23
249	Ju.Po.	69086	Freimann	Leib	01.07.05
571	Ju.Po.	69428	Freinof	Josek	05.05.24
564	Ju.Po.	69421	Freitag	Hersz	07.01.20
569	Ju.Po.	69426	Freitag	Mendel	01.10.22
624	Ju.Po.	69481	Friad	Fiszel	13.07.02
595	Ju.Po.	69452	Friemann	Bronislaw	23.10.17
737	Ju.Ung	77122	Fried	Josef	24.04.98
287	Ju.Po.	69126	Friedmann	Leon	27.04.09
608	Ju.Po.	69465	Friedmann	Pinkus	16.02.16
738	Ju.Ung	77124	Friedmann	Rudolf	01.12.28
633	Ju.Po.	69491	Friedner	Lobl	12.01.97
638	Ju.Po.	69496	Frisch	Samuel	21.04.01
81	Ju.Po.	68911	Frunnel	Leon	21.08.05
187	Ju.Po.	69021	Fuchs	Dawid	21.08.24
560	Ju.Po.	69417	Fuhrmann	Efroim	20.12.17
787	Ju.Dt	77181	Galinzki	Erich	17.04.22
615	Ju.Po.	69472	Gangel	Maurycy	17.07.09
656	Ju.Po.	69515	Garde	Adam	24.09.13
336	Ju.Po.	69181	Garde	Dawid	22.12.01
649	Ju.Po.	69508	Garde	Mieczyslaw	14.01.21
165	Ju.Po.	68998	Garfunkiel	Majlech	23.02.22
694	Ju.Po.	77007	Gartner	Meier	14.06.22
329	Ju.Po.	69174	Geiger	Lemel	27.06.05
685	Ju.Po.	74684	Gelbwerth	Aron	06.06.02
296	Ju.Po.	69135	Geller	Motio	16.12.08
417	Ju.Po.	69264	Gerstner	Leib	16.10.12
366	Ju.Po.	69213	Gewelbe	Jakob	22.09.97

Ldf Nr.	H.Art. U.Nat.	H.No	Vorname	Name	Geburts Datum
121	Ju.Po.	68953	Glassner	Henryk	06.01.10
315	Ju.Po.	69159	Gleitmann	Mojzesz	04.08.23
291	Ju.Po.	69130	Glicenstein	Abram	16.04.16
346	Ju.Po.	69193	Gluckmann	Gedalie	01.09.02
654	Ju.Po.	69513	Gluckmann	Naftali	10.02.98
250	Ju.Po.	69087	Gluckmann	Siegfried	30.12.06
303	Ju.Po.	69144	Gold	Stefan	18.11.04
399	Ju.Po.	69246	Goldberg	Berisch	17.05.13
416	Ju.Po.	69263	Goldberg	Bernard	10.10.16
279	Ju.Po.	69117	Goldberg	Efraim	03.04.17
343	Ju.Po.	69189	Goldberg	Kalman	25.05.23
651	Ju.Po.	69510	Goldberg	Marcel	11.04.15
311	Ju.Po.	69152	Goldberg	Moses	25.12.24
321	Ju.Po.	69166	Goldberg	Otto	12.03.13
739	Ju.Ung	77125	Goldberger	Arnold	29.03.29
323	Ju.Po.	69168	Goldberger	Chaskel	15.05.99
548	Ju.Po.	69405	Goldberger	Roman	10.08.22
542	Ju.Po.	69399	Goldberger	Salomon	28.07.20
341	Ju.Po.	69186	Goldblatt	Salomon	03.07.15
203	Ju.Po.	69037	Goldfarb	Izrael	15.12.08
210	Ju.Po.	69045	Goldkern	Hersch	03.10.24
643	Ju.Slo	69501	Goldmann	Alexander	06.06.15
309	Ju.Po.	69150	Goldmann	Moses	09.12.08
53	Ju.Po.	68877	Goldschmied	Aron	02.02.23
673	Ju.Po.	69690	Goldstein	Adolf	23.01.12
586	Ju.Po.	69443	Goldstein	Aron	10.10.14
295	Ju.Po.	69134	Goldstein	Bernard	05.01.03
695	Ju.Po.	77008	Goldstein	Idel	11.05.06
345	Ju.Po.	69192	Goldstein	Stefan	25.07.21
678	Ju.Po.	69833	Goldwasser	Alex	23.11.88
677	Ju.Po.	69832	Goldwasser	Marcel	15.01.20
330	Ju.Rus	99175	Gorywocki	Szulim	15.08.08

Ldf Nr.	H.Art. U.Nat.	H.No	Vorname	Name	Geburts Datum
445	Ju.Po.	69294	Gotinger	Moses	04.04.97
17	Ju.Po.	68838	Gottselig	Dawid	06.05.20
213	Ju.Po.	69048	Gottselig	Hermann	22.02.25
740	Ju.Hol	77126	Goudstikker	Henryk	16.09.27
741	Ju.Dt.	77127	Grabowski	Markus	22.03.93
280	Ju.Po.	69118	Grauer	Wilhelm	03.12.11
215	Ju.Ung	69050	Grob	Josef	10.06.14
281	Ju.Po.	69119	Grob	Oskar	23.04.14
334	Ju.Po.	69179	Grobler	Leon	02.02.12
335	Ju.Po.	69180	Grobler	Samuel	14.07.99
318	Ju.Po.	69162	Gross	Abraham	24.12.97
314	Ju.Po.	69158	Gross	Benjamin	12.05.93
359	Ju.Po.	69206	Gross	Daniel	02.08.96
319	Ju.Po.	69163	Gross	Jakob	21.06.26
328	Ju.Po.	69173	Gross	Jerzy	16.11.28
317	Ju.Po.	69161	Gross	Josef	29.05.04
333	Ju.Po.	69178	Gross	Karol	11.11.00
325	Ju.Po.	69170	Gross	Otto	30.10.26
591	Ju.Po.	69448	Grossmann	Abraham	15.07.20
642	Ju.Po.	69500	Grossmann	Moszek	15.05.24
590	Ju.Po.	69447	Grossmann	Szymon	15.05.01
260	Ju.Po.	69098	Grubner	Chaim	04.05.97
62	Ju.Po.	68888	Grun	Abraham	14.05.05
521	Ju.Po.	69377	Grunberg	Abraham	02.01.06
189	Ju.Po.	69023	Grunblum	Jakob	19.12.08
307	Ju.Po.	69148	Gruner	Emil	21.07.30
357	Ju.Po.	69204	Gruner	Salomon	01.05.10
310	Ju.Po.	69151	Gruner	Saul	27.04.00
742	Ju.Ung	77128	Grunfeld	Alexander	16.12.03
312	Ju.Po.	69153	Grunfeld	Jgnacy	03.06.04
743	Ju.Slo	77129	Grunfeld	Salomon	10.09.12
354	Ju.Po.	69201	Grungras	Chaim	01.05.10

Ldf Nr.	H.Art. U.Nat.	H.No	Vorname	Name	Geburts Datum
322	Ju.Po.	69167	Grunhaut	Adolf	29.02.24
662	Ju.Po.	69521	Grunwald	Dawid	12.05.10
34	Ju.Po.	68857	Gruss	Abraham	06.09.06
339	Ju.Po.	69184	Gruss	Leopold	02.03.07
516	Ju.Po.	69372	Grycman	Leib	14.06.14
274	Ju.Po.	69112	Gurewicz	Meilech	22.08.12
304	Ju.Po.	69145	Gurfinkel	Natan	15.05.27
657	Ju.Po.	69516	Gutherz	Adolar	22.11.15
349	Ju.Po.	69196	Gutherz	Henryk	02.03.26
348	Ju.Po.	69195	Gutherz	Josef	05.11.22
513	Ju.Po.	69369	Guttmann	Adolf	18.08.19
51	Ju.Po.	68875	Haar	David	20.12.12
71	Ju.Po.	68897	Haar	Felwel	01.07.10
284	Ju.Po.	69123	Haber	Ignacy	11.05.15
361	Ju.Po.	69208	Hahn	Dawid	20.10.97
184	Ju.Po.	69018	Haliczer	Josef	18.09.95
85	Ju.Po.	68916	Haller	Jacob	15.08.21
446	Ju.Po.	69295	Handler	Szaja	17.12.06
745	Ju.Dt	77132	Hansel	Otto	04.08.05
87	Ju.Po.	68918	Hartmann	Ferdinand	11.08.17
61	Ju.Po.	68886	Hartmann	Salomon	05.02.20
744	Ju.Dt	77133	Hartog	Fritz	23.05.13
666	Ju.Po.	69592	Hauben	Iszak	10.05.98
561	Ju.Po.	69418	Haubenstock	Jakob	29.01.16
671	Ju.Po.	69658	Hecht	Isak	15.05.12
292	Ju.Po.	69131	Hecht	Zygmunt	24.10.26
746	Ju.Ung	77134	Heller	Paul	23.07.10
627	Ju.Po.	69484	Hellmann	Henryk	03.03.08
45	Ju.Po.	68869	Hellmann	Michal L	08.05.22
747	Ju.Tsc	77135	Herrmann	Alfred	19.05.93
49	Ju.Po.	68873	Herschlag	Abraham	02.03.20
50	Ju.Po.	68874	Herschlag	Salomon	15.08.22

Ldf Nr.	H.Art. U.Nat.	H.No	Vorname	Name	Geburts Datum
186	Ju.Po.	69020	Herszkowicz	Jakob	12.01.12
748	Ju.Ung	77136	Herszkowits	Ingnaz	04.02.96
273	Ju.Po.	69111	Herz	Dawid	24.06.23
628	Ju.Po.	69485	Herz	Isak	15.09.24
42	Ju.Po.	68866	Herz	Ludwig	19.09.25
676	Ju.Po.	69789	Herzberg	Henoch	27.07.99
431	Ju.Po.	69280	Heuberger	Edward	04.01.14
69	Ju.Po.	68895	Hilfstein	Chaim	14.11.86
243	Ju.Po.	69080	Hilfstein	Edward	17.09.24
390	Ju.Po.	69237	Hillmann	Bernard	24.12.15
696	Ju.Po.	77009	Hinigmann	Moisze	10.12.19
86	Ju.Po.	68917	Hirsch	Abraham	28.05.12
449	Ju.Po.	69298	Hirsch	Leon	06.11.09
35	Ju.Po.	68858	Hirschberg	Herz	16.05.27
415	Ju.Po.	69262	Hirschberg	Szymon	23.07.08
749	Ju.Ung	77137	Hirschel	Julius	27.12.00
23	Ju.Po.	68844	Hirschfeld	Samuel	27.02.19
144	Ju.Po.	68977	Hirschhorn	Israel	08.11.26
675	Ju.Po.	69743	Hoffmann	Zdenek	20.03.14
750	Ju.Ung	77138	Holasz	Gabor	28.04.01
237	Ju.Po.	69077	Hollander	Szulim	08.02.06
30	Ju.Po.	68851	Horn	Eliasz	29.09.07
7	Ju.Po.	68827	Horn	Josef	04.02.14
701	Ju.Dt.	77014	Hornitzer	Berthold	07.05.08
19	Ju.Po.	68840	Hornung	Dawid	25.02.19
18	Ju.Po.	68839	Hornung	Josef	06.09.11
73	Ju.Po.	68899	Horowitz	Bernard	28.05.97
409	Ju.Po.	69256	Horowitz	Izydor	25.09.98
436	Ju.Po.	69285	Horowitz	Moses	18.04.04
381	Ju.Po.	69228	Horowitz	Schachne	31.12.88
124	Ju.Po.	68956	Horowitz	Wolf	02.09.98
43	Ju.Po.	68867	Hudes	Izak	26.01.16

Ldf Nr.	H.Art. U.Nat.	H.No	Vorname	Name	Geburts Datum
313	Ju.Po.	69157	Hudes	Leib	04.06.09
418	Ju.Po.	69265	Hudes	Naftali	10.07.99
578	Ju.Po.	69435	Ickowicz	Josef	08.05.14
370	Ju.Po.	69217	Immergluck	Mendel	24.09.03
362	Ju.Po.	69209	Immergluck	Zygmunt	13.06.24

Ldf Nr.	H.Art. U.Nat.	H.No	Vorname	Name	Geburts Datum
350	Ju.Po.	69197	Ingber	Bernard	06.04.17
63	Ju.Po.	68889	Inglicht	Emil	02.09.08
202	Ju.Po.	69036	Izraclowicz	Izak	11.12.23
451	Ju.Po.	69300	Jachzel	Abraham	27.11.23
442	Ju.Po.	69291	Jachzel	Salomon	23.06.99
392	Ju.Po.	69239	Jakobowicz	Chaim	10.01.19
383	Ju.Po.	69230	Jakobowicz	Dawid	15.04.26
13	Ju.Po.	68834	Jakubowicz	Jakob	13.11.27
77	Ju.sti	68905	Jakubowicz	Kurt	27.07.20
672	Ju.Po.	69666	Jakubowski	Hersz	22.12.03
679	Ju.Po.	69886	Jasse	Ascher	25.02.07
327	Ju.Po.	69172	Jazowski	Zalel	02.02.14
648	Ju.Po.	69506	Jerethh	Simon	11.01.88
412	Ju.Po.	69259	Joachimsmann	Abr.	19.12.95
344	Ju.Po.	69190	Jonas	Josef	03.11.23
751	Ju.Dt	77140	Jospe	Heinz	18.10.15
697	Ju.Dt.	77010	Juttla	Artur	24.01.07
796	Ju.Ung	77191	Kahan	Desider	13.01.24
439	Ju.Po.	69288	Kahane	Wladyslaw	06.09.09
640	Ju.Po.	69498	Kaminski	Felix	15.09.12
471	Ju.Po.	69323	Kammer-Mann	Hen.	14.02.03
356	Ju.Po.	69203	Karp	Izak Szyja	02.01.03
155	Ju.Po.	68988	Katz	Hermann	02.07.93
363	Ju.Po.	69210	Katz	Isak Josef	03.12.08
308	Ju.Po.	69149	Katz	Juda	14.07.14

426	Ju.Po.	69273	Kaufmann	Leon	06.08.20
526	Ju.Po.	69382	Kaufmann	Szaja	02.04.02
128	Ju.Po.	68960	Keil	Josef	12.09.12
171	Ju.Po.	69004	Keller	Zacharjasz	20.08.14
752	Ju.Tsc	77142	Kellner	Eugen	19.06.17
753	Ju.Ung	77143	Kellner	Josef	29.01.28
754	Ju.Ung	77144	Kellner	Soltan	13.05.03
589	Ju.Po.	69446	Kern	Szyja	05.11.06
84	Ju.Po.	68915	Kerner	Majer	23.06.04
650	Ju.Po.	69509	Kessler	Jerzy	24.04.21
660	Ju.Po.	69519	Kessler	Maximilian	06.01.95
684	Ju.Po.	74558	Kestenberg	Szya	25.08.12
801	Ju.Po.	77196	Kief	Jarum	02.12.17
38	Ju.Po.	68861	Kinstlinger	Joachim	11.11.15
167	Ju.Po.	69000	Kirschen-Baum	H.	16.04.22
166	Ju.Po.	68999	Kirschen-Baum	Izak	22.12.21
168	Ju.Po.	69001	Kirschen-Baum	J.	27.11.11
204	Ju.Po.	69038	Klassner	Samuel	08.09.17
755	Ju.Ung	77145	Klein	Eugen	12.08.98
388	Ju.Po.	69235	Kleinberg	Szaja	01.04.20
116	Ju.Po.	68948	Kleiner	Bernard	08.05.14
632	Ju.Po.	69490	Kleiner	Meier	14.10.24
302	Ju.Po.	69143	Kleinmann	Adolf	07.11.20
669	Ju.Po.	69645	Kleinmann	Feiwel	26.12.26
172	Ju.Po.	69005	Kleinmann	Jakob	10.01.12
394	Ju.Po.	69241	Klinburt	Abram	01.11.13
54	Ju.Po.	68878	Klingenholz	Aron	18.06.22
47	Ju.Po.	68871	Klinghofer	Ignacy	30.01.25
8	Ju.Po.	68828	Klinghofer	Simon	25.03.97
60	Ju.Po.	68885	Klinstilinger	Moses	21.07.06
158	Ju.Po.	68991	Klipstein	Izak Dawid	14.04.95
163	Ju.Po.	68996	Klugmann	Henryk	12.12.25

549	Ju.Po.	69406 Knobler	Moszek	27.05.20
698	BV/RD	77011 Knobloch	Leo	06.06.10
377	Ju.Po.	69224 Kohane	Chiel	15.09.25
757	Ju.Ung	77147 Kohn	Markus	07.11.02
185	Ju.Po.	69019 Kollender	Awadie	07.03.09
756	Ju.Slo	77146 Kollmann	Natan	06.03.00
294	Ju.Po.	69133 Konig	Jakob	14.09.16
391	Ju.Po.	69238 Konigl	Marek	02.11.11
797	Ju.Jgs	77192 Koniowitsch	Mirko	27.05.99
609	Ju.Po.	69466 Kopec	Samuel	12.01.11
221	Ju.Po.	69056 Kopec	Selig	01.05.06
33	Ju.Po.	68856 Kopyto	Moses	14.03.98
440	Ju.Po.	69289 Korber	Chaim	14.12.05
411	Ju.Po.	69258 Kormann	Abraham	15.01.19
367	Ju.Po.	69214 Korn	Edmund	07.04.12
278	Ju.Po.	69116 Kornblau	Jakob	29.03.08
604	Ju.Po.	69461 Kornfeld	Henryk	14.10.19
612	Ju.Po.	69469 Kornfeld	Ludwig	05.06.13
438	Ju.Po.	69287 Kornhauser	Bernard	07.06.09
453	Ju.Po.	69302 Kornhauser	Hermann	14.11.04
702	Ju.Po.	77015 Korzec	Max	15.01.15
283	Ju.Po.	69122 Koscher	Szaja	06.02.18
82	Ju.Po.	68912 Kranz	Wilhelm	06.03.05
758	Ju.Ung	77149 Kraus	Kosef	05.09.25
444	Ju.Po.	69293 Krebs	Moses	27.04.02
179	Ju.Po.	69013 Kremsdorf	Jakob	26.11.20
75	Ju.Po.	68902 Krieger	Chaskel	08.06.00
454	Ju.Po.	69303 Krieger	Szymon	12.10.04
1	Ju.Po.	68821 Krischer	Hirsch	15.08.97
25	Ju.Po.	68846 Krug	Samuel	15.12.11
699	Ju.Po.	77012 Kroger	Natan	21.02.17
700	Ju.Po.	77013 Kochler	Josef	08.09.22
437	Ju.Po.	69286 Kujawski	Jankiel	13.02.98
282	Ju.Po.	69120 Kukurutz	Roman	06.08.17

64	Ju.Po.	68890	Kukurutz	Salo	24.10.13
379	Ju.Po.	69226	Kupferberg	Izrael	04.09.98
157	Ju.Po.	68990	Kurz	Ignacy	02.11.00
32	Ju.Po.	68855	Lamensdorf	Leib	14.12.90
759	Ju.Tsc	77150	Lampel	Heinrich	09.02.98
286	Ju.Po.	69125	Landesdor-Fer	Izak	07.04.23
372	Ju.Po.	69219	Landschaft	Aron	07.07.09
760	Ju.Ung	77151	Lang	Max	28.05.95
518	Ju.Po.	69374	Langsam	Jakob	28.11.23
149	Ju.Po.	68982	Lasser	Szaja	04.04.11
566	Ju.Po.	69423	Laus	Jakob	02.12.16
407	Ju.Po.	69254	Lax	Ryszard	09.07.24
153	Ju.Po.	68986	Lebenstein	Izak	11.02.06
337	Ju.Po.	69182	Lederberger	Mojzesz	11.01.23
147	Ju.Po.	68980	Lederer	Dawid	25.06.07
152	Ju.Po.	68985	Lederer	Mendel	25.08.01
67	Ju.Po.	68893	Leibermann	Ignacy	16.07.08
68	Ju.Po.	68894	Leibermann	Mauryoy	27.08.10
143	Ju.Po.	68976	Leibler	Leon	06.09.08
10	Ju.Po.	68830	Leichter	Josef	25.11.17
465	Ju.Po.	69316	Leinkram	Eliasz	06.05.07
288	Ju.Po.	69127	Lejzon	Dawid	01.08.27
289	Ju.Po.	69128	Lejzon	Leib	15.09.29
290	Ju.Po.	69129	Lejzon	Moses	15.12.98
515	Ju.Po.	69371	Lermer	Abraham	31.07.24
105	Ju.Po.	68937	Leser	Jakob	25.02.13
106	Ju.Po.	68938	Leser	Szulim	05.05.16
48	Ju.Po.	68872	Lewertow	Jakob	10.11.08
306	Ju.Po.	69147	Lewi	Dawid	02.06.07
645	Ju.Po.	69503	Lewi	Salomon	26.06.16
567	Ju.Po.	69424	Lewin	Josek	20.11.24
406	Ju.Po.	69253	Lewkowicz	Ferdynand	12.03.09
113	Ju.Po.	68945	Lewkowicz	Hermann	29.04.09
151	Ju.Po.	68984	Lewkowicz	Icek	18.01.17

125	Ju.Po.	68957	Lewkowicz	Moses	20.03.94
110	Ju.Po.	68942	Lewkowicz	Natan	29.04.09
108	Ju.Po.	68940	Lezerklewicz	Wiktor	25.08.19
376	Ju.Po.	69223	Liban	Jan	29.04.24
154	Ju.Po.	68987	Licht	Hersch	31.01.06
78	Ju.Po.	68906	Lichtig	Samuel	20.03.98
117	Ju.Po.	68949	Lieser	Markus	12.03.04
164	Ju.Po.	68997	Lindenber-Ger	Leon	05.01.21
293	Ju.Po.	69132	Linkowski	Maurycy	23.06.05
342	Ju.Po.	69187	Lipschutz	Josef	01.11.18
150	Ju.Po.	68983	Loffler	Hermann	17.12.14
403	Ju.Po.	69250	Low	Jakob	03.03.00
402	Ju.Po.	69249	Low	Zysze	28.06.97
178	Ju.Po.	69011	Luftig	Eliasz	17.12.95
176	Ju.Po.	69009	Luftig	Leopold	07.03.26
175	Ju.Po.	69008	Luftig	Stefan	17.02.29
9	Ju.Po.	68829	Mahler	Abraham	07.04.02
160	Ju.Po.	68993	Makowski	Israel	25.11.06
299	Ju.Po.	69140	Malawer	Chaim	28.12.05
133	Ju.Po.	68965	Mandel	Hersch	17.10.04
46	Ju.Po.	68870	Manskleid	Anatol	15.05.25
142	Ju.Po.	68975	Markheim	Maurycy	14.02.23
174	Ju.Po.	69007	Marlakow	Nuchym	12.03.90
761	Ju.Tsc	77153	Massaryk	Ferdinand	09.10.16
703	Ju.Dt.	77016	Matuschak	Abraham	20.02.15
198	Ju.Po.	69032	Meisels	Kalman	05.11.20
410	Ju.Po.	69257	Meisels	Szlama	02.02.16
111	Ju.Po.	68943	Melzer	Josef	07.07.11
762	Ju.Tsc	77154	Melzer	Leo	14.06.03
169	Ju.Po.	69002	Merkrebs	Juda	28.11.21
562	Ju.Ung	69419	Mernelstein	Alex	17.04.21
57	Ju.Po.	68881	Metzendorf	Majer	01.12.14
704	Sch.Fr	77017	Michaud	Roger	22.03.22
389	Ju.Po.	69236	Miedziuch	Michael	03.11.16

456	Ju.Po.	69305	Milgrom	Josef	25.10.13
102	Ju.Po.	68934	Mindelgrun	Menasche	04.05.17
430	Ju.Po.	69279	Mingelgrun	Max	03.02.06
583	Ju.Po.	69440	Minz	Iser	08.03.18
148	Ju.Po.	68981	Mond	Dawid	16.04.91
582	Ju.Po.	69439	Monderer	Nachum	10.11.23
56	Ju.Po.	68880	Morgenbesser	Adam	05.09.27
55	Ju.Po.	68879	Morgenbesser	Kafal	09.10.00
600	Ju.Po.	69457	Mowscho-Witz	Szymon	17.09.14
705	Ju.Po.	77018	Mozek	Josef	01.10.14
103	Ju.Po.	68935	Muhlrad	Alecksander	09.09.17
479	Ju.Po.	69332	Muller	Idam	30.03.26
107	Ju.Po.	68939	Muller	Moses	23.05.10
480	Ju.Po.	69334	Muller	Zygmunt	15.12.02
112	Ju.Po.	68944	Mutzenmacher	Rubin	14.11.98
98	Ju.Po.	68930	Mutzner	Jeremiasz	15.10.10
429	Ju.Po.	69276	Nachhauser	Wilhelm	26.12.20
120	Ju.Po.	68952	Nadel	Dawid	05.06.13
161	Ju.Po.	68994	Nadel	Szymon	05.08.08
763	Ju.Ung	77155	Nadler	Miklosz	26.06.14
706	Ju.Dt	77019	Nebel	Hans	25.09.15
338	Ju.Po.	69183	Neiger	Dawid	19.03.06
123	Ju.Po.	68955	Neufeld	Henryk	14.08.20
764	Ju.Ung	77156	Neumann	Dezso	14.05.96
621	Ju.Po.	69478	Neumann	Siegmund	21.06.98
99	Ju.Po.	68931	Nichthauser	Alfred	16.07.98
353	Ju.Po.	69200	Niemiec	Josek	07.03.25
707	Ju.Po.	77020	Nusbaum	Ignaz	06.02.12
568	Ju.Po.	69425	Nussbaum	Henoch	11.09.09
95	Ju.Po.	68927	Nussbaum	Richard	22.03.30
94	Ju.Po.	68926	Nussbaum	Wilhelm	01.08.10
39	Ju.Po.	68862	Oberfeld	Adolf	24.09.11
766	Ju.Ung	77158	Obstler	Kalman	09.04.03

267 Ju.Po.	69105	Oestreicher	Jakob	07.05.17
765 Ju.Dt	77157	Offner	Erich	15.02.26
145 Ju.Po.	68978	Opoczynski	Henryk	25.07.24
91 Ju.Po.	68922	Oppenheim	Saal	04.06.98
708 Ju.Po.	77021	Ordynans	Julek	22.12.08
88 Ju.Po.	68919	Panzer	Henryk	28.01.19
109 Ju.Po.	68941	Pechner	Simon	18.07.21
135 Ju.Po.	68967	Pelzmann	Hersch	02.10.99
137 Ju.Po.	68969	Pelzmann	Natan	20.05.13
655 Ju.Po.	69514	Pemper	Mieczyslaw	24.03.20
495 Ju.Po.	69349	Pemper	Alfred	17.02.12
104 Ju.Po.	68936	Pemper	Jakob	30.08.98
96 Ju.Po.	68928	Pemper	Stefan	05.09.24
368 Ju.Po.	69215	Penner	Jonas	02.02.15
351 Ju.Po.	69198	Penner	Mieczyslaw	29.02.20
97 Ju.Po.	68929	Perl	Salomon	02.03.07
435 Ju.Po.	69284	Perlberger	Teodor	08.01.97
130 Ju.Po.	68962	Perlmann	Chaim	10.08.01
461 Ju.Po.	69312	Perlmann	Izrael	03.04.07
129 Ju.Po.	68961	Perlmann	Jakob	31.05.08
139 Ju.Po.	68972	Perlmann	Jakob	21.02.09
134 Ju.Po.	68966	Perlmann	Moses	09.10.26
767 Ju.Ung	77159	Perlmutter	Farkcas	18.08.02
173 Ju.Po.	69006	Pfefferberg	Leopold	20.03.20
768 Ju.Po.	77160	Piotrkowski	Salomon	03.07.12
769 Ju.Po.	77161	Piskorz	Max	26.11.96
136 Ju.Po.	68968	Planzer	Chaim	28.09.01
770 Ju.Dt	77162	Pollak	Robert	20.07.13
527 Ju.Po.	69383	Pomeranz	Hersz	24.03.25
799 Ju.Po.	77194	Pomerauz	Baruch	25.04.20
100 Ju.Po.	68932	Posner	Baruch	17.09.18
404 Ju.Po.	69251	Pozniak	Szloma	15.09.16
424 Ju.Po.	69271	Preiss	Isak	18.12.99
447 Ju.Po.	69296	Presser	Bernard	16.09.14

681	Ju.Po.	69931	Ptasznik	Abe	03.09.14
680	Ju.Po.	69928	Ptasznik	Chaim	11.10.09
530	Ju.Po.	69386	Pudlowski	Jacob	03.05.21
419	Ju.Po.	69266	Pufeles	Maurycy	05.10.12
205	Ju.Po.	69040	Puntirer	Mejzesz	18.06.25
473	Ju.Po.	69326	Putter	Abraham	11.04.04
469	Ju.Po.	69321	Putter	Ezriel	15.09.03
156	Ju.Po.	68989	Rabner	Artur	19.09.18
771	Ju.Ung	77163	Rade	Siegmund	02.03.16
422	Ju.Po.	69269	Radziwiller	Adolf	31.03.11
231	Ju.Po.	69067	Rath	Wladyslaw	21.03.24
405	Ju.Po.	69252	Ratz	Wolf	20.06.09
793	Ju.Po.	77188	Rawot	Abe	03.07.07
425	Ju.Po.	69272	Reben	Natan	25.07.05
386	Ju.Po.	69233	Rechin	Ryszard	30.05.21
126	Ju.Po.	68958	Rechtschafer	Moses	03.03.06
460	Ju.Po.	69311	Reich	Emil	11.05.94
177	Ju.Po.	69010	Reich	Jerzy	28.02.24
476	Ju.Po.	69329	Reich	Kalman	22.03.09
497	Ju.Po.	69351	Reich	Kalman	26.01.12
448	Ju.Po.	69297	Reich	Mendel	25.05.13
772	Ju.Po.	77164	Reichgott	Moritz	11.12.02
119	Ju.Po.	68951	Reif	Viktor	24.10.06
664	Ju.Po.	69566	Reisfeld	Baruch	24.05.20
663	Ju.Po.	69565	Reisfeld	Salomon	26.01.95
794	Ju.Po.	77189	Reismann	Aron	01.03.08
90	Ju.Po.	68921	Reismann	Leon	31.12.16
423	Ju.Po.	69270	Reiss	Abraham	03.01.23
504	Ju.Po.	69358	Richter	Juda	07.07.03
505	Ju.Po.	69360	Rimmler	Moses	05.05.07
644	Ju.Tsc	69502	Ring	Leopold	08.02.94
347	Ju.Po.	69194	Ringelblum	Arnold	27.06.20
427	Ju.Po.	69274	Rittermann	Zygmunt	18.04.06
652	Ju.Po.	69511	Rosen	Szymon	17.07.00

537	Ju.Po.	69393	Rosenberg	Juliysz	10.12.00
472	Ju.Po.	69325	Rosenblatt	Majer	15.01.10
710	Ju.Po.	77023	Rosenblum	Szaja	08.02.16
118	Ju.Po.	68950	Rosenfried	Albert	24.06.16
122	Ju.Po.	68954	Rosenkranz	Max	25.02.06
374	Ju.Po.	69221	Rosenthal	Israel	24.10.09
114	Ju.Po.	68946	Rosenzweig	Maks	13.04.98
365	Ju.Po.	69212	Rosner	Leopold	26.06.18
414	Ju.Po.	69261	Rosner	Wilhelm	14.09.25
610	Ju.Po.	69467	Roter	Siegmund	19.03.20
140	Ju.Po.	68973	Roth	Fischel	00.00.12
489	Ju.Po.	69343	Roth	Wigdor	08.03.15
12	Ju.Po.	68833	Rottenberg	Beer	09.08.20
616	Ju.Po.	69473	Rottman	Jakub	14.02.10
101	Ju.Po.	68933	Rozer	Franciszok	31.10.19
517	Ju.Po.	69373	Rubin	Osias	13.07.14
132	Ju.Po.	68964	Rumpler	Josef	01.04.98
498	Ju.Po.	69352	Ryba	Josef	09.01.19
512	Ju.Po.	69368	Ryba	Szaja	14.07.14
773	Ju.Dt	77165	Sabarsky	Siegfried	27.09.03
711	Ju.Po.	77024	Salem	Chaim	13.01.14
433	Ju.Po.	69282	Salpeter	Leib	20.12.97
503	Ju.Po.	69357	Salzberg	Jankiel	27.05.17
587	Ju.Po.	69444	Salzberg	Szmul	30.11.23
574	Ju.Po.	69431	Sauerbrunn	Dawid	15.01.10
413	Ju.Po.	69260	Sawicki	Samuel	09.04.17
326	Ju.Po.	69171	Schanz	Zew	06.01.23
573	Ju.Po.	69430	Scharf	Josef	03.11.16
15	Ju.Po.	68836	Scheck	Jerzy	25.12.17
29	Ju.Po.	68850	Scheidlinger	Markus	19.08.18
487	Ju.Po.	69341	Schein	Szymon	05.01.12
508	Ju.Po.	69363	Scheinok	Szulim	13.11.06
511	Ju.Po.	69367	Scher	Dawid	11.02.08
474	Ju.Po.	69327	Schide	Rubin	10.04.88

355	Ju.Po.	69202	Schimmel	Mojzesz	13.01.08
790	Ju.Po.	77184	Schimmel	Oskar	18.05.09
619	Ju.Po.	69476	Schindel	Samuel	11.01.05
40	Ju.Po.	68863	Schlang	Dawid	08.07.05
37	Ju.Po.	68860	Schlesinger	Abraham	02.09.10
774	Ju.Ung	77166	Schlesinger	Leopold	12.06.04
26	Ju.Po.	68847	Schlesinger	Moses	05.07.96
712	PSV/RD7702	5	Schlichting	Willy	02.06.01
776	Ju.Dt	77168	Schnapp	Harry	03.06.01
93	Ju.Po.	68925	Schneider	Israel	30.04.12
791	Ju.Po.	77185	Schoenfeld	Alfred	26.03.22
775	Ju.Stl	77167	Schonfeld	Otto	23.10.07
576	Ju.Po.	69433	Schonherz	Siegmund	20.06.14
602	Ju.Po.	69459	Schreiber	Isak	05.07.06
396	Ju.Po.	69243	Schreiber	Leopold	15.10.25
463	Ju.Po.	69314	Schreier	Roman	28.06.04
603	Ju.Dt.	69460	Schubert	Alexander	05.03.94
713	Ju.Po.	77026	Schuhma-Cher	Abra.	15.03.20
141	Ju.Po.	68974	Schuldiener	Moses	26.05.06
502	Ju.Po.	69356	Schulkind	Kopel	18.09.05
777	Ju.Ung	77169	Schwarz	Alexander	19.12.19
482	Ju.Po.	69336	Schwarz	Paul	03.12.03
457	Ju.Po.	69306	Schweber	Jzak	27.09.97
464	Ju.Po.	69315	Schweber	Mendel	10.10.02
466	Ju.Po.	69317	Schwelb	Georg	06.01.07
553	Ju.Po.	69410	Seewald	Leib	31.01.10
532	Ju.Po.	69388	Seftel	Jakob	05.11.10
36	Ju.Po.	68859	Segal	Chaim	30.03.07
382	Ju.Po.	69229	Segal	Richard	09.11.23
563	Ju.Po.	69420	Seidenfeuer	Rachmiel	10.04.04
778	Ju.Dt	77171	Seif	Siegmar	09.03.13
467	Ju.Po.	69319	Seifmann	Markus	18.01.16
127	Ju.Po.	68959	Selinger	Chaim	17.07.95
572	Ju.Po.	69429	Selinger	Lazar	04.07.24

452 Ju.Po.	69301	Selinger	Peretz	28.06.14
579 Ju.Po.	69436	Selinger	Szymon	02.09.91
408 Ju.Po.	69255	Semmel	Berek	05.01.05
541 Ju.Po.	69398	Senft	Wolf	03.07.09
378 Ju.Po.	69225	Senftmann	Dawid	06.09.09
714 Ju.Fr	77027	Silber	Isak	10.01.24
375 Ju.Po.	69222	Silber-Schlag	Hersch	07.04.12
481 Ju.Po.	69335	Silberspitz	Izak	08.07.10
599 Ju.Po.	69456	Silberstein	Hirsch	27.07.02
397 Ju.Po.	69244	Silberstein	Jakob	01.01.00
79 Ju.Po	68907	Silberstein	Max	21.07.00
613 Ju.Po.	69470	Silberstein	Max	30.04.24
779 Ju.Dt	77172	Singer	Gunther	14.01.22
522 Ju.Po.	69378	Sloma	Lankiel	01.09.08
385 Ju.Po.	69232	Smolarz	Szymon	15.05.04
547 Ju.Po.	69404	Sommer	Abraham	22.12.07
384 Ju.Po.	69231	Sommer	Josef	21.12.14
646 Ju.Po.	69504	Spatz	Natan	13.01.15
28 Ju.Po.	68849	Sperber	Chaim	07.07.03
491 Ju.Po.	69345	Sperling	Bernard	27.01.12
539 Ju.Po.	69395	Sperling	Efroim	28.10.05
475 Ju.Po.	69328	Sperling	Moritz	21.04.97
780 Ju.Sl	77173	Spiegel	Markus	30.04.11
524 Ju.Po.	69380	Spira	Aszer Edward	02.09.02
525 Ju.Po.	69381	Spira	Jerzy	12.03.30
781 Ju.Bt	77174	Stagel	Paul	15.12.12
493 Ju.Po.	69347	Stanger	Abraham	14.09.10
782 Ju.Ung	77175	Stark	Jaros	20.05.16
459 Ju.Po.	69308	Starzycki	Szymon	08.05.01
470 Ju.Po.	69322	Stein	Aron	30.12.20
510 Ju.Po.	69365	Stein	Josef	10.05.10
783 Ju.Dt	77176	Stein	Leon	06.07.98
519 Ju.Po.	69375	Steininger	Rafael	05.06.04

432	Ju.Po.	69281	Stejman	Nysel	15.07.10
546	Ju.Po.	69403	Stelzer	Alfred	17.01.07
488	Ju.Po.	69342	Stemmer	Max	06.12.12
538	Ju.Po.	69394	Stern	Aszer	29.01.08
115	Ju.Po.	68947	Stern	Henryk	19.11.96
659	Ju.Po.	69518	Stern	Isak	25.01.01
428	Ju.Po.	69275	Stern	Natan	21.04.06
58	Ju.Po.	68882	Sternberg	Jakob	16.12.99
59	Ju.Po.	68883	Sternberg	Jerzy	09.06.26
540	Ju.Po.	69397	Sterngast	Josef	27.08.13
715	Ju.Dt.	77028	Stillmann	Albert	08.10.12
501	Ju.Po.	69355	Stimmler	Samuel	13.09.23
455	Ju.Po.	69304	Strenger	Szymon	06.01.22
494	Ju.Po.	69348	Sussermann	Moses	04.01.95
535	Ju.Po.	69391	Susskind	Moniek	09.07.22
536	Ju.Po.	69392	Susskind	Salomon	27.12.24
554	Ju.Po.	69411	Sussmann	Adolf	12.12.24
462	Ju.Po.	69313	Sussmann	Jakob	22.07.10
716	Ju.Fr	77029	Szczapa	Aron	23.02.10
162	Ju.Po.	68995	Szenwic	Zenon	10.06.05
387	Ju.Po.	69234	Szlamowicz	Chaim	16.05.24
324	Ju.Po.	69169	Szlamowicz	Naftali	15.10.23
320	Ju.Po.	69165	Szlamowicz	Szulam	01.01.18
784	Ju.Po.	77177	Szydlo	Selman	22.06.12
24	Ju.Po.	68845	Taube	Emanuel	16.01.02
22	Ju.Po.	68843	Taube	Maksymilian	17.06.27
500	Ju.Po.	69354	Taubler	Wilhelm	24.12.12
687	Ju.Po.	74695	Teitelbaum	Elias	22.05.08
607	Ju.Po.	69464	Teitelbaum	Leib	12.08.13
27	Ju.Po.	68848	Tennenbaum	Izydor	01.10.20
665	Ju.Po.	69573	Tennenbaum	Szymon	13.10.18
65	Ju.Po.	68891	Tilles	Jakob	20.10.11
490	Ju.Po.	69344	Trauring	Ferdynand	15.01.92
558	Ju.Po.	69415	Turner	Henryk	20.10.20

551	Ju.Po.	69408	Turner	Moses	25.06.24
31	Ju.Po.	68853	Urbach	Dawid	18.02.96
560	Ju.Po.	69427	Urbach	Salomon	25.10.25
2	Ju.Po.	68822	Vogel	Gedale	05.07.01
492	Ju.Po.	69346	Vogelhut	Max	20.04.03
332	Ju.Ita	69177	Vogelmann	Szulim	28.04.03
66	Ju.Po.	68892	Wachholder	Baruch	29.11.08
72	Ju.Po.	68898	Wachholder	Schulim	15.04.03
634	Ju.Po.	69492	Wachsberg	Lejbusz	01.05.08
369	Ju.Po.	69216	Wachtel	Roman	05.11.05
683	Ju.Po.	69944	Wahrhaft	Moses	08.11.05
785	Ju	77179	Waldapfel	Erwin	11.03.01
786	Ju.Ung	77180	Walz	Julius	30.08.97
373	Ju.Po.	69220	Wandersmann	Markus	14.09.06
520	Ju.Po.	69376	Wasserlauf	Nachim	16.05.25
514	Ju.Po.	69370	Wasserteil	Moses	26.09.98
16	Ju.Po.	68837	Weil	Naftali	10.09.14
5	Ju.Po.	68825	Wein	Wolf	09.06.00
131	Ju.Po.	68963	Weinberger	Adolf	06.06.10
4	Ju.Po.	68824	Weinberger	Hachum	16.05.21
89	Ju.Po.	68920	Weinberger	Markus	02.03.09
686	Ju.Po.	69741	Weingarten	Jakob	18.01.18
674	Ju.Po.	69742	Weingarten	Jechiel	13.02.16
483	Ju.Po.	69337	Weingarten	Szymon	18.10.21
11	Ju.Po.	68832	Weinschel-Baum	Dawid	14.02.24
14	Ju.Po.	68835	Weinschel-Baum	Pinkus	24.09.19
667	Ju.Po.	69606	Weinstein	Berl	20.09.04
74	Ju.Po.	68901	Weinstock	Josef	06.01.17
544	Ju.Po.	69401	Weinstock	Josef	04.10.00
545	Ju.Po.	69402	Weinstock	Moniek	19.11.27
533	Ju.Po.	69389	Weinzier	Srul	25.05.02
668	Ju.Po.	69608	Weiser	Osias	10.06.06
792	Ju.Fr	77186	Weismann	Baruch	11.03.04

468 Ju.Po.	69320	Weiss	Chaim	10.10.17
485 Ju.Po.	69339	Weiss	Menachem	27.08.25
484 Ju.Po.	69338	Weiss	Symche	10.11.98
478 Ju.Po.	69331	Wendum	Salomon	16.07.09
371 Ju.Po.	69218	Wichter	Feiwel	25.07.26
443 Ju.Po.	69292	Wiener	Israel	12.01.21
441 Ju.Po.	69290	Wiener	Juliusz	09.05.04
364 Ju.Po.	69211	Wiener	Samuel	11.05.07
138 Ju.Po.	68971	Wilk	Sadek	11.11.18
555 Ju.Po.	69412	Wilostein	Hermann	21.08.16
395 Ju.Po.	69242	Wisniak	Abram	00.00.30
477 Ju.Po.	69330	Wohlfeiler	Henryk	09.01.99
21 Ju.Po.	68842	Wohlfeiler	Ignazy	01.11.99
557 Ju.Po.	69414	Wohlfeiler	Roman	15.02.18
717 Ju.Dt	77030	Wohlgemut	Horst	27.08.22
420 Ju.Po.	69267	Wulkan	Markus	30.10.10
506 Ju.Po.	69361	Zalcberg	Dawid	07.12.15
682 Ju.Po.	69937	Zimmermann	Max	07.07.17
52 Ju.Po.	68876	Zimmet	Dawid	01.06.14
593 Ju.Po.	69450	Zuckermann	Chaim	26.03.11
585 Ju.Po.	69442	Zuckermann	Isak	26.08.16

Women
Alphabetized by Surname
Gross-Rosen L.Brünnlitz/Liste D. Weibl. Haftlinge-18.4.45. Blatt 2
* indicates that the person is referred to in the text

Ldf Nr.	H.Art. U.Nat.	H.No.	Vorname	Name	Geburts Datum
1	Ju.Po	76201 *	Aftergood	Bertha	20.02.16
2	Ju.Po	76202	Appel	Gisela	28.07.21
3	Ju.Po	76203	Ast	Rachela	28.08.20
4	Ju.Po	76204	Banach	Lol	03.07.08
5	Ju.Po	76205	Barth	Helena	25.12.10

Ldf Nr.	H.Art. U.Nat.	H.No.	Vorname	Name	Geburts Datum
6	Ju.Po	76206	Begleiter	Valeria	18.06.21
7	Ju.Po	76207 *	Berger	Hilde	13.06.14
8	Ju.Po	76208	Berhang	Elka	07.04.15
9	Ju.Po	76209	Bernstein	Golda	10.11.21
12	Ju.Po	76212	Bernstein	Henja Malka	29.08.19
10	Ju.Po	76210	Bielfeld	Frania	31.03.22
11	Ju.Po	76211	Blawat	Felicia	25.12.24
14	Ju.Po	76214	Blumenkranz	Karola	19.01.14
20	Ju.Po	76220	Borenstein	Basia	20.04.26
13	Ju.Po	76213	Borger	Anna	08.03.15
21	Ju.Po	76221	Brandsilber	Charlotte	05.04.09
22	Ju.Po	76222	Brechner	Nelli	14.05.08
23	Ju.Po	76223	Breit	Giza	11.06.11
15	Ju.Po	76215	Bronner	Jetti	27.08.13
16	Ju.Po	76216	Brunnengraber	Halina	12.03.26
17	Ju.Po	76217	Brzeska	Cecilia	24.12.26
18	Ju.Po	76218	Brzeska	Hela	10.05.25
19	Ju.Po	76219	Buchsbaum	Sofia	11.03.13
24	Ju.Po	76224	Bugajer	Rachela	03.02.18
25	Ju.Po	76225	Burstiner	Hela	27.01.09
26	Ju.Po	76227	Danzig	Sara	26.07.07
27	Ju.Dt	76228	Dawidowitz	Ida	06.02.99
140	Ju.Po	76342	Dembitzer	Sara	17.06.96
28	Ju.Po	76229 *	Dortheimer	Helena	19.05.22
29	Ju.Po	76230 *	Dortheimer	Helena	08.07.20
33	Ju.Po	76234	Dresner	Danuta	24.08.27
30	Ju.Po	76231	Dressler	Marta	13.06.96
31	Ju.Po	76232	Dressler	Susi	01.10.14
32	Ju.Po	76233	Dressner	Chaja	08.04.06
34	Ju.Po	76235	Duklauer	Anna	20.12.22
35	Ju.Po	76236	Durst	Szyfra	03.04.14

Ldf Nr.	H.Art. U.Nat.	H.No.	Vorname	Name	Geburts Datum
36	Ju.Po	76237	Eisen	Erna	27.02.19
37	Ju.Po	76239	Feigenbaum	Necha	16.01.02
38	Ju.Po	76240	Feingold	Mina	27.07.10
39	Ju.Po	76241	Feldmann	Lola	01.08.22
40	Ju.Po	76242	Feldmann	Rosa	04.09.26
41	Ju.Po	76243	Feldstein	Felicia	10.04.24
42	Ju.Po	76244	Ferber	Rena	24.02.28
43	Ju.Po	76245	Ferber	Rosa	14.09.05
44	Ju.Po	76246	Fertig	Gustawa	21.12.22
45	Ju.Po	76247	Feuereisen	Eleonora	12.06.24
89	Ju.Po	76291 *	Finder	Eugenia	13.07.15
46	Ju.Po	76248	Flinder	Fela	15.08.09
49	Ju.Po	76251	Frankel	Frieda	14.04.24
48	Ju.Po	76250	Freilich	Rosa	01.03.15
47	Ju.Po	76249	Frey	Cecilia	11.11.21
51	Ju.Po	76253	Friedmann	Estera	01.12.20
50	Ju.Po	76252	Friedmann	Eugenia	18.06.23
52	Ju.Po	76254	Friedmann	Felicia	02.01.23
53	Ju.Po	76255	Friedmann	Helena	03.09.04
55	Ju.Po	76257	Friedner	Ada	16.01.21
54	Ju.Po	76256	Friedner	Franciszka	05.07.06
57	Ju.Po	76259	Frisch	Ella	04.03.01
56	Ju.Po	76258	Frisch	Stefania	20.04.27
58	Ju.Po	76260	Gams	Genia	01.09.14
60	Ju.Po	76262	Garde	Irena	02.04.18
59	Ju.Po	76261	Garde	Mira	07.08.99
61	Ju.Po	76263	Geller	Anna	08.09.12
62	Ju.Po	76264	Geminder	Fela	18.07.14
63	Ju.Po	76265	Geminder	Helene	16.05.10
64	Ju.Po	76266	Geminder	Lore	05.01.23
65	Ju.Po	76267	Gerner	Eidla	22.11.96
66	Ju.Po	76268	Gerner	Pola	17.01.21

Ldf Nr.	H.Art. U.Nat.	H.No.	Vorname	Name	Geburts Datum
67	Ju.Po	76269 *	Getzler	Syda	15.05.13
68	Ju.Po	76270	Ginter	Ernestine	16.03.10
69	Ju.Po	76271	Glockenberg	Rosa	04.01.20
70	Ju.Po	76272	Goldberg	Salomea	18.12.18
71	Ju.Po	76273	Goldberg	Syda	08.03.22
72	Ju.Po	76274	Goldmann	Hinde	06.07.92
73	Ju.Po	76275	Goldstein	Cypera	15.01.99
74	Ju.Po	76276	Grajower	Sara	30.07.23
81	Ju.Po	76283	Gronner	Gustawa	22.10.08
82	Ju.Po	76284	Gross	Cypora	26.03.16
83	Ju.Po	76285	Gross	Selma	26.06.12
84	Ju.Po	76286	Grossbard	Paulina	03.08.25
75	Ju.Po	76277	Grunberg	Leonie	23.10.19
171	Ju.Po	76374	Grunberg	Miriam	01.12.20
76	Ju.Po	76278	Gruner	Hanka	03.11.05
77	Ju.Po	76279	Gruner	Helena	20.12.27
78	Ju.Po	76280	Grunspan	Sabina	24.01.18
80	Ju.Po	76282	Grunwald	Sabina	26.11.11
86	Ju.Po	76288	Guntherz	Augusta	18.09.97
85	Ju.Po	76287	Gunz-Sperling	Bronia	21.05.16
88	Ju.Po	76290	Haubenstock	Maria	12.04.17
87	Ju.Po	76289	Haubenstock	Sofia	14.05.21
90	Ju.Po	76292	Heilmann	Sara	20.11.10
91	Ju.Po	76293	Hendler	Lea	10.05.08
92	Ju.Po	76294	Henig	Chana	06.06.02
94	Ju.Po	76296	Herzog	Estera	15.06.99
93	Ju.Po	76295	Herzog	Lea	12.12.22
95	Ju.Po	76297	Heublum	Nina	11.01.97
96	Ju.Po	76298	Hilfstein	Miriam	25.01.97
98	Ju.Po	76300	Hirsch	Anna	29.03.15
97	Ju.Po	76299 *	Hirsch	Helena	03.09.11
99	Ju.Po	76301	Hirsch	Helga	01.07.23

Ldf Nr.	H.Art. U.Nat.	H.No.	Vorname	Name	Geburts Datum
100	Ju.Po	76302	Hirschberg	Sali	18.05.03
101	Ju.Po	76303	Hirschfeld	Polda	21.04.21
102	Ju.Po	76304	Hollander	Rachela	23.03.17
103	Ju.Po	76305	Holzmann	Perl	14.03.10
109	Ju.Po	76311	Horowitz	Bella	10.03.20
105	Ju.Po	76307 *	Horowitz	Bronislawa	22.04.30
106	Ju.Po	76308 *	Horowitz	Halina	13.03.29
107	Ju.Po	76309 *	Horowitz	Roma	15.05.12
108	Ju.Po	76310	Horowitz	Ruchel	14.12.06
110	Ju.Po	76312	Horowitz	Sara	24.06.88
111	Ju.Po	76313	Hudes	Estera	10.03.10
112	Ju.Po	76314	Ickowicz	Pola	21.02.18
113	Ju.Po	76315	Israeli	Stella	04.03.10
114	Ju.Po	76316	Jerethh	Chaja	12.07.92
115	Ju.Po	76317	Karmel-Poss	Adela	05.04.21
116	Ju.Po	76318 *	Karp	Celina	28.05.29
117	Ju.Po	76319	Karp	Feiga Raza	15.09.05
118	Ju.Po	76320	Katolik	Cyla	14.05.14
119	Ju.Po	76321	Katz	Cecilia	12.08.22
121	Ju.Po	76323	Katz	Gabriela	17.03.19
120	Ju.Po	76322	Katz	Ruth	25.08.20
122	Ju.Po	76324	Kaufmann	Regina	23.12.20
125	Ju.Po	76327	Kerner	Estera	20.08.05
126	Ju.Po	76328 *	Kinstlinger	Chana	15.08.13
127	Ju.Po	76329	Kiwetz	Fradel	06.05.21
128	Ju.Po	76330	Kleinmann	Paula	18.02.27
129	Ju.Po	76331	Klinger	Sara	03.04.14
130	Ju.Po	76332	Klipstein	Rosalie	17.10.99
131	Ju.Po	76333	Kohn	Ruth	10.02.26
123	Ju.Po	76325	Konigsberg	Anna	26.11.90
104	Ju.Po	76306	Korn	Estera	24.11.18
132	Ju.Po	76334 *	Korn	Rachela	08.04.00

Ldf Nr.	H.Art. U.Nat.	H.No.	Vorname	Name	Geburts Datum
133	Ju.Po	76335 *	Kornhauser	Rosalia	24.07.14
134	Ju.Po	76336	Kraus	Czeslawa	17.08.23
135	Ju.Po	76337 *	Krumholz	Lola	10.01.17
124	Ju.Po	76326	Kuhn	Helena	06.02.22
136	Ju.Po	76338	Kupferberg	Ala	18.10.18
137	Ju.Po	76339	Kurz	Tauba	18.06.03
138	Ju.Po	76340	Kuzmer-Lewkowicz	R	06.12.15
141	Ju.Po	76343	Lampel	Anita	26.05.28
142	Ju.Po	76344	Lampel	Celina	14.03.07
143	Ju.Po	76345	Landsberger	Helene	12.07.08
139	Ju.Po	76341	Laufer	Rosa	16.10.24
144	Ju.Po	76347	Leder	Paula	01.01.21
148	Ju.Po	76351	Lehrer-Handler	Bella	08.12.19
145	Ju.Po	76348	Lejzon	Chana	15.06.00
147	Ju.Po	76350	Lejzon	Pesia	03.05.26
149	Ju.Po	76352	Lermer	Anna	10.01.13
150	Ju.Po	76353	Leser	Perla	13.07.11
155	Ju.Po	76358	Lewinska	Natalia	22.04.14
156	Ju.Po	76359	Lewkowicz	Ital	22.11.06
159	Ju.Po	76362	Lichtig	Anna	20.10.04
157	Ju.Po	76360	Liebermann	Salomea	06.03.98
158	Ju.Po	76361 *	Liebgold	Etka	04.09.14
160	Ju.Po	76363	Linzer	Lusia	08.09.27
161	Ju.Po	76364	Lipschutz	Debora	08.04.17
162	Ju.Po	76365	Lis	Eda	15.05.00
163	Ju.Po	76366	Lis	Henryka	22.07.20
146	Ju.Po	76349	Loffel	Sabina	22.02.13
151	Ju.Po	76354 *	Low	Dr.Matilde	06.01.99
152	Ju.Po	76355	Lowenstein	Ruth	18.07.18
153	Ju.Po	76356	Lowi	Adela	29.11.10
154	Ju.Po	76357	Lowi	Maria	28.05.95

Ldf Nr.	H.Art. U.Nat.	H.No.	Vorname	Name	Geburts Datum
166	Ju.Po	76369	Mandel	Perla	06.02.12
79	Ju.Po	76281	Mandelbaum	Mala	24.07.17
164	Ju.Po	76367	Manne	Tauba	13.10.88
165	Ju.Po	76368	Markia	Maria	05.01.12
167	Ju.Po	76370	Markin	Tilla	06.06.08
170	Ju.Po	76373	Mischel	Maria	07.07.17
168	Ju.Po	76371	Muller	Berta	06.03.07
169	Ju.Po	76372	Muller	Stella	05.02.28
172	Ju.Po	76375	Nadel	Doba	27.02.93
173	Ju.Po	76376	Nadel	Felicia	26.06.17
174	Ju.Po	76377	Nass	Roma	09.01.06
175	Ju.Po	76378	Nessel	Gisela	20.07.28
176	Ju.Po	76379	Nessel	Paulina	09.07.22
177	Ju.Sl.	76380	Neumann	Irena	29.11.12
178	Ju.Po	76381	Neumann	Mina	04.12.14
179	Ju.Po	76382	Nussbaum	Herta	28.07.22
180	Ju.Po	76383	Nussbaum	Rosalia	14.11.12
181	Ju.Po	76384	Offmann	Henryka	01.05.27
182	Ju.Po	76385	Offmann	Hermina	15.05.27
183	Ju.Po	76386	Offmann	Steffa	16.06.08
184	Ju.Po	76387	Opoczynska	Olga	17.09.98
185	Ju.Po	76388	Orbach	Sara	22.12.19
186	Ju.Po	76389	Pariser	Cecilia	14.04.15
187	Ju.Po	76390	Peller	Rega	15.01.20
188	Ju.Po	76391	Peller	Sara	06.12.18
189	Ju.Po	76392 *	Pelzmann	Gusta	21.02.02
190	Ju.Po	76393	Penner	Fanny Debora	27.09.15
192	Ju.Po	76395	Penner	Franciszka	27.01.24
191	Ju.Po	76394	Penner	Maria	03.12.96
193	Ju.Po	76396	Perlberger	Dora	14.11.07
194	Ju.Po	76397	Perlmann	Ewa	16.06.98

Ldf Nr.	H.Art. U.Nat.	H.No.	Vorname	Name	Geburts Datum
195	Ju.Po	76398 *	Pfefferberg	Ludmila	15.07.20
196	Ju.Po	76399 *	Pinkas	Estera	06.02.24
197	Ju.Po	76400	Presser	Bronislawa	09.03.23
198	Ju.Po	76401	Presser	Frania	12.11.01
199	Ju.Po	76402	Presser	Rosa	22.04.19
200	Ju.Po	76403	Rath	Dora	05.09.19
201	Ju.Po	76404 *	Ratz	Ewa	05.03.30
202	Ju.Po	76405	Ratz	Fela	29.04.12
203	Ju.Po	76406	Redlich	Irena	08.12.21
204	Ju.Po	76407	Reich	Anna	14.09.20
205	Ju.Po	76408	Reicher	Bluma	07.12.22
206	Ju.Po	76409	Reismann	Lola	26.06.17
209	Ju.Po	76412	Ring	Hanka	16.01.28
208	Ju.Bo.	76411	Ring	Rena	12.01.05
210	Ju.Po	76413	Ringelblum	Eugenia	25.10.18
211	Ju.Po	76414	Rittermann	Elzbieta	05.07.10
212	Ju.Po	76415	Rittermann	Jadwiga	18.04.16
213	Ju.Po	76416	Rosen	Estera	18.03.05
214	Ju.Po	76417	Rosen	Mira	05.11.25
215	Ju.Po	76418	Rosenberg	Hanka	20.12.18
216	Ju.Po	76419	Rosenberg	Sara	07.01.16
217	Ju.Po	76420	Rosenbluth	Felicia	22.07.19
218	Ju.Po	76421	Rosner	Helena	14.08.09
219	Ju.Po	76422	Rosner	Helena	31.07.22
220	Ju.Po	76423 *	Rosner	Marianne	21.10.10
221	Ju.Po	76424	Rothberg	Erna	31.12.15
222	Ju.Po	76425	Rottenberg	Ratael	21.04.16
207	Ju.Po	76410	Ruckel	Gustawa	06.06.25
223	Ju.Po	76426	Safier	Rita	26.06.26
224	Ju.Po	76427	Sauerbrunn	Sulamith	31.12.15
228	Ju.Po	76431 *	Scheck	Irena	20.02.21
225	Ju.Po	76428	Schein	Meta	02.09.21

Ldf Nr.	H.Art. U.Nat.	H.No.	Vorname	Name	Geburts Datum
226	Ju.Po	76429	Schenierer	Hella	15.08.06
227	Ju.Po	76430	Schenker	Ryfka	08.01.88
231	Ju.Po	76434	Schiffer	Ruth	02.07.20
232	Ju.Po	76435	Schlafstein	Malwina	25.01.16
233	Ju.Po	76436	Schlesinger	Hania	24.07.18
234	Ju.Po	76437	Schmidt	Hanka	12.07.26
235	Ju.Po	76438	Schmidt	Toni	16.01.23
236	Ju.Po	76439	Schneeweiss	Anna	25.08.10
237	Ju.Po	76440	Schonherz	Erna	18.06.25
238	Ju.Po	76441	Schonherz	Helena	13.09.99
239	Ju.Po	76442	Schonherz	Stefania	01.03.16
229	Ju.Po	76432	Schonthal	Bella	06.10.00
230	Ju.Po	76433	Schonthal	Regina	27.10.25
240	Ju.Po	76443	Schwarzmann	Bella	24.09.04
241	Ju.Po	76444	Schwarzmann	Salomea	27.05.28
242	Ju.Po	76445	Schwed	Dora	24.07.21
243	Ju.Po	76446	Schweizer	Estera	15.06.25
245	Ju.Po	76448	Seelenfreund	Feiga	18.01.09
246	Ju.Po	76449	Selinger	Syda	22.04.22
247	Ju.Po	76450	Semmel	Regina	17.03.22
248	Ju.Po	76451	Sichermann	Blima	20.05.02
250	Ju.Po	76453	Spira	Franciszka	04.01.09
251	Ju.Po	76454	Srebrna	Gisela	25.12.18
252	Ju.Po	76455	Steinhardt	Ruth	31.11.23
253	Ju.Po	76456	Steinhaus	Rescha	29.12.10
254	Ju.Po	76457	Stern	Leontyna	06.08.11
255	Ju.Po	76458	Stern	Sala	10.02.07
256	Ju.Po	76459 *	Sternberg	Klara	23.03.00
257	Ju.Po	76460	Sterngast	Adela	02.03.11
260	Ju.Po	76463	Sternlicht	Bronislawa	03.05.22
261	Ju.Po	76464	Sternlicht	Helena	25.04.25
262	Ju.Po	76465	Sternlicht	Sydonia	24.02.20

Ldf Nr.	H.Art. U.Nat.	H.No.	Vorname	Name	Geburts Datum
258	Ju.Po	76461	Stiel	Laura	28.06.12
259	Ju.Po	76462	Stiel	Syda	08.08.20
263	Ju.Po	76466	Strom	Adela	26.11.27
249	Ju.Dt.	76452	Susskind	Ewa	06.11.16
244	Ju.Po	76447	Szypiacka	Frajda	12.01.20
267	Ju.Po	76479	Tanzer	Anna	28.10.08
268	Ju.Po	76471	Tanzer	Berta	07.09.10
264	Ju.Po	76467	Tauss	Teofila	03.03.12
265	Ju.Po	76468	Teitelbaum	Toni	15.09.18
266	Ju.Po	76469	Tennenbaum	Salka	25.08.98
269	Ju.Po	76472	Tilles	Tauba	17.01.17
272	Ju.Po	76475	Trauring	Stefania	14.12.08
270	Ju.Po	76473	Turk	Lola	15.07.15
271	Ju.Po	76474	Turk	Rosalia	11.01.09
273	Ju.Po	76476	Urbach	Salomea	25.06.07
274	Ju.Po	76477	Wachsberger	Chana	06.08.13
275	Ju.Po	76478	Wadler	Ester	10.10.10
276	Ju.Po	76479	Wahl	Sara Estera	22.10.16
277	Ju.Po	76480	Wasserteil	Cecilia	28.05.21
278	Ju.Po	76481	Weinstock	Balka	17.12.05
279	Ju.Po	76482	Weitmann	Carmen	15.01.15
280	Ju.Po	76483	Wiener	Maria	28.12.21
281	Ju.Po	76484	Wohlfeiler	Chaja	04.06.97
282	Ju.Po	76485	Wohlfeiler	Eugenia	18.05.26
283	Ju.Po	76486	Wohlfeiler	Halina	03.01.26
285	Ju.Po	76488	Wohlfeiler	Krystyna	09.05.28
284	Ju.Po	76487	Wohlfeiler	Rena	29.01.27
286	Ju.Po	76489	Wohlfeiler	Rosa	07.07.03
287	Ju.Dt.	76490	Wolf	Hannelore	16.10.23
288	Ju.Po	76491	Wortszmann	Sara	20.03.97
289	Ju.Po	76492	Wulkan	Chaja	16.12.13
290	Ju.Po	76493	Zimmerspitz	Elsa	18.12.13

Ldf Nr.	H.Art. U.Nat.	H.No.	Vorname	Name	Geburts Datum
291	Ju.Po	76494	Zimmerspitz	Jetti	16.07.08
292	Ju.Po	76495	Zoldan	Cecilia	29.01.18
293	Ju.Po	76496	Zucker	Fela	20.11.18
295	Ju.Po	76498	Zuckermann	Estera	10.11.20
294	Ju.Po	76497	Zuckermann	Jetti	10.11.20
296	Ju.Po	76499	Zweig	Bronislawa	28.03.06
297	Ju.Po	76500	Zwetschen-Stiel	Junta	08.07.08

Appendix H: Collaboration with Herbert Steinhouse

The collaboration between the author and Herbert Steinhouse over many years when the author submitted to him his early draft of the Schindler story, "The Man from Svitavy".[322]

Herbert Steinhouse, Montreal 1994, when he received the author's draft
manuscript of the Schindler story.

The article written by Steinhouse 50 years earlier supports *Schindler's Ark* by Keneally, who never met Schindler. The Steinhouse documentation makes Schindler even more extraordinary than either the book or the film, both of which depict him as someone who started out wanting cheap labor to make money and who became a humanitarian in the process. The Steinhouse papers wrestle with the answer to the question that we all want to know: What made Schindler tick? Why did he do what he did? Herbert Steinhouse's interviews would appear to have more validity than the speculative writing of both the book and the film.

The Steinhouse documentation is important for several reasons: for the corroboration it gives to the established record; for the additional details and anecdotes not contained in either Keneally's novel or Spielberg's film; and, most importantly, for the direct access it gives us to Schindler himself.

Steinhouse refers to his 'ancestral estate' in the note below. He is referring to Stonehenge, a prehistoric monument near the author's residence in Wiltshire. Since a boy he had conjured-up the thought of living there.

NOTE:

"For Robin O'Neil, relentless tracker of the truth, unlike us too easily satisfied purveyors of semi-demis, we "factual" journalists and "semi-fictional novelists". Take good care of The Steinhouse ancestral estate!

Herbert Steinhouse

Oskar Schindler

· · · · · · · · · · · · · · · · · · ·

AND HIS LIST

For Robin O'Neil, relentless
Tracker of the truth, unlike us
too-easily satisfied purveyors of semi-demis, we
"factual" journalists and "semi-fictional"
novelists.

    Take good care of the Steinhouse
ancestral estate!

               [signature]
          Montreal, August '95

Notes

---

[1] Viktor was born in Krakow on September 16, 1918. He died aged 81years on May 8, 2000. One of three sons (Michael, David and Viktor) of Herman and Fransisca Dortheimer. Michael was killed in fighting with the Polish army at the outbreak of war. When the Krakow ghetto was established in March 1942, both brothers married local Jewish girls both named Helena. See Schindler women's list: Helena Dortheimer 76229 and Helena Dortheimer 76230. Because of their identical names both women were the subject of some difficulty when the Schindler women were rescued from Auschwitz. When the Krakow ghetto was liquidated on March 13 1943, Herman, Viktor and David were sent to Plaszow concentration camp. In Plaszow Viktor, a qualified painter and decorator, was selected by Amon Goeth to paint his villa. Viktor's father, Herman, was sent to Mathausen camp where he was killed with a lethal injection of benzene. Viktor's brother Michael was shot by Amon Goeth when he was caught with concealed food on his person. Viktor was sent to Schindler's factory where he struck up a personal relationship with the Director. Schindler repaid Viktor for loyal service by selecting him and the two Helena Dortheimers for Brünnlitz. On the last day of the war Oskar Schindler offered a memento to Viktor. Viktor chose a signed photograph of the Director which shows him relaxing in a deckchair (Figure 83). Viktor subsequently came to England, residing in North London, where he met and joined the author in a world-wide journey of re-discovering the Schindler story. Viktor Dortheimer's obituary written by the author was published in *The Times* newspaper on May 16, 2000.

[2] Moshe Bejski, a former Israeli Supreme Court justice and Holocaust survivor who was saved from the Nazis by Oskar Schindler, died Tuesday at the age of 86

[3] Josef Bau was trained as a graphic artist at the University for Plastic Arts in Krakow, Poland. His education was interrupted by World War II and he was transferred to the Plaszow concentration camp in late 1941. Having a talent in gothic lettering, he was employed in the camp for making signs and maps for the Germans. While in Plaszow, Bau created a miniature – the size of his hand – illustrated book with his own poetry. He also forged documents and identity papers for people who managed to escape from the camp. During his imprisonment, Bau fell in love with another inmate, Rebecca Tennenbaum. They were secretly married, despite prohibition by the Germans, in the women's barracks of Plaszow. After Plaszow, Bau was transferred to Gross-Rosen and then to Oscar Schindler's, camp where he stayed till the end of the war. After liberation, Josef Bau graduated from the University of Plastic Arts in Krakow. In 1950, he immigrated to Israel together with his wife and three-year-old daughter, where he worked as a graphic artist at the Brandwein Institute in Haifa and for the government of Israel

Chapter 1

[4] Certified extract from Registrar of births, deaths, and marriages – Svitavy.

[5] Johann Schindler (born September 5, 1883, Svitavy) described by Emilie Schindler as often drunk and absent from the family home at 24 Iglaustrasse,

Svitavy (now 24 Polieska Street). Johann died in the Kisslau camp in Eichstadt on February 19, 1947.

[6] Francizka Schindler (née Luserova), was born on February 15, 1884, Svitavy. Within the family she was called Fanny. Described by Emilie Schindler as a very pleasant and elegant woman who was always ill. Francizka Schindler died at age 53 years (1935). Their marriage took place on October 12, 1907.

[7] Emilie Schindler's memoir describes Elfriede looking like her father: ugly, with chestnut hair and large brown eyes. According to Emilie she was ignored by everyone.

[8] An interesting newspaper clipping found by the author in Svitavy town archive. No date, but probably early thirties. The document is a half-page section for advertisements by local businesses. There are two of particular interests: (1) Hans Schindler, Zwittau, (Svitavy) Iglaustrasse 24 (Schindler family address). 'Insurance Business; all insurances catered for, fire, theft and personal insurance.' Immediately after this section there is a motif, then, 'All farm machinery of the highest quality supplied; (2) A similar advertisement with the same motif but headed 'Franz Schindler, Zwittau (Svitavy) Lotschnau 187.' According to the translator there is no connection. The motif was used by similar allied trades.

According to Emilie Schindler, Johann Schindler specialized in the selling of electrical generators for domestic and farm purposes. He had previously traded in insurances but the business had collapsed.

[9] After primary school, Schindler attended the Realgymnasium, Svitavy.

[10] Thomas Keneally's, *Schindler's Ark*, London, 1982, 37. Hereafter, Keneally.

[11] Thomas Fensch, *Oskar Schindler and His List*, Vermont, 1995, 13. Hereafter, Fensch/Steinhouse. Also included in this letter were references about Schindler by Herbert Steinhouse. (Spielberg commences his portrayal of Schindler as of 1939.) This disclosure by Steinhouse is very interesting as it corroborates many instances from other sources of Schindler's interest in Jewish culture from a very early age. One of Schindler's favorite images of Jewish life in Krakow was the sight of a Hassid scurrying across the square with a goose tucked under his arm ready for Shabbos (as related to the author by Mrs. Sophia Stern, wife of Itzhak Stern).

[12] Schindler's local drinking house was the Hotel Ungar in the main street of Svitavy. The place where, at age 16, he would taste his first pint of Pilsner beer, where he would celebrate his wedding, conduct his Abwehr activities and the place where he would be arrested for spying and later sentenced to death. The hotel is still functioning and has retained that mysterious atmosphere where small groups of people still conduct their business at all hours of the day and night. The hotel is now called the Hotel Slavia.

[13] List of previous convictions for minor offenses taken from the police files at Svitavy and Brno Magistrates Court Office and the opinion of local people who knew Schindler at the time.

[14] Wundheiler refers to twin girls in Brecher's introduction, p.xxxiii, of her book *Schindler's Legacy*. There is a photograph of Schindler: Oskar Schindler with female companions, apparently twins, taken about 1940 (photo by courtesy of Pola Yogev).

[15] Wundheiler: After Keneally had written *Schindler's Ark* he was approached by a big blonde man who claimed to be Oskar's illegitimate son: "First I thought this guy was a con," said Keneally, "but he had too much information, and he sure looked like Oskar. He said his mother had him and his sister by Oskar, and they had lived a block away from Emilie and Oskar in Svitavy." Source

from American press report. In Mrs. Schindler's memoir she confirms that an illegitimate son of her husband lived in Australia.

[16] Official program number 624457, Zavod Brno-Sobesice 13. Kvetna. On May 19, 1928, in the magazine *Sport,* the results of the trials on May 12 are shown. First: Jaraslav Tichy, riding a Terrot, 2.58.6; second, Mirko Wagner, riding a Terrot, 3.17.1; and third, Oskar Schindler, riding a Motor-Guzzi, 3.22.5. Source material from the Svitavy museum. Verified by the author, 1995. See also Keneally, 38-40.

[17] Herbert Steinhouse, "The Real Oskar Schindler," *Saturday Night,* April, 1994, 77.

[18] Moravska Elektrotechnica (M.E.A.S.). Brno.

[19] Mahren-Schonberg is halfway between Svitavy and Ostrava. It was during this period of employment that he was to meet Ilse Pelikan, agent of the Abwehr.

[20] All genealogical documents were lost in the Second World War.

[21] Emilie Schindler, 42

[22] Emilie also stated that there were other things that the gypsy would not elaborate on. She was not to tell her husband about this incident until after the war when they were en route to Argentina. It has all come true.

[23] Keneally refers to this incident but names the girl as Rita Reif. 41.

[24] Keneally states that she was killed in 1942.

[25] Emilie states that her mother was a just woman, which was passed on to her.

[26] Verified by the author, Svitavy 1996 (town records).

[27] Emilie Schindler, 36

[28] *People Newspaper,* Buenos Aires, 1994, 7 (date of article mislaid). Interview with Emilie Schindler by journalists David Gardner and Corinna Honan.

[29] Since the Spielberg film, Mrs. Schindler has been the center of media attention. She has always given frank observations about her relationship with her husband. The author interviewed Mrs. Schindler on three occasions at the King David Hotel, Israel, in 1994. She has remained the main source of information regarding Oskar Schindler. Her involvement with her husband in his Abwehr duties and her direct action at the Brünnlitz camp cannot be underestimated. Her relationship with Oskar was always strained.

[30] Ball-Kaduri. See also Keneally, 41.

[31] Czech Security Police Documentation/C.J.1553/1/pros.-30. Dated 19.7. 38. Interrogation of Oskar Schindler by Inspector Kirbek of the Security Police Department, Brno. This document is one of a series, and obtained by the author in Prague, Svitavy, and Brno, dealing with the surveillance and arrest of Schindler during his spying activities in July, 1938. Under interrogation Schindler admits his association with the Abwehr, and his methods and contacts used during his activities. It also gives us further information about his personal life. The documentation contains 30 pages of reports and statements, including a full set of Schindler's fingerprints, photograph, and description. Hereafter, Czech Security Document - Schindler.

Chapter 2

[32] Czech Security Document - Schindler.

[33] There are a number of sources where Schindler's character is analyzed by witnesses who were present during these partying activities with Wehrmacht and SS officers.

Mrs. Emilie Schindler, who hosted entertainment evenings at their flat in Krakow.

Henry Rosner (69212), prisoner in Plaszow. Seconded by Goeth to play the violin during entertainment evenings in Goeth's villa. See Elinor J. Brecher, *Schindler's Legacy* 1-5. Rosner interviewed by the author, King David Hotel,

Jerusalem, 1994. The opening scenes in the Spielberg film portray the personality of Schindler accurately.

[34] Author's interview with Mrs. Sophia Stern, Israel, 1995. Although this is very much hearsay evidence I have no reason to believe that this statement is not correct. Subsequent clarification of the statement made by Mrs. Stern is in some way corroborated. See Robert S. Wistrich, *Who's Who in Nazi Germany*, London, 1995, 29. (Canaris was born on 1.1.1887 and was appointed Chief of the Abwehr on 1.1.35.) Perhaps this was a Schindler story but it would explain his subsequent cover and protection.

[35] Mrs. Schindler: "In 1935/6 Oskar traveled to Krakow where he met and seduced a woman. She worked for the counter-intelligence service and recommended him to her superiors in Berlin. Oskar enjoyed his new job, tracking down foreign spies on the Czech/Polish border."

[36] Czech Security Documents - Schindler.

[37] A very good analysis can be found in the book by Bloch, M., *Ribbentrop*. London, 1992. Ch. 15. See also Henderson, Sir Neville, *Failure of a Mission*. (Berlin 1937-1939) London 1941.

[38] Austria annexed March 13, 1938; 183,000 Jews are alerted to the danger.

[39] Report by Henlein, March 28, 1938: German Foreign Policy, series D, 11, No. 107, as cited in A.J.P. Taylor, *Origins of the Second World War*. London, (Penguin) 1963, 192.

[40] See AJP Taylor below.

[41] Keneally, 42. Czech Security Documents - Schindler.

[42] Ziegenhals 514.

[43] (1) Czech Security Document - Schindler. (2) Keneally, 43 refers to the Abwehr agent as Eberhard Gebauer and that Schindler's introduction into the Abwehr took place on the Czech/Polish border. Keneally's account is similar but the names and location are contradicted by the evidence of the Czech Security Document.

[44] Czech Security Document.

[45] Ibid.

[46] Ibid.

[47] Czech Security Officers of the Counter Intelligence Branch.

[48] Ibid.

[49] Jon Blair interview with Mrs. Schindler, Slates 165-186, interview Blair/Emilie Schindler, Buenos Aires, 1981, for the film documentary, *Oskar Schindler*. 165/Take 1. 7. Hereafter, Mrs. Schindler. In the 1994 memoirs she refers to the documents being found behind a mirror in the bathroom.

[50] Ibid.

[51] Czech Security Document CJ.Z - 416/1946 - Relate to the extradition and interrogation of Joseph Aue, alias Sepp Aue, born 13.5.1907. Interviewed by the CSO in Ostrava on August 6, 1946. Re Aue's wartime activities and involvement with the Abwehr during the period 1938/9. This material is significant as it gives us new evidence of the Schindler/Stern relationship.

Chapter 3

[52] C.J. 7219/1946 - 11-1. Moravska Ostrava, 9.8.1946. Interrogation of Joseph Aue by the Czech Security Service after the war. A crucial twelve-page document which deals with detailed information of the Abwehr in Moravska Ostrava and Krakow, Aue's involvement with Schindler and the Higher Officers of the SS, SD, and Wehrmacht. Also included is the official position of Treuhänder in the offices of the Jew, Salomon Bucheister at 15 Stradon Street, Krakow. Hereafter, Czech Security Document - Aue.

[53] The Abwehr also had offices in Oprava.

[54] Up until the end of September 1939, all the security departments of the Nazi State were working independently. By the decree of September 29, 1939, all existing German police forces were merged under one umbrella organization – the Reichssicherheitshauptamt (Reich Security Office). There were numerous changes in the RSHA over the years, but essentially the structure was kept until the end of the war.

[55] Jon Blair/Mrs. Schindler interview, 1981, 166/1-8.

[56] Ibid.

[57] Emilie Schindler, 49.

[58] Ibid. See also Blair/Mrs. Schindler interview note, Argentina 1982.

[59] SD Headquarters - Hohenzollern Palace, 102 Wilhelmstrasse, backing onto the Prinz Albrechtstrasse Gestapo building where Himmler also had offices. (After Heydrich's assassination he was succeeded by Dr. Kaltenbrunner.) The bureaucracy had grown and the RSHA offices sprawled all over Berlin occupying no fewer than 38 buildings. See Butler, *Gestapo*, 131.

[60] SS-Obersturmbahnführer Dr. Werner Best.

[61] Rupert Butler, *Gestapo*, London, 1992, 77/8.

[62] Aleksander B. Skotnicki, *Oskar Schindler In the eyes of Cracovian Jews Rescued by him. Krakow,* 2008, 49.

[63] Czech Security Document - Aue. Joseph Aue, alias Sepp Aue, was the son of the Jew, Emily Goldberger. Mother – German National, née Kamily. Parents were not married. Aue's mother married Charles Lederera who died in 1937. Aue was brought up as a Catholic German and was able to avoid persecution. His father died in Auschwitz in 1942.

[64] Ibid.

[65] Ibid.

[66] Ibid.

[67] Ibid.

[68] Sicherheitsdienst: the SD, on paper at least, was the intelligence organ of the Nazi Party, whereas the Gestapo was the Secret State Police. In fact, the two worked so closely together that, at times, they were indistinguishable. The SD laid heavy emphasis on pursuing ideological and racial enemies.
Rupert Butler, *Gestapo*, London, 1992, 96-8.

[69] Ibid.

[70] (1)Mrs Schindler. (2) The Jon Blair/Emilie Schindler interview in 1981 makes interesting reading with regard to *Operation Himmler*. She mentions meetings at about this time of high ranking SD, SS, and Wehrmacht officers, at their apartment in Moravska Ostrava. She speaks of the Polish uniforms being delivered, and boxes which filled her rooms. Mrs. Schindler mentions that her husband was paying cash on delivery for these items. The Schindlers' main concern was the Polish Abwehr, who had been keeping their movements and apartment under observation. She stated that they had already been burgled. She concluded that whoever entered the premises was looking for papers but all that was taken was her wristwatch. Emilie Schindler was part of the Abwehr in Moravska Ostrava but only in a nominal role. She never undertook operational duties but remained privy to all her husband's activities. Mrs. Schindler returned to Svitavy shortly after September 1, 1939. Author's interview with Emilie Schindler. King David Hotel, Jerusalem 1995.

[71] Emilie, 32.

[72] Rupert Butler, *Gestapo*, 98.

[73] Ibid.

[74] Ibid.

[75] Jon Blair, film documentary, *Oskar Schindler*.

[76] Czech Security Document - Aue. See also, Martin Gilbert, *The Holocaust*, London, 1987, 94/5.

[77] Czech Security Document – Aue.

[78] Ibid. The woman, Marta, was to become a trust administrator for Schindler in the controversial Wiener Affair.

[79] Schindler's NSDAP record card shows his personal details including changes of residence. He is shown as Member No. 27 Zwittau/Svitavy (6,421,477). Residence on 28.3.40, Parkstra. Moravska Ostrava, 25, 6.3.40. 4.4.40 Westring, inner Stadt 23/111, Krakow.

[80] Fensch/Steinhouse, 13.

Chapter 4

[81] Dr. Frank began his political career in the Third Reich as a Dragoon in the Sturmabteilung (SA). A lawyer by profession, he gave free legal service to Nazi Party members. He was rewarded by being appointed as the first Bavarian Minister of Justice, then Reichsminister without portfolio. In October 1939, Hitler charged him with exemplary powers to oversee Poland being cleansed of Jewish culture and the suppression of the civilian population. Dr. Frank was answerable to Hitler directly over all matters. Frank was a moody autocrat who displayed sentimentality and brutality. He was powerful but vain. He was one of the principal architects of the destruction process in Poland.

[82] After the outbreak of war with Russia (June 22, 1941), the German army overran Galicia and this area became the fifth district. (Raul Hilberg, *The Destruction of the European Jews*, London, 1985, [3 vols.] Vol. 1, 197. Hereafter, Hilberg.)

[83] Otto Gustav Freiherr von Wächter, born 1901, was the son of General Josef Freiherr von Wächter, an Austrian Minister of the Army. He joined the Austrian Nazis and took part in the futile Nazi attempt of July 1934 to seize power in Austria. He fled to Germany where he dropped his title of nobility and became a German citizen. After the invasion of Russia in 1942, Wächter moved to Lvov where he remained until being dislodged by the Russians in 1944. He presided over the "ghettoization" of the Jews in the Krakow and Galicia districts and over the deportations of the Jews in Galicia and Italy. Wächter died in Italy in 1949 under the protection of Bishop Alois Hudal. (Raul Hilberg, *Perpetrators, Victims, and Bystanders, the Jewish Catastrophe*. London, 1991, 46/47. See also Hilberg, Vol. 3, 1108.)

[84] Replaced in 1943 by Koppe. Rumored killed on the Eastern Front. No trace post-1945.

[85] Rupert Butler, *Gestapo*, London, 1992, 168/9. One of the powers behind the throne of Heydrich was Walter Schellenberg (1910-1952), who rose to be head of SS Foreign Intelligence. As such, he was charged with drawing up the Sonderfahnungliste-GB (Special Search List for Great Britain). It was Schellenberg who had engineered the downfall of Canaris after the attempt on Hitler's life, the so-called bomb plot. Schellenberg knew that the concept of a unified intelligence service was favored by Kaltenbrunner (Heydrich's successor). The bomb plot on Hitler was the green light for the SD to go for Canaris. Himmler and Kaltenbrunner, in their furor of vengeance, soon unearthed damning evidence against Canaris. Their investigators had found a safe in the basement of the Abwehr headquarters at Zossen. They unearthed meticulous notes written in Canaris's own hand. Here were details of the Vatican exchanges, together with a sensational revelation that Oster

(Canaris's deputy) and others had betrayed the plans of the German High Command for the invasion of France and the Low Countries.

[86] Coded message from Schindler's secretary (Viktoria Klonowska) was sent directly to Canaris Headquarters. See Keneally 70.

[87] After the invasion of Poland, Heydrich issued a decree dated September 21, 1939, in two parts: (1) under heading – *The Jewish Question in Occupied Territories* – set out preliminary measures against the Jews; (2) dealt with the establishment of the Jewish Council of Elders (Judenrat) to facilitate the evacuation of Jews from countryside to town. Document marked "Secret." See Gutman, *Pattern of Jewish Leadership*, 169.

[88] See Hilberg, Vol. 1 250, 214. Entries by Czerniakow for October 19-20 and November 2, 1939, in Hilberg, Staron, and Kermisz, eds., *Warsaw Diary*, 84, 86-87.

[89] Source - Alexander Biberstein (brother of Mark), *Extermination of Krakow's Jews*, Warsaw, 1946. Extract translated by Leo Aftergood, London, 1995 (brother of Bertha Aftergood [76201]). See also Keneally, 88/9. He has got it exactly right.

[90] (1) Keneally 88. (2) The Holocaust raised some of the most acute moral issues ever faced by humanity. Moral judgments and dilemmas can be seen in their most striking form in connection with the Judenrat. For a comprehensive appraisal of the Judenrat, see Isaiah Trunk's *Judenrat*, New York, 1972.

[91] Ball-Kaduri, 17. See also Keneally 63. Keneally suggests that Schindler obtained his information from like-minded sympathizers in the offices of the SD and SS.

[92] Krakow, Westring, inner Stadt 23/111.

[93] Mrs. Schindler's memoir: Schindler had a long-term relationship with Klonowska. Oskar appears to have got his women's loyalties mixed up, i.e. Klonowska, according to Mrs. Schindler, was with the Gestapo (anti-Canaris) and the lady Amelia was with the Abwehr. I think we must accept that even love can override individual loyalties. Who was spying for whom?

[94] Ibid.

[95] The term *Treuhänder* appears to have been an innovation brought in by the Germans at the outbreak of hostilities. From the many regulations published in occupied Poland between 1939 and 1944, there appear to be no directives directly concerning the characteristics of a Treuhänder. The only requirements for this position were that the person had to be capable of guardianship according to the general principles of the time. Only German and Austrian citizens, and later the volksdeutsche were acceptable for this position. Hereafter, Trust Administrator - Treuhänd Office/Trust.

[96] Ball-Kaduri.

[97] Ibid.

[98] Czech Security Document –Aue.

[99] Ball-Kaduri.

[100] It was the policy of the RSHA to Aryanize not just the ownership of companies, but also the management and workforce. The sooner the Trust Administrators filtered out the skilled Jewish employees, the better. Ball-Kaduri, 16. Keneally, 51. For further information on the policy of Aryanization and the procedures, see Raul Hilberg, *Documents of Destruction*, London, 1972, 25.

[101] Ibid.

[102] Within a matter of months, Schindler had bought the factory outright for a reported sum of 300 RM. Victor Dortheimer interview with the author, 1996.

[103] Yitzhak Stern (69518). His account of the times and, in particular of his dealings with Schindler, are of utmost importance. He was born in Krakow, Poland, January 25, 1901 to Menachem and Perla, née Hirschberg. He was the chief accountant for the Jewish-owned export-import firm of J.L. Bucheister and Co., 15 Stradon Street, Krakow, a position he had held since 1924. He lived until the war at Gruene Gasse 28, Krakow. He married a solicitor, Sophia Backenrot, in 1945. Stern was the vice-president of the Jewish Agency for Western Poland and a member of the Zionist Committee in Krakow. He survived the war with Schindler and, for a time, lived with him in Paris. He immigrated to Israel in 1948. He was interviewed in 1948 by Herbert Steinhouse about his war experiences, which were later published in the book by Thomas Fensch, *Oskar Schindler and His List*, Vermont, 1995, 270 pages. Stern also published a small booklet, *Oskar Schindler the Humanist*, Tel Aviv, 18 pages, written shortly before his death in the summer of 1967.

[104] Mrs. Stern to the author, 1995.

Chapter 5

[105] The Wiener papers and statements are in the archives at Yad Vashem. Translated from Hebrew into English by Yaël Reicher, Tel Aviv, for the author. See also Keneally, 86/87. Working independently on this issue, I find that Keneally got it just about right. He changed the names probably on advice from his publishers. Keneally's research is very thorough.

[106] The share of Jewish workers employed by Schindler at Emalia 1940-1944. 1940-150; 1941-190; 1942-550; 1943-900; 1944-1,000; 1945 (Brünnlitz)-1,100.

[107] Jon Blair, film documentary, *Schindler*, 1982.

[108] Author interviews Richard Rechen, Israel, 1992. Rechen played an important part in Schindler's escape from Brünnlitz after the war. He was also the man who, when Schindler died in 1974, was nominated to go to Germany and bring Schindler's body to Jerusalem.

[109] See Hilberg Vol. 208/10.

[110] Dr. Arieh L. Bauminger. *The Fighters of the Krakow Ghetto.* Yad Vashem, 1990, 23.

[111] Courtesy of the Historical Museum of the City of Krakow.

[112] Tadeusz Pankiewicz. *The Krakow Ghetto Pharmacy* (2nd ed. 151), Israel, 1987. 1-10. This edition was translated from Polish into English by Henry Tilles. This is an excellent book, by far the most descriptive account from a person on the spot and who saw everything.

[113] Bauminger, 26.

[114] Ibid.

[115] Pankiewicz, vii.

[116] Jon Blair, film interview with Mrs. Emily Schindler, 1982. B.A.

[117] See Wundheiler 4, also Ball-Kaduri documentation.

Chapter 6

[118] Julius Madritsch, *Menschen in Not* (People in Distress). Wien, 1963, 1-28.

[119] The clothing factories of F.A. Strassberg & Co. and F.A. Hugo. The takeover as a Trust Administrator was very similar to that of Joseph Aue's. Madritsch gave comfort to the Jews in his employment and made conditions as comfortable as possible.

[120] Working for Madritsch were: Raymond Titsch and Dr. Adolf Lenhardt, both from Vienna; Anneliese Pipgorra from Berlin; Maria Herling from Vienna.

Also on the books was Oswald Bousco from Vienna, the police sergeant in the ghetto.

121 (1) Ball-Kaduri documentation. (2) Madritsch documentation secured by the author, Vienna 1995.

122 Raul Hilberg, *Documents of Destruction*, London, 1972, 89/90.

123 Benjamin B. Ferencz, *Less Than Slaves*, London, 1979, 18.

124 Oswald Pohl, who had joined the Party in 1926 and had risen to the rank of Obergruppenführer, was to be the man in charge of the new RSHA. Glueck's Department D, which was in charge of all concentration camps, was made subordinate to Pohl. Department D11 handled the commitment of inmates for labor and was headed by Standartenführer Gerhard Maurer, who was assisted by Karl Sommer.

125 Hilberg, *Documents of Destruction,* 290.

126 The specialists for Jewish matters who belonged to the Sicherheitspolizei were: SS Obersturmführer Becher, SS-Oberscharführer Siebert, Untersturmführer Brand. These officials appeared in the ghetto from time to time. SS-Sturmscharführer Kriminalsekretar Wilhelm Kunde, Olde, and SS-Obersturmführer Hermann Heinrich were permanently stationed there.
The Gestapo were: SS-Obersturmführer Theodor Heinermayer, Specialists SIPO Korner and Paul Mallotke. The SSU Polizei were: SS-Oberführer Schermer (Schermer was the highest authority for Jewish affairs in the Krakow district), Sturmbanführer Hässe, SS-Unterscharführer Horst Pilarzik, SS-Rotteführer Wiktor Ritschek,and SS-RotteführerZugsberger.
The Main office of the SSU Polizei was located at Oleanders. See Pankiewicz, 69.

127 Dr. Arieh L. Bauminger. *The Fighters of the Krakow Ghetto.* Yad Vashem, 1990, 26.

128 Chris Webb collection.

129 Tadeusz Pankiewicz. *The Krakow Ghetto Pharmacy*. New York, 1985 (English translation), Chapter 2, 29-52. Still the most credible book that deals specifically with the Krakow ghetto. Victor Dortheimer (69124). Interview with the author 1996.

130 Only in May 1942 did the Nazi regime begin the systematic mass deportations of Reich Jews that Hitler had decided upon the previous autumn. A similar fate befell the transports from Slovakia and Western Europe soon thereafter. Between May 4 and 15, 12 transports containing 10,000 Reich Jews were deported to Chelmno where they were gassed. Jews from Vienna were deported to Maly Trostenets on May 5, followed by a further 17 transports June 1942. On June 22. 1942, it was pointed out by Dr Frauendorfer, the Director of Labor in the Generalgovernment, that expulsions of Jewish labor from the ghettos was causing economic difficulties. Frauendorfer explained that Jews were part of the 100,000 skilled workers employed in the armaments industry; 800,000 workers were sent to Germany, and a further 100,000 (including Jews) were employed by the military. He further pointed out that he was solely dependent on Jewish labor and, therefore, Jewish skilled labor should be used and not be fodder for the SS resettlement program. While Globocnik was pulling one way to exterminate the Jews, the military were pulling the other way to retain Jewish skilled labor. A compromise was reached in September/October 1942.

131 County of Krakow (Krakow): Martin Gilbert (MG), 'Map of the Holocaust', Map 128 (7,000), Yad Vashem Archives (YVA); YA (5,000, 1 - 6), TB, table 7, two very large transports between June 1 and 6, 1942. See also YVA KK/1, 6,000 on June 1,1942, and 4,000 on June 6,1942. From all other sources 10,000

is the probable number. See also Tadeusz Pankiewicz, Krakow Ghetto Pharmacy, NY, 1985, 40-53.

[132] County of Lviv (Galicia): YVA, this transport from Janowska camp joined up with the Kolomyja transport for Belzec in mid June. See also YVA LL/1, June 24, 1942, 4,000 deported to Belzec. Lviv was spared further transports until 12 August 12, 1942.

[133] County of Tarnow (Krakow): MG, Map 128, YVA, YA, 11-18 June 1942, these were very large transports. See also YVA KK/3, June 11-18,1942, 12,000. SS-Oberführer Scherner, Police Leader, Krakow, personally directed these transports. These were the first big deportations since the Krakow transports. 40,000 Jews in the open ghetto faced 30 Schutzpolizei, 100 Polish police officers, 150 Gendarmerie, a unit of Sonderdienst and the Polish labor service (Baudienst). Two separate operations were taking place simultaneously: örtliche Aussiedlung (local resettlement) where thousands were either taken to the forests or to the local cemetery, where they were shot into pits. The residue, some 11,500, were deported to Belzec. These actions stalled on June 18, when the remaining (some 20,000) work Jews were sealed into the ghetto. Further actions of this kind took place in August, September and November 1942. When this transport arrived at Belzec on June 13, 1942, there was a spontaneous act of resistance. When the work Jews were removing the bodies from the gas chambers and they saw the situation, they attacked the German and Ukrainian guard. It was reported four Germans and nearly all the Jews were killed. See Archives of PZPR (Polish United Worker's Party), Documents for 1942 - Sikorski Archive London.

[134] Pankiewicz, 48.

[135] Ibid. Ch 2.

[136] Ibid, 48.

[137] The Madritsch papers from Vienna obtained by the author, 1995.

[138] Pankiewicz, 103.

[139] Mrs. Sophia Stern's recollection of her husband. Interview with the author. See also Wundheiler.

[140] Keneally, 135-138. See also Ball-Kaduri documentation.

[141] Affidavit by Lesser, Yad Vashem, dated 1962.

[142] Pankiewicz, 58.

[143] Madritsch documentation, Vienna, 1995.

[144] (1) Bauminger/Pankiewicz.

Chapter 7

[145] See: Piper, *Auschwitz,* 9 who quotes *Wspomnienia Rudolfa Hoßa - Komendanta obozu oświęcimskiego,* Warsaw 1965, 18, 204; T. Cyprian, J. Cyprian and Sawicki, *Sprawy polskie,* 438-439.

[146] PRO, File No. FO 371/50971/85681. British Intelligence report dated 16 March 1945.

[147] Ibid. See also Alexander Skotnicki, *Oskar Schindler*, Krakow 2008, 331

[148] Trial notes and indictment of Amon Leopold Goeth. Although only hearsay, in 1995 I interviewed Sofia Stern (wife of Yitzhak Stern, collaborator with Oskar Schindler in Krakow) when she stated that Schindler, on hearing Bachner's story, went to Belzec to verify the details but was turned back by the SS-guards at Sobibor Lubelski.

Chapter 8

[149] Joseph Bau (69084), interviewed by the author over several weeks in 1993-6. Recollections of Bau come from a detailed diary of events immediately after the war.

[150] Interviewed by the author.

[151] The Ferber shooting was witnessed by Victor Dortheimer (69124). Interviewed by the author in London 1995.

[152] This hanging was witnessed by the entire camp. Moshe Bejski (69387) related the facts to the author in 1995.

[153] Julius Madritsch and Raymond Titsch witnessed the aftermath of the liquidation. The only Jews to survive from Tarnow were the Jews employed in the Madritsch factory, who were transferred to the Madritsch factory in Plaszow. Madritsch paid well for this concession.

[154] Mieczyslaw Pemper (69514) was employed by Goeth as a secretary. Some of the most secret information was obtained by Pemper, including details of the transport of the Hungarian Jews in 1944. I will be referring to Pemper's activities later. Interviewed by the author in Augsburg, Germany, 1995.

[155] I am still strongly of the opinion that the Canaris/Schindler connection is standing firm.

[156] Mrs. Schindler's memoir, my observation.

[157] R. Fikejz, *In Search of the Star of David.*

[158] Adam Guard (69515) interviewed by the author in Jerusalem, who confirmed this transfer.

[159] Blair interview with Mrs. Schindler 1982.

[160] Ball-Kaduri documentation. See also Benjamin B. Ferencz, *Less Than Slaves,* Harvard 1979, 191-192. Even Jews who worked nearby for Siemans-Bauunion at Krakow/Plaszow described how they could sometimes warm their hands by the fire in the Schindler work hall, where they dared to cook a potato that they had managed to hide or steal.

Chapter 9

[161] The Judenrat, and Gutter at its head, tried for several successive days to postpone the date of the liquidation, using whatever means possible. All attempts failed. Haase refused to agree to a delay of even one day.

[162] Ibid, 106.

[163] Goeth and Haase could not stand each other. (Krakow archive record 2586/76) Pankiewicz, from his observation post, noted other SS officers; W. Kunde, K. Olde, Heinrich, K. Heinemayer (Chief of the political division of the Gestapo and his deputy, specialist SIPO Koener), and, of course, Goeth's personal body-guard, Oberscharführer Albert Hujar, who was personally responsible for shooting all the patients in the main hospital at Jozefinska Street, as Pankiewicz noted, "Hujar was running amok like a rabid animal through the entire building, leaving a trail of blood and corpses, he shot the guard at the gate and the dog cowering in the dog house."

[164] Part of a 150-person Jewish detail sent to Plaszow to help build the new camp were the Bejski brothers – Israel (69385), Moshe (69387), and Uri (69384).

[165] The headstone was still in-situ; June 1996.

[166] Pankiewicz, 113. Dr. Aleksandrowicz's escape from the ghetto is related in a book, *Pages from the Diary of Dr. Tough,* published in 1962 by the Literary Publishing House.

[167] Ibid, 107.

[168] Pankiewicz, 39

[169] Interviewed by the author, 1995. Dortheimer Sr. was later taken to Mathausen where he was killed with a lethal injection of benzene. A doctor Eigenholtz from Haifa, a prisoner in Mathausen, told Victor of the fate of his father.

[170] Jon Blair documentary film, *Schindler* (1982).

[171] Interviewed by the author at the King David Hotel, Jerusalem. Also Jon Blair film, *Schindler* (1982).

[172] Pankiewicz, 42.

[173] Madritsch documentation.

[174] Bousco, sickened with the Nazi policies, fled to the forest dressed as a Polish farmer. He was caught and summarily tried for treason and shot. The date was September 18, 1944.

[175] Henry and Olek Rosner interviewed by the author at the King David Hotel, Jerusalem. See also Jon Blair film *Schindler* (1982).

[176] Madritsch documentation – statement of Raymond Titsch.

[177] Martin Gilbert, *The Holocaust*, 367.

[178] Pankiewicz, 114-5.

[179] Unkelbach took over as manager of the factory "Progress." which manufactured cutlery. When all the Jews were moved to Plaszow, Unkelbach, like Schindler, got special dispensation to march his men from the camp to the factory each day and return in the evening. Later Schindler was to reap the benefits of his new barracks when his Jewish labor remained at Emalia, guarded by a very small SS detachment.

[180] Dr. Karl Eberhardt Schoengarth, SS-Standartenfüher (Commander) of the Befehlshaber der Sicherheitspolizei und des SD (BdS) in the Netherlands and then the General Government, had much experience in tracking down and killing Jews. He organized three Kommandos. In the middle of July 1941 these Kommandos moved into the Eastern Polish areas and, with headquarters in Lwow, Brest-Litovsk, and Bialystok, respectively, killed tens of thousands of Jews. (See note 26, Hilberg, 296, Vol. 1,) Schoengarth also present at Wannsee on 20.1.1942. A drinking partner of Schindler's, he was a main source of information, which was filtered by Schindler to selected Jews on a need to know basis. He was addicted to alcoholic oblivion. (Rupert Butler, 180)

[181] Interviewed by the author in Tel Aviv 1995.

[182] Another influential Jewish leader that immediately comes to mind, who also had these qualities, was Dr. Elachanan Elkes of the Kovno Ghetto.

[183] Rabbi Lewertow will be remembered in Spielberg's film as the factory worker who was "timed" by Goeth in the making of hinges and then taken out where several attempts were made by Goeth to shoot him. Keneally incorrectly (page 223) refers to the Peltzmann family as Perlman.

[184] See the Bejski papers.

Chapter 10

[185] Wundheiler.

[186] Irene Schek (76431) statement in the Blair film.

[187] Wundheiler.

[188] Leopold Pfefferberg (69006) Blair film.

[189] In 1945, Florenz met Lamus, who asked for Schindler's address and asked Florenz to give his regards and thank Schindler for saving his life (statement by Florenz in Yad Vashem).

[190] Roman Wohlfeiler (69414) and Halina Wohlfeiler (76486), both interviewed by the author. See also Ball-Kaduri documentation. Here, as elsewhere, when Schindler's own report is mentioned, the author is referring to Schindler's

report of his activities that can be inspected in the archives of Yad Vashem and that are published in Grossmann, K.R.: *Die Unbesungenen Helden*. Frankfurt: Ullstein, 1989.

[191] See Keneally, 235/6.

[192] Author's interview with Dr. Bauminger and Shlomo Schein, Israel, 1995.

[193] Recollections by Wohlfeiler and Dortheimer of the incident as told to the author.

[194] Ball-Kaduri documents. See also statement of Stern, Yad Vashem, and Keneally page 243.

[195] Ball-Kaduri documents and statement by Stern at a Schindler gathering in 1962 in Tel Aviv.
Keneally, 243.

[196] *The Times*, dated July 8, 1996. – "Review of Plotting Hitler's Death" by Joachim Fest.

[197] Author's interview with Adam Garde 1995. See also Keneally, 292.

Chapter 11

[198] Ball-Kaduri, 18.

[199] Ibid.

[200] Wundheiler.

[201] Mrs. Sophie Stern.

[202] Ibid. See also Ball-Kaduri, 48.

[203] Interviewed by the author in Tel Aviv, 1995.

[204] Interviewed by the author in Germany, 1995.

[205] Mrs. Schindler – Jon Blair interview.

[206] Bejski documents to the author.

[207] Ball-Kaduri.

[208] Wundheiler, 13.

[209] Ibid, 14.

[210] Interview by the author with Moshe Bejski, 1995.

[211] Wundheiler, 11.

Chapter 12

[212] Tarnow ghetto final deportations on January 9, 1943. The only survivors were the Madritsch factory personnel who were sent to Plaszow.

[213] Personal memoir of Madritsch.

[214] Ibid.

[215] Ibid.

[216] Interview with Pemper. See also Ball-Kaduri document.

[217] Ball-Kaduri.

[218] Pemper's open access to confidential files in Goeth's office was the subject of charges when Goeth was arrested by the SS investigation team.

[219] Plaszow held over 30,000 Jewish prisoners in early 1944.

[220] See also Keneally, 280-1.

[221] Mrs. Chana Kinstlinger (76328)

[222] Recollection by Joseph Bau, interviewed by the author.

[223] Ibid.

[224] Ibid.

[225] Original wagons can still be seen in a siding at Plaszow railway station. On a visit there I was shown the wagons, which were all sealed. The stationmaster very kindly broke the seal on one wagon and allowed me to inspect the interior. The small narrow window covered by barbed wire was still intact.

[226] Statements of these two doctors can be seen in the archives of Yad Vashem.

Chapter 13

[227] Keneally, 299. On today's maps, Gross-Rosen is shown as Rogoznica (to the left of Wroclaw).

[228] Blair film 1982, interview with Urbach.

[229] Letter to the author from Group Captain C. Russell, Commandant, RAAF College, RAAF Williams. Point Cook Vic 3028 under reference AF94/2813 Pt 2 dated 2.11.95.

[230] Ibid.

[231] Ibid.

[232] Interviews by the author with Victor Dortheimer and Richard Rechin.

[233] As stated, Bousco was found guilty as a traitor and executed by the SS on September 18, 1944.

[234] Colonel Lang was well known to Schindler, having previously sanctioned the Emalia armaments contract.

[235] Schindler's own assessment of his feelings, as shown in a letter to Ball-Kaduri.

[236] Moshe Bejski's interview with the author.

[237] Detailed overview of events by Schindler to Ball-Kaduri.

[238] Madritsch was never happy with Schindler over this incident.

[239] Bejski papers to the author.

[240] Madritsch's personal memoir.

[241] Alexander Biberstein, *Extermination of the Krakow Jews,* 143. Also interview with Moshe Bejski.

[242] Dr. Alexander Biberstein's memoir.

[243] One of the most curious aspects of the list is that nowhere is Doctor Gross shown. We know he went to Gross-Rosen and that he was in Brünnlitz and later returned to Auschwitz. Nowhere is his name recorded. I find this most odd and when I sought a reason from Yad Vashem (whose expertise is questionable), they were unable to offer a reason. I am not persuaded that we have the final answer to this.

[244] Ibid.

[245] Ibid. Dr. Schindel and his brothers were the last prisoners to leave KL Plaszow. Dr. Schindel landed up in Auschwitz but would survive the war. The brothers were forced to march to Flossenburg. One was shot, the other survived.

[246] The Gross-Rosen concentration camp was originally established in 1940 as a branch camp of Sachsenhausen in the vicinity of a quarry. Gross-Rosen became an independent camp on May 1, 1941 and remained so until February 1945. During the period of camp liquidation the number of prisoners reached 100, 000. These were prisoners of various nationalities, though predominantly Jewish. Nearly 50 smaller camps fell under the administration of Gross-Rosen. One of these was Schindler's labor camp at Brünnlitz. While the number of people who died at Gross-Rosen is difficult to establish, it is estimated that because of the inhumane conditions one-third of the 125,000 people who passed through the camp and its branch units during the Second World War perished.

[247] Ibid.

[248] Ibid.

[249] Ibid.

[250] Gross-Rosen (Rogoznica) near Scheidnitz in Lower Silesia had been a concentration camp since May 1941. In 1944, it contained 12,000 prisoners. It was one of numerous subsidiary camps scattered throughout the occupied

land. On March 21, 1945, the camp was evacuated and moved to Reichenau in Bohemia where it was finally liberated on April 5, 1945.

Chapter 14

[251] Statement of Maurice Finder (76291) can be seen in Yad Vashem.

[252] Mrs Emilie Schindler's memoirs sent to the author.

Chapter 15

[253] It was only in the last stages of the war that the railway spur entered the well-known archway. The usual procedure was for transports to terminate before the archway and the prisoners would walk under guard into the camp.

[254] Stella Müller-Madej, *A Girl from Schindler's List*, London, 1997.

[255] The author interviewed a number of the women survivors, who gave vivid recollections of what happened in Birkenau: Irena Schek (76431), Ludmilla Pfefferberg (76398), Bertha Aftergood (76201), Rachel Korn (76334), Manci Rosner (76423), Regina Horowitz (76309), Klara (76459), and others.

[256] In the Spielberg film, Stern is shown waiting with the other men as the women marched into the camp. As the last woman passed Stern realized that his mother had not returned. This scene was vividly displayed.

[257] Emilie Schindler, 66.

[258] Ibid, 68.

[259] Emilie Schindler, 90- 91.

[260] The woman was Hela Goldfinger, the sister of Gena Turgel (née Goldfinger), whom the author interviewed in London, 1993.

[261] Emilie, 69.

Chapter 16

[262] See David Crowe, Schindler biography, 423.

[263] Recollections of Moshe Bejski – interview with the author.

[264] Emilie, 101-103.

[265] Keneally, 355, cited in the Wundheiler documentation. Mrs. Schindler gives a full graphic account of the Golleschau tragedy in her film interview with Jon Blair, 1982.

[266] Moshe Bejski interviewed by the author.

[267] Alexander Biberstein recollections in archive at Yad Vashem.

[268] Interviewed in London by the author, 1995.

[269] Moshe Pantirer interviewed by the author.

[270] Information source – Ball-Kaduri documentation.

[271] Recollection by Moshe Bejski in interview with the author.

[272] Ibid.

[273] I am in correspondence with Schoenfeld, who now lives in Paris. He gives a graphic and interesting account of his rescue by Schindler.

[274] Statements by Breslauer and Wilner can be seen in the archives of Yad Vashem.

Chapter 17

[275] The Germans had set up a new army, a million strong, comprised of Russians, Ukrainians, and Russian prisoners of war. A Soviet general, Wlassove, who was captured by the Germans at Stalingrad, had been designated the commander of the new army.

[276] Ball-Kaduri documentation. Recollections by Moshe Bejski, Mietek Pemper, and Richard Rechen in interviews with the author. Schindler's own defense

team was apart from other defense activity in the camp. He was unable to control some of the Budzyn prisoners who were starting to act independently.

[277] I found this recollection by some of the survivors incredible. I double checked the archive material and translation documents of Ball-Kaduri and it appears from the evidence that there is much substance in it.

[278] Witnesses to Leipold's departure were given by Eduard Heuberger (69820) to the French Military Authorities after the war. See also the Ball-Kaduri documents. The witness Bronia Guns-Sperling (76287) refers to the prisoners digging their own graves in the camp and the confrontation with Leipold. This episode is well documented in Yad Vashem.

[279] The Jews Arthur Rabner (68989) and Selman Szydlo (77177), both radio technicians, had been receiving news from the front for some time. Schindler had supplied the radio, and the information received was used on a large scale map showing the front coming nearer and nearer. On a visit to the factory in 1995/6 I noticed that radio speakers were still in situ. The present director of the factory told me that they had been there since the war.

[280] Dr. Alexander Biberstein, *Extermination of the Cracow Jews*, 1955 (Polish; translated by Leo Aftergood).

[281] Moshe Bejski recollects this incident and says that he never agreed with hanging Willi. See also Dr. Alexander Biberstein (note 6) 154.

[282] I met Hirsch Licht and his daughter in Jerusalem where Hirsch gave me his personal account of that day.

[283] Mrs. Schindler states that this vehicle had been custom-built for the Shah of Persia, but the war impeded delivery. The vehicle was originally light blue but had since been re-sprayed grey. See Mrs. Schindler's memoir. Schindler bought the vehicle in Berlin soon after he took over the Rekord factory (Emalia). He took one of his Polish (non-Jewish) secretaries to Berlin and paid cash for the vehicle. The money had been given to him by the Abwehr. Statement of Eva Kiza, Jon Blair film, 1982.

[284] Marta-Eva Scheuer remained with the Schindlers throughout the peace.

[285] Moshe Bejski with his length of cloth went to Prague where he exchanged it for his first suit of clothes. He had last worn a suit in 1939.

[286] Refer: *Star of David*.

[287] Aleksander Skotnicki, *Schindler*, 47 (edited).

Chapter 18

[288] Acknowledgement to the Jerusalem Report 2 June, 1994.

[289] Ibid.

[290] Emilie Schindler, 110.

[291] Hersch Licht in conversation with the author 1995.

[292] The Jerusalem Report June 2 1994, photograph attributed to David Rubinger/ASAP.

Chapter 19

[293] A German Government was established in Krakow under Dr. Hans Frank (the Governor) who was legally entitled, based upon a law of the Führer from 12 October 1939, to fulfill the civil authority of those parts of Poland that at first did not belong to the Soviet Union or were not attached to the German Reich. The entire area was called the General Government.

Chapter 21

[294] In December 1941, during the evacuation of the Riga ghetto, the 81-year-old historian Simon Dubnow was shot. The story is told that Dubnow's last

words were an admonition to his fellow Jews: 'Write and record!' (Yidn, shreibt un farschreibt). It was a phrase written on walls and scraps of paper thrown out of deportation trains in a last desperate act of defiance when the victims saw their immediate demise. These 'last words' were also recorded in the last transport carriages bringing the Jewish workers of the 'death brigade' from Bełżec to Sobibor where they were all shot.

[295] This assessment was taken in conjunction with the findings of Dr. Wundheiler and Rosalia Kornhauser (76335), now Pechthold and living in Raanana, Israel, interviewed by the author 1992.

[296] Raul Hilberg. *The Destruction of the European Jews.* London 1985, 8.

[297] Dr. R. Ball-Kaduri: References to this document are to the English translation, 1-103. If one takes a cynical view of this letter one could be forgiven for thinking, *"He would say that, wouldn't he."* Ten years after the war Schindler was down and out and grasping for survival, what should one make of this letter in the context of what actually happened during the war period? My own view, which I think is supported by the evidence presented, is that Schindler's testament is an understatement of his activities. It is a summary of his feelings. It gives one a glimpse of the true Schindler, an ordinary human being with ordinary successes and failures.

[298] Dr. L.N. Wundheiler, *Oskar Schindler's Moral Development during the Holocaust.* Humbolt Journal of Social Relations, Vol.X111, No. 1-2 (1985) 1-20.

[299] Dr. Moshe Bejski's interview with the author. Jerusalem/London 1995.

[300] Thomas Fensch, *Oskar Schindler and His List.* Vermont, 1995, 45. *Schindler's author gives the film a standing ovation.* The Orange County Register, January 2, 1994, Valerie Takahama.

[301] In January, 1944, Plaszow's status changed from labor camp to concentration camp, indicated by the letters KL (*Konzentrationslager*). Hereafter, all camps are referred to by name only.

[302] The number shown after the individual is the number shown on the 'list' from Yad Vashem, Ref. 01/164.

[303] Prior to 1939, the factory premises at 4 Lipowa Street were known as 'Rekord'. Schindler renamed the factory '*Deutsche Emailwaren Fabrik*' (D.E.F). To this day the former Jewish employees at the factory refer to it as Emalia.

[304] Elinor J. Brecher, *Schindler's Legacy*, London 1995, 68. Schindler's personal selection came in different guises; e.g. Helena (Susan) Sternlicht (76464) domestic servant to Amon Goeth. "In September 1944, Goeth was arrested for corruption. Schindler came to me and said, 'Susanna, you're coming with me. I have a list. I built a factory in Czechoslovakia and I'm taking all the people with me'. Schindler took down the names of Sternlicht's family and kept his word. The Sternlicht family survived with Schindler."

[305] Dr. Moshe Bejski, interviewed by the author in Israel, 1995, re corruption in Plaszow (the list: compiled by Marcel Goldberg).

[306] Alexander Biberstein, *Zaglada Zydow w Krakowie* (Extermination of Krakow's Jews). Krakow 1985, 143.

[307] Emilie Schindler, *Where Light and Shadow Meet*, 45.

[308] R. Ball-Kaduri, *Protocol and interview with Itzhak Stern (695518)*, Yad Vashem (01/1643) 1956, 1-80. Also includes observations on Schindler, and correspondence with Schindler, certified documentation and depositions with witnesses and interested parties. Hereafter, 'Ball-Kaduri'.

[309] The stranger was Frantisek Sperka, hotel receptionist at the Hotel Slavia, Svitavy (previously known as the Hotel Ungar where Schindler was arrested in 1938).

[310] Dr. R. Ball-Kaduri, *Protocol and interview with Itzhak Stern (69518),* Yad Vashem, (01/1643) 1956.

[311] Personal documentation from Steinhouse to the author. See also, Thomas Fensch, *Oskar Schindler and His List* (Vermont 1995) 3-19; hereafter, Fensch.

[312] Julius Madritsch, *Menschen in Not*, 2nd ed., (Vienna 1962) 28; hereafter, Madritsch. The information at the author's disposal also referred to Schindler and the slave labor system and factory administration in Krakow and Tarnow and his dealings with the German WVHA (Wirtschafts-und Verwaltungshauptamt); the Economic and Administrative Main Office of the SS, formed in 1942 and headed by Oswald Pohl to administer the concentration camps and economic enterprises of the SS.

[313] Raymond Titsch, a non-Jew from Vienna. Factory manager for Julius Madritsch in Krakow and Tarnow.

[314] Oswald Bousco, a non-Jew from Vienna. He was an Oberscharführer (police sergeant) in the Krakow ghetto.

[315] Photographs of the Plaszow camp taken by Raymond Titsch were preserved under dramatic conditions. Today the photographs are in the archives at the Yad Vashem Holocaust memorial in Israel.

[316] Police report of Brno, Czech Republic, found in the police archives in Prague by the author in 1995. Deals with the arrest of Oskar Schindler in Svitavy on July 18, 1938, and notes of his interrogation, fingerprints and photograph. Further documentation deals with the arrest of Joseph Aue (Treuhänder) at the premises of Salomon Bucheister and Co., 15 Stradom Street, Krakow in Czechoslovakia in 1946, and his extradition to Poland and interrogation. The material exposes Schindler as a spy for the German Security Services, his activities around Moravska Ostrava in 1938/9, and the setup of the Abwehr in Krakow where Stern was employed. The documentation was in the Czech and German languages and translated by Dr. Yitka Viklova, Massaryk University, Brno, Czech. Republic. Read by the translator onto tape (probably a summarized account) and then filtered by the author for factual information.

[317] Emilie, 33.

[318] Moravska Ostrava; hereafter, M. Ostrava.

[319] Although Stern had worked at the Bucheister Company since 1924, he was never aware of the fact that the premises were a front for the Abwehr and that his new German employer, Aue, was an agent and a half-Jew planted there by Schindler in 1939. Stern was not to know about this until after the war, when he was called to give evidence on behalf of Aue, who was on trial in Krakow as a German collaborator in Krakow. Much of this background information comes from many interviews by the author with Mrs. Sophia Stern, née Backenrot (now deceased), in Israel. In 1938, Stern and Sophia Backenrot were engaged and later married in 1945. Sophia was able to survive in the Drohobcyz ghetto due to her Aryan appearance. Although Mrs. Stern's recollections are mostly hearsay, they are very important when piecing together the facts. More substantial were the many documents that were made available to the author for scrutiny.

[320] Mrs. Schindler always refers to her husband as "Schindler".

[321] Following the Munich Agreement many Jewish families from the town moved away and 152 local Jews perished in Nazi camps. One of the labor camps for Jewish men from Poland and the Protectorate was located at the Barthel Company in Svitavy. In 1944 the prisoners were deported to Wroclaw.

[322] Unknown to Keneally or Spielberg, another writer—Herbert Steinhouse--had stumbled on the Schindler story nearly forty-six years ago. Herbert Steinhouse, a Montreal-born journalist, novelist, and broadcaster, flew with the RCAF during the war and afterwards became an information officer for the United Nations Relief and Rehabilitation Administration (UNRRA). While stationed in Paris, he signed on with Reuters but in 1949 jumped to the CBC as its Paris bureau chief.

It was a few months earlier, in Munich, that Steinhouse first met Schindler. He had already fallen in with some of the Holocaust survivors Schindler had saved--the so called *Schindlerjuden*--and they had begun telling him some of their stories. Given his work at UNRRA, Steinhouse was suspicious of "good German" tales, but he was sufficiently intrigued this time to begin looking for independent verification.

Steinhouse was led to Schindler himself by two Polish Jews who had decided that their rescuer's security and best hope for the future lay in maximum publicity for his remarkable wartime story. This was especially so since he was still classified as a "former Nazi," which severely limited his chances of emigrating to most countries. "Schindler charmed him as he did everyone," Steinhouse recalls. "Our wives also hit it off. We dined together and drank together. He talked, I made notes."

The story continued to strike Steinhouse as "far-fetched," but he found more and more corroboration both in survivors' recollections and in underground and resistance files. Finally, after a half-dozen sessions with Itzhak Stern, who was his principal source, four interviews with Schindler, and professional pictures taken by a close friend the late Al Taylor, Steinhouse set to work and wrote his exclusive in the form of a magazine article which he published in 1994: 'Saturday Night; Herbert Stenhouse's account of Oskar Schindler, had been sitting unread in his files for most of half a century...

Bibliography

Bauminger, A. L., *Fighters of the Cracow Ghetto*. Jerusalem, 1986.

Bau, Josef, *Dear God, Have You Ever Gone Hungry?* New York, 1998.

Bejski, Moshe, *Notes on the Banquet in Honor of Oskar Schindler*. Tel Aviv, 1962.

Bieberstein, Alexander, *Zaglada Zydow w Krakowie*. Krakow, 1985.

Brecher, Elinor J., *Schindler's Legacy*. London, 1994.

Crowe, David M., *Oskar Schindler - die Biographie.* Frankfurt am Main, 2005.

Elon, Amos, *Timetable (the story of Joel Brand).* London, 1982.

Fensch, Thomas, *Oskar Schindler and his List*. Vermont, 1995.

Fikejz, R., *Oskar Schindler (1908 - 1974).* Svitavy, 1998.

In Search of the Star of David, Svitavy, 2008.

Gruntova, J., *Legendy a Fakta, o Oskaru Schindlerovi*. Svitavy, 2002.

Keneally, Thomas, *Schindler's List*. London, 1982.

Madritsch, Julius, *Menschen In Not!* Vienna, 1962.

O'Neil, R., *Belzec: Stepping Stone to Genocide*, NY, 2008: (An analysis of the action of Oskar Schindler within the context of the Holocaust in German-occupied Poland and Czechoslovakia).

The Man from Svitavy, London, 1994.

Schindler: Stepping Stone to Life, NY, 2010.

Pankiewitz, Tadeusz, *The Cracow Ghetto Pharmacy*. New York, 1987.

Piper, F., *Auschwitz - Nazi Death Camp*. Oświetim, 1996.

Schindler, Emilie, *Where Light and Shadow Meet*. NY, 1997.

Silver, Eric, *The Book of the Just.* London, 1992.

Skotnicki, Aleksander B., *Oskar Schindler*. Krakow, 2008.

Stern, Itzsak, *Oskar Schindler der Mensch*. Tel Aviv, 1968.

Wundheiler, L. N., "Oskar Schindler's Moral Development During the Holocaust." In: *Humboldt Journal of Social Relations*, Vol. XIII, 1985.

Index

G

Personal montage of the Schindler story